Marlborough's Wars

Eyewitness Accounts 1702–1713

Marlborough's Wars
Eyewitness Accounts 1702–1713

James Falkner

Foreword by His Grace the Duke of Marlborough

Pen & Sword
MILITARY

First published in Great Britain in 2005 by
Pen & Sword Military
an imprint of
Pen & Sword Books Ltd
47 Church Street
Barnsley
South Yorkshire
S70 2AS

ISBN 1-84415-170-0

A CIP catalogue record for this book is
available from the British Library

Typeset in 11/13pt Plantin by Mac Style Ltd, Scarborough, N. Yorkshire
Printed and bound in England by CPI UK

Pen & Sword Books Ltd incorporates the Imprints of Pen & Sword Aviation,
Pen & Sword Maritime, Pen & Sword Military, Wharncliffe Local History, Pen
& Sword Select, Pen and Sword Military Classics and Leo Cooper.

For a complete list of Pen & Sword titles, please contact
Pen & Sword Books Limited
47 Church Street, Barnsley, South Yorkshire, S70 2AS, England
E-mail: enquiries@pen-and-sword.co.uk
Website: www.pen-and-sword.co.uk

Contents

List of maps

Foreword by His Grace
The Duke of Marlborough

It is the sense of realism in this book which strikes me. Not only does James Falkner give a detailed and accurate account of the progress of the War of the Spanish Succession but his frequent inclusion of eye-witness reports invests his account with a vividness, drama and humanity which at times verge on the painful. The events of 300 years ago seem to unfold before our eyes:

> 'Each discharge of the cannons stretched some of my men on the ground. I suffered agonies by seeing these brave fellows perish without a chance of defending themselves – but it is absolutely necessary that they should not move from their posts.'

Thus, Colonel De La Colonie describes his French infantry on the slopes of the Schellenberg exposed to the Allied artillery; we are sharply aware in real terms of that worst of military dilemmas – the need to accept casualties.

However, while basing his story on eye-witness accounts the author astutely recognises that contemporary interpretations are not necessarily the best interpretations and so he skilfully weaves these accounts into his own substantial, detailed and accurate narrative.

The actual eye-witness accounts are drawn from wide-ranging resources. In describing the events of the Battle of Blenheim alone James Falkner weaves into his story current descriptions and judgements from over twenty contemporary sources, thirteen from the Allied side and eight from the French.

There is an equally wide range in terms of rank, from the highest to the lowest on both sides, from Marshal Tallard to Private John Dean of the Foot Guards.

This book creates a welcome degree of understanding beyond mere historical narrative and I recommend it.

Marlborough

Introduction

The War of the Spanish Succession raged across Western Europe in the years between 1702 and 1713. It was fought to decide whether a French or an Austrian prince should sit on the throne in Madrid, and the eventual outcome of the war satisfied no one, becoming the cause of recrimination between Great Britain and her Allies, Holland and Austria. Still, the principal result was an effective limitation on the martial power of France. Not for another ninety years or so, with the rise of Napoleon, would that country's military capability fully recover and enable her, once again, to bully and intimidate her neighbours with near impunity, as King Louis XIV had done throughout the late 17th and early 18th century.

This remarkable achievement was largely the work of England's Captain-General, John Churchill, the 1st Duke of Marlborough. His campaigns, fought between 1702, when he took command of the English and Dutch armies, and the end of 1711, saw a whole series of astonishing victories against France and her allies, both in open battle and siege. Louis XIV was in despair at the ruin he faced, but the Duke fell from favour and was dismissed by Queen Anne at the end of 1711. The Allied effort limped on, half-heartedly, for a couple of years, but France was able to recover much of what had been lost in the Low Countries and along the Rhine. When peace came, the French claimant to the throne in Madrid, Louis XIV's grandson, the Duc d'Anjou, remained there as King Philip V, while the Austrian contender, Archduke Charles, became Emperor in Vienna on the untimely death of his older brother.

The story of these exciting events, when Marlborough dominated the European military scene, has often been told, not least by the Duke's illustrious descendant, Sir Winston Churchill. In addition to such later histories, it is possible to find a surprising number of memoirs, diaries and reminiscences left by those who took part in the campaigns, or were observers of those momentous times. Those stories (some remarkably lurid, others a little dull) are well worth the effort to find, and it is pleasantly surprising that so many ordinary soldiers at that time had considerable, if sometimes fairly simple, literary skill. At the one extreme, with the wordy correspondence of those who dealt with matters of grand strategy or affairs of state – the letters sent by monarchs to their generals, messages from the commander of one army to another, or the voluminous and immensely valuable official correspondence of the Duke of Marlborough himself – it is possible to see guiding hands at work in waging Continental war. At the other end of the scale are the intimate, often very amusing, accounts of the life of the trooper or soldier of the day – the minute details of camp life, the labour of marching in mud or dust, and wreathed in flame and smoke in the teeming line of battle.

Those accounts that have been published (and in some cases revised, translated and republished) often allow the veteran to 'speak for themselves' and this can limit their effectiveness. Sometimes the eyewitness narrator was standing just a little too close to the action, and smoke, noise, fatigue and fear got in the way; events, dates and timings became jumbled in the memory. The resulting accounts of momentous deeds, written in some cases years later, often intended only for family members and friends to read, can be rather dry and, in a way, too safe. The veterans will have done their best to recount events of great importance to them, but few would wish to admit that, some time afterwards, they simply didn't remember a certain detail, a date or a time, a name or a rank, or a place-name, which might be important to the story. Sticking to the standard and accepted account of a battle neatly avoided having to make such an admission. Those diarists who kept a daily journal (as quite a few did), had the freshness of memory as an aid, but their own familiarity with those same daily events could lead to mundane repetition. Therefore, without wishing to unduly embellish what are already valuable accounts, I have tried to tell the tale of Marlborough's wars between 1702 and 1713 as a genuinely exciting story, using my own narrative of the campaigns, linked, far more importantly, with extensive edited extracts from the memoirs of those veterans who took part, and those who watched from the sidelines.

All dates given are in the New Style (N.S.) unless it is stated otherwise. This was in use on the Continent, where almost all the action in this book takes place, and from 1700 onwards was eleven days later than the Old Style (O.S.) which was still used, at that time, in Great Britain. Therefore, war was declared by the Grand Alliance on 15 May 1702 (N.S.) in Holland and Austria, but the same day was known as 4 May 1702 (O.S.) in London.

Where necessary a certain pruning of the contemporary accounts has been undertaken, I hope sensitively, to avoid undue verbosity and needless repetition. Short explanatory comments, where they seem necessary and helpful, are included in square brackets in the text. As most of the printed memoirs that are available have already been put into modern grammatical form by others, I have extended this practice to those few accounts that still exist in the rather idiosyncratic style and erratic spelling of the early eighteenth century. This aims at achieving greater consistency, and to help the narrative to flow more freely, but changes have been kept to a minimum. Where this would seem to alter the meaning of the text unduly, however, I have left well alone, and some variations in syntax and spelling were so widespread – as with such examples as Douai/Douay, Sensée/Senset, Marshal/Marechal – occasionally both styles being used willy-nilly in the same letter, that some inconsistency between quotations and text may still be noticed.

Chronological table of the main events of the War of the Spanish Succession
NB: All dates are in New Style.

1700
1 November	Death of King Carlos II in Madrid
16 November	Louis XIV recognises grandson as Philip V of Spain

1701
February	French troops occupy Barrier Towns in Spanish Netherlands
18 February	Phillipe, Duc d'Anjou, enters Madrid
8 August	Marlborough appointed to command 'British' troops in Holland
7 September	Grand Alliance agreed between Britain, Holland and Austria
17 September	Louis XIV acknowledges 'Old Pretender' as King of England

1702
19 March	Death of King William III, accession of Queen Anne
15 May	Grand Alliance declares war on France and her allies
11 June	French drive Dutch back into Nijmegen
15 June	Dutch capture Kaiserswerth
1 July	Marlborough takes command as Allied Captain-General
23 August	Dutch prevent Marlborough's attacks at Heaths of Peer
25 September	Allies capture Venlo
September	Bavaria and Liège ally themselves to France
October	Spanish treasure fleet captured at Vigo
7 October	Allies take Ruremonde
26 October	Allies capture Liège

1703
15 May	Marlborough captures Bonn
30 June	Dutch army mauled at Eckeren by Marshal Boufflers
26 August	Allies take Huy
13 September	Archduke Charles declared King Carlos III of Spain
27 September	Allies capture Limburg
November	Duchy of Savoy joins Grand Alliance
December	Portugal joins Grand Alliance (2nd Methuen Treaty)

1704
May	Abortive offensive from Portugal into Spain
19 May	Marlborough begins march up the Rhine
30 May	Allies fail to capture Barcelona

2 July	The Schellenberg battle
6 August	Anglo–Dutch force captures Gibraltar
11 August	Baden begins siege of Ingolstadt
13 August	Battle of Blenheim
29 October	Marlborough occupies Treves (Trier)
11 November	First Franco–Spanish attempt to recapture Gibraltar
28 November	Allies capture Landau
20 December	Allies take Trarbach

1705

5 May	Death of Emperor Leopold, succeeded by son, Joseph
10 June	French capture Huy
11 July	Marlborough retakes Huy
18 July	Battle of Elixheim and passage of the Lines of Brabant
18 August	Abortive battle on River Yssche, near Waterloo
6 September	Allies capture Leau
September	Allied forces land in eastern Spain under Peterborough
14 October	Barcelona captured by Allies
29 October	Marlborough captures Sand Vliet
December	Valencia occupied by Allies

1706

19 May	Marshal Villeroi moves out to challenge Marlborough
22 May	Barcelona relieved of French siege by Royal Navy
23 May	Battle of Ramillies
28 May	French abandon Brussels
17 June	Antwerp submits to Marlborough
23 June	Allies capture Cartagena
27 June	Madrid entered by Allies
9 July	Allies capture Ostend
4 August	Madrid evacuated by Allies
22 August	Menin captured by Marlborough
7 September	Prince Eugene victorious at Battle of Turin
9 September	Allies take Dendermonde
13 September	Majorca and Ibiza submit to Allied occupation
1 October	Allies capture Ath
11 November	Cartagena retaken by Marshal Berwick

1707

13 February	France and Austria agree to neutralize northern Italy
25 April	Allies defeated at Almanza in Spain
22 May	Marshal Villars storms Lines of Stollhofen
22 August	Failure of Allied attempt to take naval base at Toulon
14 November	Berwick captures Lerida

1708

30 April	Imperial army under Stahremberg arrives in Catalonia
5 July	French capture Bruges
7 July	French take Ghent
11 July	Marlborough defeats Vendôme at Oudenarde
August	Sardinia occupied by Allies
29 August	Stanhope captures Minorca
August–December	Siege of Lille (citadel capitulates 10 December)
28 September	Battle of Wynendael

1709

2 January	Allies recapture Ghent (French abandon Bruges)
9 April	Louis XIV declares intention to remove French troops in Spain
7 May	Allies defeated at Val Gudina in Portugal
3 September	Marlborough captures Tournai
11 September	Battle of Malplaquet
20 October	Mons capitulates to Allies
29 October	1st Anglo–Dutch Barrier Treaty agreed

1710

25 June	Allies take Douai
27 July	Allied victory at Almenara
20 August	Allied victory at Saragossa
28 August	Allies capture Bethune
September	Carlos III enters Madrid
29 September	Allies take St Venant
8 November	Allies capture Aire
9 December	Stanhope defeated at Brihuega near Madrid
10 December	Vendôme's army mauled at Villaviciosa

1711

25 January	Berwick takes Gerona
17 April	Death of Emperor Joseph, accession of Charles
7 August	Marlborough passes Lines of Non Plus Ultra
14 September	Allies take Bouchain
22 September	Charles (Carlos III) leaves Spain
31 December (O.S.)	Marlborough removed from all offices and posts

1712

4 July	Allies capture Le Quesnoy
16 July	British troops removed from operations
19 July	Dunkirk handed to Britain by the French

24 July	Villars defeats Dutch at Denain
2 August	Dutch and Imperial troops fail to capture Landrecies
30 July	French capture Marchiennes
8 September	French retake Douai
2 October	Suspension of hostilities in Spain
3 October	French retake Le Quesnoy
8 October	Peace preliminaries signed between France and Britain
19 October	Villars retakes Bouchain
3 November	Suspension of hostilities in Portugal

1713

30 January	2nd Anglo-Dutch Barrier Treaty agreed
11 April	Treaty of Utrecht agreed between main parties in the war
9 July	Barcelona declares allegiance to Carlos III
13 July	Anglo-Spanish Treaty agreed

1714

6 March	Treaty of Rastadt agreed between France and Austria
26 June	Treaty agreed between Holland and Spain
31 July	Death of Queen Anne, accession of King George I
17 August	Marlborough reappointed as Captain-General
7 September	Treaty of Baden agreed between France and the Empire
	Barcelona taken by Berwick

1715

6 February	Treaty between Spain and Portugal agreed
15 September	Death of Louis XIV, accession of King Louis XV (as a minor)
15 November	Barrier Treaty signed between Holland, Empire and France.

Chapter One

The Coming of the War for Spain 1701–1702

'Gentlemen' said he, indicating the Duc d'Anjou, 'this is the King of Spain'. In this dramatic way, the Duc de St Simon described how, on 16 November 1700, King Louis XIV of France introduced his young second grandson, Philippe, to the assembled courtiers in the palace of Versailles. The news of the death of sickly and childless King Carlos II of Spain had come a week or so earlier, together with confirmation, long looked for, that the now vacant throne in Madrid was to be offered to the young French prince. The Spanish Envoy to France, Castel del Rey, was now introduced to his new King, and invited to kiss his hand, then the whole Court went to hear prayers in Louis XIV's private chapel.

Archduke Charles of Austria, younger son of the Habsburg Emperor Leopold I, was also a claimant to the Spanish throne (Leopold set aside his own claim in favour the Archduke); a young Bavarian prince, whom everyone had agreed should succeed to the throne, having died some years' earlier. Louis XIV hoped to buy off Austrian outrage at the French prince's impending accession with territorial concessions in Northern Italy. However, concern was felt throughout the Protestant states of western Europe at this increase in French influence, particularly as the Spanish empire, although moribund and with no real military power, extended across wide parts of the Mediterranean, Italy, the Low Countries and the Americas.

Two Barrier Treaties, negotiated in the late 1690s, had brought to a tired end the seemingly interminable series of French and Dutch wars, and contained provisions that the thrones of France and Spain should always be kept separate. This important matter was now in some doubt. Louis XIV was well aware of this: 'Whatever I do someone will blame me' he had commented on giving consent to Anjou's acceptance of the offered throne. The King took some care to reassure his near neighbours, in particular England and Holland, that their own interests would not be jeopardised by the presence on the throne in Madrid of a French Prince of the Blood. Both countries at first seemed inclined to accept things as they stood – certainly no one wanted a renewal of war – but experience made them wary, and the Sun King, usually so astute, made a series of almost inexplicable mistakes, perhaps through over-confidence, that caused alarm in both London and the Hague.

By these two treaties, the Dutch had secured a 'barrier' against future French aggression comprising a series of strongly held towns in the Spanish, or Southern, Netherlands (present-day Belgium). This territory was a province of the new Spanish King, and Louis XIV, urged on by his military engineer genius, Marshal Vauban, felt compelled to occupy those same towns with French troops, ostensibly on behalf of his grandson. This he did in February 1701, and the Dutch took both alarm and offence at the move, and had to negotiate with the French to obtain the release of the interned Dutch garrisons. Earnest diplomatic efforts continued, to avert a new war, although it seems that William III, King of England and Dutch Stadtholder, knew in advance of Louis XIV's intentions and kept the information to himself, apparently quite content that trouble between the French and the States-General should be the result. William did, however, complain in a letter to Parliament: 'For twenty-eight years I have tried unceasingly to preserve this barrier for the States [General of Holland] and now I have to watch it being swallowed up in one day without a single blow being struck.' The Dutch garrison commanders had yielded the towns rather quickly when summoned to do so, but Maastricht was different, and the Governor there resolutely refused to admit the French, and they drew off.

Matters grew worse, for in September 1701 James II, the exiled King of England, was dying. 'That unhappy prince's troubles' as John Evelyn said in his diary 'were at an end.' Louis XIV stood at the death bed, and told his old friend that he considered his son, the Chevalier de St George, to be the rightful heir to the throne in London. Louis XIV was almost certainly overcome with the emotion of the moment and spoke incautiously, but this clumsy acknowledgement of the Pretender by the French monarch was yet another infringement of the Barrier Treaties, and great offence was taken in London; the Duc de Tallard, the subtly skilful French Ambassador, was promptly expelled. It seemed to all concerned that, despite the assurances to the contrary, mighty France was once again intent on becoming an intolerable threat to her neighbours, and something would have to be done to curtail her power.

During this tense period, William III negotiated a Treaty of Grand Alliance between England, the States-General of Holland and Imperial Austria, to try and limit what was seen as the burgeoning ambition of Louis XIV. The treaty was concluded on 7 September 1701; John Churchill, the 51-year old Earl of Marlborough (as he still was at this time) signed for England. Five days later Louis XIV learned the details of the treaty from the Swedish Ambassador to London. In one of his addresses to Parliament in London, William had set out the threat, both real and imagined, which resulted from the recent extension into the Spanish Empire of France's power and influence:

> By the French King's placing his grandson on the throne of Spain, he is in a condition to oppress the rest of Europe, unless speedy and effectual measures be taken. Under this pretence he is become the master of the whole Spanish Monarchy; he has made it to be entirely depending on France, and disposes of it as his own dominions; and by that means he has

surrounded his neighbours in such a manner, that though the name of peace may be said to continue, yet they are put to the expense and inconveniences of war. This must affect England in the nearest and most sensible manner ... it is fit I should tell you, the eyes of all Europe are upon this parliament.

Parliament, although always suspicious of both the risk and the cost of foreign entanglements, was convinced and moved by the King's frank speech. The necessary funds were voted to the put the army and navy, so recently and imprudently reduced to slender peacetime strength, on a war footing.

William III died after a riding accident at Hampton Court the following spring. Donald McBane, a rascally grenadier serving with Orkney's Regiment, was in camp in Holland at the time and remembered that 'We hear the sad news of the death of King William.' The King was mourned less by those who did not appreciate his soldierly qualities. His sister-in-law the Princess Anne, James II's youngest daughter, came to the throne: 'A bright day, and everyone much pleased and satisfied' as John Evelyn remembered. England once again had an English monarch. The new Queen proved to be just as resolute as her deceased Dutch brother-in-law, and she wrote to encourage and reassure the Elector Palatinate and the Directors of the Imperial Circle of the Upper Rhine, on 17 March 1702:

> Doubtless, very well known to your Highnesses Elect is the ancient and insatiable desire of the French King to dominate; notorious are the wrongs, the cunning and the fraud by which he is scheming to aggrandise the limits of his empire until satiated. Indeed, when we consider his grandson, quite recently thrust upon Spanish soil, the sanctity of the Imperial oath with regard to the Succession, so often and so solemnly confirmed, now forsworn, the faith of treaties despised, the provinces of the Spanish Netherlands occupied with arms, the Duchy of Milan likewise besieged, and also the very bulwark of the Empire usurped by force and fraud – these sufficiently and completely demonstrate how formidable an enemy threatens the lives of all, and to what straits not only peace and tranquility, but also the public liberty, has been reduced. When, moreover, we see that the Kingdom of France is about to unite with the Spanish Indies, and both to be governed wholly by the will and counsel of one person.

This was overstating things to a certain degree, but the new Queen was at pains to ensure that her allies, and the French, should know that the resolve to confront Louis XIV was quite as firm as that under King William.

Meanwhile, France too was preparing for war, and Louis XIV began a rapid expansion of the army, with more than 100 new regiments being raised; some, it must be said, of rather questionable quality. Commands and commissions were liberally dispensed to the courtiers and half-pay officers who clamoured at Court, but the Duc de St Simon, whose own regiment had been broken up at the close of the wars in the late 1690s, was to be disappointed:

Some colonels junior to myself were given back their commands, but this seemed only reasonable, since they were all veterans, who had obtained their appointments through length of service ... My whole heart was set on having a regiment and commanding it in the campaign that was about to open, so as to avoid the humiliation of acting as a kind of supernumerary aide-de-camp ... the general promotion [appointment of new commands] was made at last and everyone was astonished at the length of the list. As I eagerly searched through the names of the new cavalry brigadiers, vainly hoping to find my own, I was humiliated to see five of my juniors included in the list.

With no notion of why he had been excluded, St Simon could not contain his bitterness and resigned from the army. 'I wrote a short letter to the King, not in any way complaining, not mentioning my disappointment, nor even hinting at regiments and promotions, but merely regretting that my health obliged me to leave his service.' He thus incurred the displeasure of the King, who commented tartly 'here we have another deserter.' Although he continued to serve at Court, St Simon was cast rather into the shadows, but his wife remained favoured and the couple retained the entrée to the royal circle.

War was declared on France simultaneously by England, Holland and Austria on 15 May 1702. Marlborough was appointed Captain-General and Commander in Chief of Queen Anne's armies. He was also made commander of the Dutch armies when on campaign (although this caused some resentment in Holland). This friction with the Dutch was smoothed over, due in great measure to the confidence that they had in Marlborough; he had largely negotiated the terms of the Treaty of Grand Alliance with them, and they were used to his ways, and trusted his abilities. Soon after the Earl arrived in the Low Countries, the Dutch confirmed his appointment. Adam Cardonnel, his secretary, wrote in a postscript to a letter sent to the Earl of Nottingham on 1 July 1702 'The States [General] have given directions to all their generals and other officers to obey my Lord Marlborough as their general.'

Over-shadowing all of Marlborough's campaigns – some of them the most stunningly successful in all military history – was his own increasing ill-health. At 52 years of age at the outbreak of the war, he was getting to be an old man by the standards of the time. An instance of the Earl's own appreciation of his physical infirmity is seen in a letter sent to his good friend the Lord Treasurer, Sidney Godolphin, a year or so after his appointment as the Captain-General, while attempting to pursue an effective military campaign against the French amidst all the procrastination and objections of the Dutch: 'My eyes are so extremely sore with the dust and the want of rest for these two days, that it is very great trouble to me to write ... I am almost mad with the headache.' Despite such fatigue and recurrent migraines, the Earl had a great capacity for hard work and could apply brilliant attention to small detail. His never-failing urbanity of manner when dealing with both high and low around him, and ability to focus on the task in hand while never losing sight of what lay in wait on the far horizon, was stunningly effective through the years of turmoil and war that lay ahead.

Chapter Two

There Was Once a War – A Glimpse at the Eyewitnesses

The quite wide range of journals, diaries and reminiscences that are available, show how very literate many soldiers were in the armies that took part in the War of the Spanish Succession. This is not at all surprising among the officers and noblemen who went on campaign, for they were plainly educated men; but the non-commissioned officer and the private soldier, wielding a musket in the ranks, are also well represented, although a number of these, such as the Hampshire farm labourer, Thomas Kitcher, recounted their stories after the war to others; in his particular case to the rector of the parish where he had returned to live after his campaigning days were over. The memoir, the 'memory' of the soldier of the adventures which befell them, whether stationed high or low, is the backbone of this book. Reminiscences of camp life, the labours of the hot and dusty march, the terror and exhilaration of the day of battle, the rigour of being under the surgeon's knife, the daily details of feeding, clothing and moving an army, all make absorbing reading. Often the most intriguing details come out of accounts, not of the soldiers riding the lightning in the battle-line, but when embroiled with their families and camp followers in the homely drudgery of life in camp and on the march.

The letters and official correspondence of senior officers provide a mine of valuable detail and information. Prominent among these are *The Letters and Despatches of the Duke of Marlborough*. Fifty-two years old at the outbreak of the war, John Churchill, as Queen Anne's close friend, adviser and Captain-General of her armies, oversaw the enormous military and, to a significant degree, the diplomatic effort of England (Great Britain from 1707 onwards) throughout most of the conflict for the throne of Spain. In so many ways, this was Marlborough's war. Major campaigns, expensive in men, money and materiel alike, took place in the Tyrol, Spain, Portugal and Italy, on the Rhine frontier, in the Balearic islands, in the Caribbean, on the high seas and, latterly, in north America; but the army led by the Duke, in the Low Countries and in Bavaria (for a short season), was the epicentre of the Allied effort to limit the power of France. Marlborough was not only the Captain-General for England, he was also field commander of the Dutch armies, and as such he had under his hand the ground forces of the two main powers in the Grand Alliance. At the same time, he conducted, almost single-handedly, the foreign policy of Queen Anne and her governments, often turning aside from the reeking field of battle to attend to some princeling or potentate whose continued support for the war effort against France had to be secured or nurtured, or whose ruffled feelings, over some imagined slight, had to be smoothed over. On a larger scale, Marlborough fostered the continuance of good relations, by and large, between the awkward Dutch and the devious Imperial court in Vienna. He also persuaded the mercurial and exceptionally dangerous warrior king, Charles XII of Sweden, to stay out of the war, a strategic coup of enormous worth.

The Letters and Despatches, a monumental and immensely valuable work, are taken from fair-hand copies of the Duke's original correspondence, found by chance in a storage chest in Blenheim Palace, then edited by General George Murray (a stalwart of the Duke of Wellington's campaigns), and published in 1845. They are indispensable for the student of Marlborough's campaigns. It is immediately apparent what a mass of detail, often quite minor, the Duke had to attend to on a daily basis; he might turn from drafting a letter to Queen Anne or their 'High Mightinesses', the States-General of Holland, announcing the successful result of a great clash of arms, to dictating a note to a junior officer concerning the manner of escorting prisoners along a hazardous stretch of road, or urging one of his generals to have a particular care for the horses, as forage was likely to be hard to find on the road ahead. On occasion, Marlborough was engaged in the diplomatic courtesies, exchanged between senior officers in the opposing armies, which made life a little more comfortable while on campaign. Although reading very strangely today, such civilities enabled generals to move relatively freely about, secure from the danger of being snapped up by an enemy patrol while on the road. In October 1703, the Duke wrote to his nephew, the Duke of Berwick, from his camp at Alderbeesten:

> I take this opportunity of returning the pass, to repeat my wishes for your good journey, and should be glad in the mean time, if you think it proper, and not otherwise, that you should desire the Marechal de Villeroi to give me a pass for twenty pieces [casks] of burgundy or champagne to come to Huy or Liege.

Always, hanging over the Duke's head, was the need to encourage the hearts, stiffen the resolve and allay the fears of politicians in both London and the Hague. Soon after the breakdown of apparently promising peace negotiations early in 1709, at a time when bitterly fought siege operations were daily in progress, and costing the lives of many of his veteran soldiers, the Duke wrote 'I wish that the whole House of Commons took their turn at the citadel of Tournai. I am apt to believe they would be much tamer creatures when they came back again.'

Much of the Duke's correspondence is, of necessity, of a formal and, to modern eyes, long-winded nature. That was the custom of the time, and flowery compliments and lengthy descriptive passages were what was expected.

His competent and urbane manner, in addition to an eye for detail, shines through, and the letters sent to close friends, such as the Lord Treasurer, Sidney Godolphin, or his beloved wife, Duchess Sarah, are warm and intimate. *The Letters and Despatches* do not, regrettably, very often contain the replies to the Duke's correspondence, and so we can see only one half of the picture; but what a vivid picture it is all the same, and with good reason free use has been made of these papers in preparing this book. Occasionally, however, it is possible to find letters of reply and instruction from Queen Anne to her Captain-General; often these are written in her own handwriting 'All my strange scrawls' as she would modestly describe them. Her concern for Marlborough is evident, as in her reply to the momentous news of the victory at Blenheim in the high summer of 1704: 'The good news Colonel Parke brought me yesterday was very welcome, but not more, I do assure you, than hearing you are well.' Even when their friendship had cooled, and Marlborough was very ill-advisedly pressing the Queen to make him Captain-General for life, her letters to him remained courteous and her refusals, when so inevitably given, were phrased as to spare the feelings of her old friend, as far as was possible.

The tale of Marlborough's wars from a far humbler British perspective is to be found in *A Journal of Marlborough's Campaigns During the War of the Spanish Succession 1704–1711*, the day to day journal of John Marshall Deane, a private 'centinell' in Her Majesty's 1st English Foot Guards. This valuable work, evidently written by an educated man with some, slightly archaic, literary ability, was known as the 'Hunter Journal' and came to the attention of the Society of Army Historical Research in the 1970s. David Chandler undertook to edit the journal, and this was then published by the Society in 1984 as SAHR Special Publication No.12. Copies are scarce, but can be found with diligent searching, and give an intriguing insight into the life on campaign of the foot soldier in Marlborough's time. Deane's account of the battles in which he participated is sketchy; this is not surprising, as the common soldier's view of what was going on during a teeming battle is understandably limited, and he is to be commended for not 'inventing' what he did not actually see in order to embellish his tale, a temptation that others, on certain occasions, seem to have been unable to resist. Deane's ability to record quite minor detail is valuable, throwing light on events that are otherwise made murky with the passage of time. It can be seen, for example, that at least one British battalion, his own, approached the battle at Oudenarde in July 1708 through the town itself, rather than by using the pontoon bridges laid over the Scheldt earlier in the day. This was no doubt expedient, but Marlborough's inability to complete the destruction of the French right Wing at the battle was due to in large part to Overkirk's failure in getting his Dutch and Danish corps into place in good time. They, too, had to use the route through Oudenarde town, and if they had to share that road, as Deane states, with British troops trying to get into position in the line along the Diepenbeek and Marollebeek streams, then, perhaps, the Veldt-Marshal's delay is more understandable than is otherwise the case.

The Irish marching captain, Robert Parker, whose *Memoirs* appeared in the 1740s and were republished (together with those of the Comte de Merode-Westerloo – see below) in 1968, also have a rather dry flavour to them. This does not detract from the value of the reminiscences, although the rather portly veteran in the well-known portrait of the captain gives few clues as to the nature of the man as a dashing young officer, making his way in an uncertain world. Parker's service with the Royal Irish Regiment took him, under William III, to the storm of Namur and the carnage of Landen; then, with the Great Duke, to the triumphs of Blenheim, Ramillies and Oudenarde; so he was witness to monumental events. Parker's accounts are not by any means always dull, as when he describes the manoeuvres to try and catch the French on the heaths of Peer in 1702:

> Both armies were drawn up on a large heath, within less than half an English mile of each other, and it was thought impossible for us to part without blows. The cannon on both sides fired with great fury, and killed a number of men. Here I narrowly escaped a cannon-ball, which I plainly saw coming directly to me, but by stepping nimbly aside, had the good fortune to escape it.

A great admirer of Marlborough, as were most of his comrades, Parker wrote of the bitterness and consternation in the army at the Duke's dismissal. He goes on to complain of the numbering system allotted to the regiments that survived to serve on at the end of the war, feeling that the Royal Irish should have been given a more senior number than the 18th. This was of particular importance to the officers of the regiment, as the disbanding of units would affect the higher (and therefore more junior) numbered regiments first; unemployment and destitution would result. Parker missed the battle of Malplaquet in 1709, as he was in Ireland at that time at the request of Lieutenant-General Ingoldsby, on recruiting and training duties. His colleagues recounted to him their experience in the battle, and he wrote in detail of the close-range contest in those awful woods between the Royal Irish and their émigré Roman Catholic countrymen serving with the French-recruited Régiment Royal d'Irlandaise, when the superior firepower and musketry techniques of the British regiment prevailed.

Another stalwart in the ranks of Marlborough's army was Donald McBane, whose salty, and often rather disreputable, memoirs were published in Edinburgh in 1728, as part of his treatise on fencing techniques: *The Expert Swordsman's Companion*. While some memoirists and diarists of the time can be said to be a little dry in their tone, this charge cannot be levelled at McBane, who tells a racy story, spiced with entertaining anecdotes and exciting events. It is tempting to think that he embellishes his story rather too much, assuming for himself a more prominent part in the events than might be truly the case. However this may be, much of his tale has the ring of truth, whether in minor, but bloody, skirmishes with French dragoons while out on patrol, engaged in throwing hand grenades for eight hours without a pause during the storming of a breach, or recounting the seamier side of life to be found when in camp. McBane was not bashful in describing activities in which he took part, such as his involvement in running one of the many brothels which accompanied the Allied army, and the rather cavalier way in which he treated the girls he employed: 'They stripped our wives and sent them to us. Many of us would rather they had kept them'. As a noted swordsman he was not slow to pick fights, often for a large wager, with those he knew to be less skilled with the blade than himself, and thus was able to profit from the unequal encounter. He comes across as rather an unpleasant character, but he was a veteran soldier, wounded and left for dead at Blindheim village in 1704, and a valuable witness to those stirring times. Soldiers are not required to have engaging personalities and charming manners, and McBane's account of his life in Marlborough's army, for all its rather sordid content, is a valuable original resource.

The story of the Irish-woman Mrs Christian (or Catherine) Davies, Christian Walsh/Welsh or Mother Ross (as she was variously known) is intriguing. Enlisting in the army in order to follow her errant husband, who had sauntered out for a drink one day and never come back, having 'gone for a soldier', this intrepid female masqueraded successfully as a man for some twelve years, serving through many campaigns, until receiving a head wound at Ramillies in 1706. She then served on as a sutleress with the army until demobilised at the end of the War of the Spanish Succession in 1713. Her lively reminiscences, thought at one time to have been related to Daniel Defoe when she was an elderly in-pensioner at the Royal Hospital in Chelsea, contain considerable embellishment and padding, apparently thought necessary for a 'history' of her services. Some of this is tedious stuff, leading to the suspicion that this is, in fact, a work of pure Defoe fiction, a sort of military *Moll Flanders*. This is not, on examination, really credible, as Defoe would have made a better job of a plain fictitious work. The eminent military historian, Sir John Fortescue, accepted their worth when he edited the 1929 version *The Life and Adventures of Mrs Christian Davies, commonly called Mother Ross*. In any case, Kit Davies undoubtedly existed, and certainly served as a soldier – she was granted a pension, and admitted to the Royal Hospital in Chelsea on 19 November 1717: 'A jolly, fat breasted woman, received several wounds in the service, in the habit of a man.' In time she was buried with full military honours and her tale, while undeniably lurid in parts, has much that is plausible about it. Her memory of minor events, the officers with whom she served, and the various exploits to which her adventurous nature led her rings very true, as in the case of the subaltern who fouled his pants in fright during a siege late on in the war 'and never recovered his reputation'.

Any account of the war for Spain would be curiously incomplete without some telling of the arduous and hazardous soldiering and desperate battles fought on the peninsula itself. These, in a strict sense, are not Marlborough's campaigns, as the Duke never went there, although the thought occurred to him more than once that he should do so. However, an anonymous private soldier, serving with Raby's (The Royal) Dragoons, left an extensive and informative account of his service in Spain. This work was published as *A Royal Dragoon in the Peninsular War*, and edited by C.T. Atkinson for the Society of Army Historical Research in 1936. It provides us with a fascinating account, from a plain soldier's view, of life in those terrible campaigns, scorched by the fierce sun in summer and frozen by the Iberian frosts of winter, in a way that would be familiar to many of the soldiers in the Duke of Wellington's army a hundred years or so later. Once again, as with John Deane, the rather odd grammar used by this soldier can occasionally be disconcerting, but his tale of this far-off campaign is both entertaining and illuminating of the hardships endured by the common soldier in camp, on the march to victory at Saragossa, or, following the calamity at Brihuega, when held in *durance vile* as a prisoner of war. Among other things, we see the privation that had to be endured, and the extraordinary patience that had to be employed, when taking ship to cross to the Iberian peninsula 'On Saturday the 30 of August 1703 we went on board the *Samuel* ... on 13 March we landed at Belem.' The condition of the troops (their horses did not, perhaps fortunately, accompany them) on at last setting foot on dry land, after seven months on board ship, may well be imagined.

Another campaigner in Spain to leave an account of his exploits was Captain George Villiers Carleton, whose *Military Memoirs* were originally published in 1727. He was a great admirer of the Earl of Peterborough, the brilliant and erratic English commander in chief during the early years of the war in Valencia and Catalonia, and much of his account comprises a eulogy of his patron's apparent qualities and achievements. Charles III, the Habsburg claimant, and the Huguenot Earl of Galway, who commanded for Queen Anne in Portugal (both of whom were thoroughly glad to see the back of Peterborough when he was recalled), may well have taken exception to some of Carleton's rather uncritical comments. Still, Sir Walter Scott, who composed an erudite introduction for 1830 reprint of the memoirs, wrote that Carleton's account was 'Plain and soldier-like, without any pretence or ornament' and this is so. His story of the brutal guerrilla campaign waged by the largely unsympathetic population of Aragon and Castile against the Allied soldiers is graphic and horrifying, with an unmistakable off-hand ring of truth. It is interesting that one modern author, who left an otherwise very useful account of the Spanish wars between the two young kings and their proxies, stated that the memoirs were a work of fiction, but then went on to quote from them all the same. Well, it is not possible to have things both ways, when choosing sources from which to quote, and there is no doubt that Carleton, who was born in Oxfordshire in 1652, served in Spain with Peterborough as a volunteer, in the capacity of an engineer officer, having been cashiered early in the century after forcing a duel on a junior officer, contrary to standing orders.

Both Carleton's reminiscences and those of the anonymous dragoon of the Raby's Dragoons, allow us an insight into this arid and thankless theatre of war, far from the glory of the campaigns waged by the Duke of Marlborough in Germany and the Low Countries. The luckless soldiers who strove in the cause of Charles III were kept short of money, supplies, ammunition and reinforcements, and led by commanders who chose, as often as not, to argue among themselves when not engaging in combat with opponents who were able to deploy greater resources, and more finely developed skills, than they themselves could muster. In this particular connection, it is worth pausing to comment that the Duke of Marlborough, when at the height of his power and influence, and while pressing that such a campaign must proceed, failed to ensure that the Allied effort in Spain was properly financed, provisioned and manned. This must count against him as one of his few strategic errors.

At least of equal interest, and possibly more, than the tales of the soldiers who fought in Marlborough's armies, are the memoirs left by those who served Louis XIV. These soldiers were by no means always French, as the complicated political landscape of the time obliged many men to seek their fortune with their swords, and in the service of a foreign monarch. This was not looked down upon, or considered, as it would be to later generations, as treachery, as long as the service was regular, properly recorded, and done in the open. Little mercy was shown to spies and informers, and sometimes to deserters, if an example was thought necessary to be made – as recorded by the dragoon in Spain who saw ten men face the firing squad in one day, or when Donald McBane wrote of the daily hanging of deserters from the Allied army.

In this way, 'Captain' Peter Drake, an impoverished and exiled Irishman of Roman Catholic persuasion (and thus unable to secure a commission with the army of Queen Anne), was able to seek his fortune as a gentleman volunteer in one of the Jacobite Irish regiments in the service of France. His rather verbose *Memoirs* were published in 1755, and edited and republished in 1960 with the title *Amiable Renegade – The Memoirs of Captain Peter Drake*. Among other exploits, he heard the gunfire coming across the fields from the fight at Elixheim in 1705, while marching to re-enlist in the French army. He was able to write vividly of the chaos that engulfed the French and Bavarian armies at Ramillies in May 1706, and of the headlong and panic-stricken flight from the field of battle of Marshal Villeroi's forces. When it suited Drake, though (usually in winter), he switched his allegiance and went back home; once actually taking up a career as a privateer on the high seas. In this venture he did not prosper, and he was convicted of piracy in 1708, in London. Drake managed to talk his way out of trouble, so that, by autumn 1709, he was able to fight in the ranks of the French Maison du Roi cavalry at the murderous battle of Malplaquet, where he was severely wounded and soon afterwards met the Duke of Marlborough, who ordered that his injuries be tended to. Drake's graphic account of how his wounds were treated by the surgeons makes grim reading, but he survived. He subsequently took service in the Duke's army, and wrote with bitter feeling of the suffering of the troops in the seemingly interminable siege operations, which often attended the latter campaigns in the war.

Colonel Jean-Martin De La Colonie, born a younger son of the minor French nobility, was, like so many of his kind, to try and make his fortune as a soldier. His memoirs were first published in 1737, but were edited, sympathetically translated and republished in 1904 by Walter Horsley, under the title *The Chronicles of An Old Campaigner*. De La Colonie had learned his trade in the Cadet Company at Charlemont, and, despite a terrible inclination to take easy offence and fight duels with his brother officers, he was in action at both Landen and Namur in the Williamite wars. He survived these, and the duels, to be able to tell of an adventurous life as an officer of dragoons, before being seconded to the Bavarian army shortly after the outbreak of the War of the Spanish Succession. De La Colonie was given the command of the Grenadiers Rouge, a rather mixed bag of French, Italian and Savoyard deserters who sought to avoid the noose or the firing squad by offering to serve on, in what might at a later date be termed a penal battalion: 'This kind of regiment was not always a success, owing to the difficulty of keeping the men in hand.' Despite such unpromising material – De La Colonie was occasionally at his wits' end to how to keep them in good order; he repeatedly comments on their lack of discipline, and their inclination to maraud and plunder whenever the chance arose – time, firm handling and good training had their effect, and the grenadiers eventually proved to be sturdy fighters, highly regarded, and as good as any that the French could put in the line of battle.

De La Colonie was present at the Schellenberg fight in 1704, and his account of the fighting, and the panic that gripped the defenders on the hill as Baden's Imperial troops swept in from an unprotected flank, is among the best and most graphic to be found. The Colonel missed the battle of Blenheim, his reconstituted regiment being in garrison at the time. As a participant he was able to describe the scrambled fighting for the small village of Taviers, the loss of which unhinged the right flank of Marshal Villeroi's army at Ramillies in May 1706: 'I shouted every epithet I could think of to my grenadiers, I seized the colonel's colour; planted it by me … I gradually rallied my French grenadiers and several companies of the Cologne Regiment … very much shaken.' His comment on the closing hours of the dramatic encounter battle at Oudenarde, two years later, are particularly interesting, as his regiment evidently held their position well into the early hours of the following morning, indicating that the French army did not flee away from the field of battle that night in quite the indecent haste that is so often reported. De La Colonie's account of the desperate fighting in the woods at Malplaquet in 1709 also illustrates the danger that Marshal Villars ran, and at which the Colonel protested in vain, when stripping his infantry away from the centre of the French army to bolster his left flank, as Henry Wither's surprise attack came pounding in across the cornfields at La Folie farm. The closing chapters of the memoirs give an account of De La Colonie's later career when, once again in the Bavarian service, he took part in the victorious campaign against the Turks at Belgrade in 1717. He then returned to France, where his apparently numerous and impecunious relatives lost no time in looking to him for support and assistance.

Eugene-Jean-Philippe, the Comte de Merode-Westerloo, was a Walloon nobleman who valiantly served his sovereign lord, the King of Spain, in whatever guise, Habsburg or Bourbon, that the monarch should appear. So, his earlier memoirs of the war find him in the service of Philip V, taking an active part with Tallard's cavalry in the Blenheim campaign. However, after the victory at Ramillies, when virtually the whole of the Spanish Netherlands thought it timely to declare for Archduke Charles, Merode-Westerloo changed his own allegiance. This was perfectly legitimate, and the Comte had, in fact, resigned his commission under Philip V before the battle took place. Misunderstandings did occasionally occur over such transfers of allegiance, as when the Comte had to rescue some of his missing troopers from the noose; a French officer, who had captured the men, mistakenly thought they had not been legally remustered into the service of the Austrian claimant. The Comte's memoirs make very entertaining reading; the keen sense of his own worth, and his acid tongue, contrast nicely with the perfectly frank accounts of his adventures when he, at times, cuts a rather ridiculous figure – as when he was trampled into the mud by his own soldiers at the battle of Eckeren in 1703, or on the famous occasion when he was raised from his slumbers on the morning of 13 August 1704, to see from his own camp bed that the Allied cavalry were pouring out onto the plain of Höchstädt.

As an officer of some rank and standing, Merode-Westerloo was familiar with many of the senior commanders in the armies, and we get a useful picture from him of the higher direction of the war, although the Comte is always at pains to stress his own valuable contribution to events. His advice was not always appreciated, as can be seen from the scant regard given by Marlborough to his perfectly valid warning that Ghent and Bruges were to be surprised by the Duc de Vendôme in the summer of 1708. Merode-Westerloo was careful, also, to stress the acute personal cost of the service he provided, as after Blenheim, when he bemoaned that 'Since the battle I had lost more than sixty horses, all my baggage had been burned; my personal expenditure during the campaign had been frightful.' Eventually he was made a Field-Marshal of the Empire and a member of the Supreme War Council, but he seems to have done little active campaigning in the later years of the war. His unfinished *Memoires de Feld-Maréchal Comte de Merode-Westerloo* (the Comte dropped dead in mid-sentence in 1732) were first published by his great-grandson in Brussels in 1840. These were translated and edited by David Chandler, and republished in *The Marlborough Wars* in 1968, as a companion to the Captain Robert Parker memoirs.

Louis de Rouvroy, Duc de St Simon, was born in 1675, and became a keen observer of the goings on at the court of Louis XIV, whether at Fontainebleau or Versailles. His diaries were translated and edited in 1876 by Bayle St John as *The Memoirs of the Duke of St Simon*. In 1958 an abbreviated version was published by Lucy Norton, but she omitted much of the military content. St Simon was a witty writer with a sharp and very often sarcastic tongue, and his temper was not improved by being denied the command of a regiment, without explanation from the King, at the commencement of the war. The Duc had fought well in the Williamite wars towards the end of the seventeenth century, so his exclusion from command by the King was, and always remained, a mystery. He had written of the fighting near Neerwinden in 1693: 'We attacked at dawn the Prince of Orange (William III), and after twelve hours, entirely routed him. I was of the 3rd squadron of the Royal Rousillion Régiment, and made five charges.' St Simon was well acquainted with the senior officers in the French army – Tallard, Marsin, Catinat, Boufflers, Villeroi, Villars – while having a particular dislike for the boorish Duc de Vendôme . His favourites received his unstinting support, and these preferences do shine through his otherwise erudite accounts of those days.

Rather unkindly described by a later commentator as a drone at the French court, St Simon was in fact a keen and talented observer of the glittering scene around him. His sharp tongue, and perfect inability to keep it under control, brought St Simon into repeated disfavour with Louis XIV, who did not appreciate his barbed comments. The King tolerated him though, as he had a fondness for the rather skittish Duchess, and the reminiscences of St Simon are an interesting, topical and remarkably frank resource from the French Court, in many ways the heart of the French war effort. As an experienced soldier, his comments on the progress of the campaigns were well-informed, as with his critical description of the tactical disadvantage that the French infantry laboured under, in the opening exchanges of the fighting in the lanes and orchards in front of Oudenarde in the summer of 1708. Coming on in column, the French soldiers were confronted by Prussian infantry already in line of battle, and the time it took to sort out the resulting confusion may, in part at least, explain the inability of the French commanders to properly grip the situation at this crucial stage in the action. St Simon's later career, during the regency of Louis XV's minority (he was the great-grandson of Louis XIV), is of interest, as he was influential in securing the exclusion of the illegitimate offspring of the Sun King from the succession to the French throne.

In addition to the eyewitnesses already mentioned, I have also quoted on occasions from others, both military and civilian, where it seems that their recollections add to the story of these exciting times. In this way we find contributions from such participants as the taciturn Marshal Marsin and the stalwart Dutch Veldt-Marshal Henry of Nassau, Count Overkirk. Marlborough's chaplain, Francis Hare, left an account of the battle of Blenheim which is among the most descriptive and detailed to be found (the precise authorship of this account has been subject to some debate, with suggestions that it was, in fact, written by Josias Sandby, chaplain to Charles Churchill, Marlborough's brother and his General of Infantry). Either way, the value of this contemporary account is not in question. Samuel Noyes, another chaplain (this time with Orkney's Regiment) had a lengthy correspondence with his family, particularly useful being those accounts relating to the often ill-reported marches of the Allied armies in the earlier campaigns in the Low Countries. Marching soldier Matthew Bishop left an interesting account of his service, as did Marlborough's private secretary, Adam Cardonnel, although his heart failed him at one point in the Blenheim campaign, when he wrote: 'God grant that I may get safely out of this country.' John Millner's *Compendious Journal*, published in 1733, is full of interest, and I have also occasionally quoted from the *Memoirs* of Marlborough's nephew (by his sister Arabella and James II, when he was Duke of York), James Fitzjames, Duke of Berwick.

Almost certainly uniquely, as an English-born soldier, he rose to become a Marshal of France and was one of Louis XIV's greatest and most formidable field commanders. The magnificently named Captain Blackader wrote about his service with Fergusson's Regiment (The Cameronians) and seems to have been a rather grim character, while the private correspondence of the Marquis de Montigny-Langost contains interesting comments on the topography of the plain of Höchstädt, particularly the unexpected (and usually unreported) dryness of the Nebel stream after the hot August weather. The veteran diarist, John Evelyn, no obvious admirer of Marlborough, provides interesting comment on the social and political scene in London. The list of diarists, correspondents and memoirists that can be used is quite lengthy, but I have tried to resist the temptation to quote from too wide a range, for fear of unduly fragmenting the text. Accordingly, the bulk of the book comprises the memories and writings of a relatively few participants, some of high station, some of low, whose brief pen-portraits I have tried to give here.

It is noticeable how many of the concerns and complaints of the soldier of the 1700s are mirrored by those of the servicemen and women of today – it should be remembered that numbers of women served and fought in the ranks in Marlborough's days too. Mrs Christian Davies, for all the 'ghost-writing' of her memoirs and the sifting through her tall tales that is required, is a well-known figure, but she was by no means the only one of her kind. Marie Mouron, a French girl, served as an infantry soldier with Captain Destone's company in the Régiment de Wallonie, and subsequently absconded only to re-enlist with the Régiment de Biez. On leaving that unit too, and being apprehended by the provost-marshal, she escaped execution as a deserter on the legally nice point that she should never have been enlisted in the first place, but was gaoled for fraudulently accepting more than one enlistment bounty. Matthew Bishop, referring to the night before the awful battle at Malplaquet in September 1709, also wrote that 'A sergeant that belonged to my Lord Hartford's Regiment had a sister in the French service'. Quite how this came about can only be guessed at. Perhaps she was a sutleress rather than a *fantassin* standing in the firing line, as Kit Davies had many times done as a dragoon; but there the sister was, enlisted into the French service somehow or other.

The Duke of Marlborough was particularly fortunate to have a well-placed confidential informant in the very heart of the court of Louis XIV. This shadowy and slightly sinister individual, whose identity is not known with any certainty, passed to the Duke some hundreds of written reports during the course of the war, containing information, gossip and informed anecdotes relating to the King and his circle. This was of enormous value to the Duke as he pursued his campaigns, both military and diplomatic. However, Marlborough was as staggered as anyone at the refusal of the French to agree to terms in the appalling aftermath of the fall of Lille late in 1708, so his informant's news was, quite understandably, both limited in its scope and delayed in transmission. It is not suggested, in any way, that one of the diarists in the service of France, mentioned here, was that informant.

Chapter Three

To See the Enemy Pass – The Borders of Holland, 1702–1703

Marlborough understood the need to fight decisive battles and, early in the war when they expected to win, so too did the French Marshals who opposed him. Largely as a result of Dutch caution, understandable enough but frustrating, the years 1702 and 1703 proved to be an unproductive period for the Earl. He was unable to force an open battle on the French in the Low Countries. The general pace of military activity was by no means slow, however, and Marlborough (soon to be made a Duke for his efforts) managed to clear the line of the lower Maas and Rhine rivers, and thus gain a measure of security for Holland. The Dutch field deputies who accompanied Marlborough on campaign hamstrung his plans; the Earl was the Captain-General of the troops in English pay, and he was commander of the Dutch troops when they were in the field. The terms of his commission were such that he exercised his authority only with the continued approval of the deputies. These were cautious men, with limited horizons, concerned mostly with the safety of their southern border, and set firmly against any hazardous or unduly adventurous operations. Captain Robert Parker, of the Royal Regiment of Ireland, wrote of this arrangement:

> That wise state [Holland] always sent into the field with him, two of the most experienced of their Council of State, who were to be consulted on all occasions. They therefore sent at this time with the Lord Marlborough, the Baron de Heyd, and the Herr Guildermaison, which his lordship could not take amiss, since he knew it had been their constant practice.

The French commander in the Spanish Netherlands, Marshal Boufflers, was hampered by a lengthy and indifferent supply line. He also got the irritating news that the Dutch, under their brilliant engineer General van Coehorn, were taking the offensive against Middelburg and Bruges (thus tying down the Marquis de Bedmar's troops there). The weather was unseasonably bad but, in June 1702, the Marshal skilfully out-manoeuvred the Allied army, commanded by Ginkel, the Earl of Athlone, and a good position at Cranenberg near to Cleves was prematurely abandoned. Robert Parker wrote of Boufflers' early morning dash

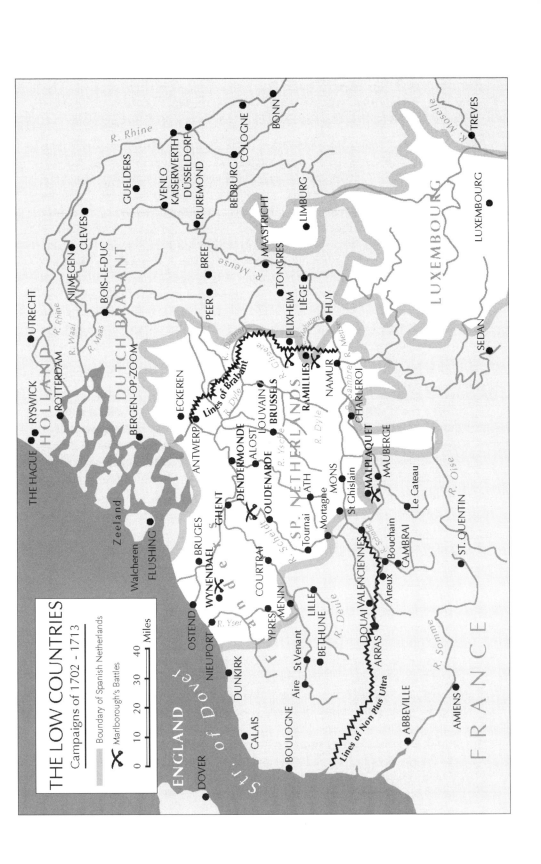

THE LOW COUNTRIES
Campaigns of 1702 - 1713

Boundary of Spanish Netherlands
✗ Marlborough's Battles

0   10   20   30   40
Miles

ENGLAND

DOVER

Str. of Dover

CALAIS

DUNKIRK

BOULOGNE

NIEUPORT

OSTEND

Walcheren

FLUSHING

Zeeland

THE HAGUE

RYSWICK

ROTTERDAM

HOLLAND

UTRECHT

R. Rhine

R. Waal

R. Maas

NIJMEGEN

CLEVES

BOIS-LE-DUC

DUTCH BRABANT

BERGEN-OP-ZOOM

ANTWERP

ECKEREN

R. Demer

Lines of Brabant

R. Dyle

BRUSSELS

LOUVAIN

R. Yssche

R. Dyle

ELIXHEIM

RAMILLIES

R. Mehaigne

NAMUR

R. Sambre

CHARLEROI

R. Meuse

HUY

LIÈGE

TONGRES

MAASTRICHT

LIMBURG

R. Meuse

ELIXHEIM

PEER

BREE

VENLO

KAISERWERTH

DÜSSELDORF

RUREMOND

GUELDERS

R. Rhine

BEDBURG

COLOGNE

BONN

LUXEMBOURG

LUXEMBOURG

SEDAN

R. Moselle

TREVES

DENDERMONDE

ALOST

SP. NETHERLANDS

ATH

R. Scheldt

OUDENARDE

GHENT

BRUGES

WYNENDAEL

Flanders

COURTRAI

MENIN

YPRES

R. Yser

LILLE

R. Deule

BETHUNE

Aire

St Venant

ARRAS

DOUAI

VALENCIENNES

Arteux

Bouchain

R. Scheldt

CAMBRAI

Le Cateau

MAUBERGE

MALPLAQUET

R. Sambre

St Ghislain

MONS

Mortagne

Tournai

R. Scheldt

Lines of Non Plus Ultra

FRANCE

R. Deule

ST. QUENTIN

R. Oise

AMIENS

R. Somme

ABBEVILLE

that 'By daylight the enemy's horse began to appear on both sides of us. This made us mend our pace.' Marlborough's nephew, the Duke of Berwick, who was serving with Boufflers at this time, wrote of the pursuit of Athlone's troops:

> The enemy retired in good order, until they came within about cannon shot of Nijmegen, where they made a show of standing their ground, supported by some infantry they had thrown into the houses, and behind the hedges. Our cavalry then ranged itself in order of battle; and the battalions of the enemy having in the mean time thrown themselves into the covered way, their cavalry posted itself on the glacis. Our infantry then coming up, we approached them within musket shot, and we might have charged their cavalry at this instant; but this was not done, of which I know not the reason. Some cannon was brought forward, which was fired upon them, without disturbing them in the least; but at length our grenadiers advancing within pistol shot, they broke their ranks, and the cannon of the place now firing upon us, and molesting us very much, we retired out of reach.

Berwick went on to comment on the hectic nature of the French pursuit of the disordered Allied army as it scampered from Cleves to Nijmegen:

> It is a thing without example, that an army should have pursued another for two leagues, and should have driven it into the covered way of a fortification, almost without striking a stroke. It may be wondered at that we did not charge them, having been so long in sight; but military men will readily comprehend, that in a flat country, without ditch, ravine or rivulet, it is not an easy matter to come to a defile, and moreover the infantry was not yet arrived.

Donald McBane, a noted swordsman serving in Orkney's Regiment who had complained of 'A heavy snowfall' some weeks earlier in the campaign, wrote now with feeling about the scrambled retreat of the Allied army as the French cavalry advanced:

> We were attacked by the French, likewise they endeavoured to get betwixt Nijmegen and our army, which obliged us to march all night until we came in sight of the town, then we halted a little time upon our arms, then we espied sixty squadrons of the French horse and dragoons, commanded by the Duke of Berwick, upon this Lord Cutts drew up his army upon the top of an hill in order to fight them, Boufflers who commanded the French Foot fell behind, in which time the Dutch General called for my Lord Athlone where my Lord Cutts was, he asked them what they were minded to do? Cutts answered with courage bold, he was willing to fight, my Lord, says he, you have too many to lose, and too few to fight for which reason I desire you to make the best of your way with the army, until you get under the walls of the town. He obeyed orders; he left several companies of grenadiers to guard the rear, my Lord Orkney's

company of Royal Grenadiers was one, in which I was one: The French horse pursuing so hard, we were obliged to get in to the walls, but the cannon playing upon the French horse obliged us to lay down, until the cannon stopped a little. The French tarried until their Foot and Train came up, we retired under the pallisades of the town, by this time, our baggage and wives were all taken by the French horse; then they raised a battery and cannonaded us very hard, one of the balls carried away the half of my cape and half of my gun, but I received no more damage.

McBane, who ran a profitable sideline selling drink to his comrades, and was not above acting as a pimp as well, wrote rather callously of the fate of his 'wife' during this affair: 'They continued their cannon firing upon us until the next day, then they stripped our wives and sent them to us, many of us would rather they had kept them.'

One of the soldiers facing McBane across the field that day was Peter Drake, an exiled Irish Roman Catholic soldier of fortune, now in the service of the French King as a gentleman volunteer. He would fight for whoever was willing to pay his wages, so much in arrears was the pay of the French army at this particular time. Drake was not slow to spot an opportunity however, and wrote that:

I was an eye-witness to this engagement, and the advantage fell to the French, having driven the confederates army to the gates of Nijmegen. At my return towards Cleves after the battle, I perceived numbers of marauders running in and out of a castle [chateau] about a half a mile distant from me. Thither I sped in hopes of meeting something to my advantage, and found several soldiers returning loaded with plunder. I entered, but could discover nothing worthwhile. There were indeed many sacks of corn, but that was neither valuable, nor easily portable. However, I took out my knife, and cut a sack of wheat from top to bottom, from which proceeded a leather bag. This I lifted unperceived of any, and marched off, thinking my fortune made, for it was bulky as well as heavy. I repaired straight to my quarters at Cleves, and opening my bag, found, to my great surprise, but a hundred silver ducatoons, value about five shillings and ten pence each, near thirty pounds sterling, a pretty good bounty but much inferior to my expectation.

Despite his very obvious disappointment at not making his fortune that day, the silver must have been a very welcome addition to Drake's soldierly lean purse.

Now, penned into Nijmegen, the Allied army faced a sorry fate unless something was done. An officer in Meredith's Regiment, frustrated at the lack of drive in the Allied campaign so far, wrote at this point 'It was not worth the coming. I could have better put my time in the granary at home.' The Earl of Marlborough arrived from the Hague soon afterwards to take the field command. Athlone was, not surprisingly, rather affronted at being passed over by an Englishman who, by many estimates, had less experience in war.

However, the Earl's easy charm won the crusty old Dutch veteran around in time; Athlone wrote candidly: 'The success of this campaign is solely due to this incomparable Commander in Chief, since I confess that I, serving as second-in-command, opposed in all circumstances his opinions and proposals.' Athlone proved a good subordinate, and his death a few months later was a blow to Marlborough.

The French had now outrun their supplies in their enthusiasm to crowd the Anglo-Dutch back towards their own border, and while this lack was being remedied, Boufflers put his army into the area around Cleves. An Imperial army was laying siege to the Marquis de Blainville in Kaiserswerth, and the Marshal was urged by Louis XIV to save so important a fortress, but it fell on 15 June, despite the earnest efforts of the Duc de Tallard, who was sent to save the place. In the meantime, Marlborough was building the strength of his army, which was soon 60,000 men strong, slightly more numerous than the French army opposed to it. Boufflers now began an attempt to manoeuvre to intercept Marlborough's communications and lines of supply with Holland, by occupying the town of Eindhoven. Berwick described the action that followed, as French cavalry chanced upon a large and inviting Allied convoy, trundling forward on its way to the Allied camp:

> I learned on my arrival [at Eindhoven] that a considerable convoy was set out from Bois-le-Duc, and I saw M. de Tilly coming from the Allied army to meet it. Instead of making the convoy pass on the other side of the Aa [river], he encamped openly on the heath of Goldorp, the distance of a league and a quarter from my camp. He had about thirty squadrons and twelve battalions. At ten o'clock in the evening, I sent to acquaint Marshal Boufflers of this, and at the same time proposed to him to order the left wing of the army to join me; by means of which we might fall upon M. de Tilly at day-break. The courier did not deliver my letter until four o'clock in the morning, so that the left wing could not begin its march until six. The Marshal having arrived, did not think it proper to attack, being apprehensive that the enemy's army might march straight to Eindhoven, while we were engaged with M. de Tilly.

So, the opportunity to snatch this rich prize, with the potential to inflict a serious setback on Marlborough's plans, was lost, to Berwick's great irritation. The younger man had no doubt that the convoy could have been taken, with Tilly's escort dispersed, and the French safely back in their encampment before Marlborough could react to the sudden attack. Boufflers was concerned, however, that, while their attention was on the rich pickings of the wagons, Marlborough could counter-march around the French army and cut them off from their own supplies. A kind of stalemate was reached, and the two armies settled back into a superficially comfortable routine of observing each other while trying to pick off their opponent's detachments. In one of these skirmishes between the lines, Peter Drake, temporarily attached to a group of French foragers, wrote of a bloody encounter. He and his comrades, their immediate duty done, were taking the opportunity to refresh themselves in an ale-house when:

> Our sentry alarmed us, by saying that a party of horse was just at hand. We ran to arms, fixed our bayonets, and drew up before the door, in the street not above sixty paces from the enemy, who halted on seeing us. The fight began, the Dutch officer ordering his people to give no quarter, which our commander hearing, gave the same, and advancing boldly, was killed instantly at my side. By this time we were mixed, and much slaughter ensued, insomuch, that in less than ten minutes, we had twenty out of twenty-five killed on the spot, and three wounded. And now being commander-in-chief of an army of five men, three of whom were wounded, I thought it prudent to retire.

The Irishman and his fellows got away by throwing down their muskets and running headlong across a muddy meadow, while the Dutch dragoons fired, without further success, at their fleeing backs.

It had become apparent to Marlborough that Marshal Boufflers's forward position, well ahead of adequate magazines and depots, was his weakest point. On 26 July 1702, the Earl struck with quite unexpected speed, aiming his army at the French lines of supply and communication running back into Limburg and Brabant. Rather taken aback, Boufflers was obliged to withdraw to protect these lines, and Marlborough hoped to bring the Marshal to battle and ruin his army on the bleak heaths of Peer. It was not to be, as Parker tells us:

> As his lordship judged the thing so it happened; for the enemy upon beating Tattoo decamped, and marched all night with the utmost expedition. By the time it was day, their front had entered the heath and my Lord Marlborough had his men under arms, and just ready to march, when the Field-Deputies came to him, and prayed him to desist. This greatly surprised him, as they had agreed to his scheme the night before; but being a man of great temper and prudence, and being determined not to do anything this first campaign without their approbation, at their earnest entreaty he desisted. Whereupon the tent and baggage were sent for, and the army pitched their camp again.

The Dutch deputies had initially consented to give battle, but then changed their collective mind. Marlborough was determined that the deputies should understand fully what an opportunity they had so carelessly cast away in their excess of caution, and he took them to a vantage point, from where they could see the fleeing French army:

> He desired they would ride out with him to see the enemy pass the heath, which they and most of their general officers did, and saw them hurrying over it in the greatest confusion and disorder imaginable; upon which they all acknowledged, that they had lost a fair opportunity of giving the enemy a fatal blow.

The Duke of Berwick remembered the narrow escape that the French army had experienced that day: 'It was very fortunate for us that the deputies of the States would not consent to an attack upon the heath. We were posted in such a manner that we should have been beaten.' The French were in this way forced away from the vulnerable Dutch border, and in the process important towns would fall to Marlborough's advance. Donald McBane remembered the exhaustion of the troops after such efforts:

> We marched along the river side until we came to Maastricht. I being up all night before, in the march, I fell drousy, and fell into the river where I lost my gun, and very narrowly escaped my self; the army halted for an hour, as I was coming along the line I took up one of the Hollanders firelocks and came to our company in the front.

McBane then tells of the awful fate that awaited French spies and saboteurs if they were caught near the Allied camp. One evening, he remembered:

> I came by the gallows, where a great many were hanging in chains, one of them cried in French, give me a drink of water; hearing the voice and thinking they were all dead, when I told my story to my comrades, they could not believe it; next morning we went to see the truth of it, and there we found a man hanging in the chains alive, with a penny loaf hanging within a little of his mouth. When he would snatch at it, it fled from him and then would hit him in the mouth. He lived this way eleven days, he eat the flesh off both his shoulders; he was a spy from the French, and was designed to blow up the magazine of that garrison, the Governor ordered this death for him.

The grenadier goes on to recount that 'Many of our men deserted to the French, but as soon as we caught them they were hanged.'

In the course of this campaign, large areas of Guelderland and Limburg were secured by Marlborough, giving the Allied armies valuable room for manoeuvre should the French commander try a renewed and stronger advance towards the southern border of Holland. Instead, by late summer, much of the line of the Meuse river had been secured, and the clearing out of the French garrisons there could proceed. Boufflers appeared baffled by Marlborough's confident campaign. A few weeks later, Marlborough had another chance to maul the French, but they managed to slip away. The camp bulletin for Sunday 27 August 1702 ran:

> On Thursday night resolutions were taken and all necessary preparations for attacking the French the next morning early, but we had notice in the night that they were retired in great disorder, whereupon, as soon as it was day, His Excellency [Marlborough] followed them with twenty squadrons of the right [Wing], as the Earl of Athlone did with a like number from the left; but the enemy were already so advanced that it was impossible to overtake them, only Brigadier Wood, with some squadrons of the right, fell in with three or four squadrons of the household [Maison de Roi], which had their rearguard [duty], and entirely broke them.

Given that Marlborough and Athlone were following the French with little more than 4,000 troopers and dragoons between their two detachments, it is plain that they expected to do no more than inflict some losses on the rearguard of the enemy, rather than to bring on a general action. So slim a force could not hope to force their opponent to stand and fight against his will. Anyway, the Earl soon had other plans for action, and, the bulletin went on:

> Yesterday morning, M. de Opdham marched away with the detachment for Venlo, and is to invest the place on this side the Meuse tomorrow night, as the Prince of Nassau is to do at the same time on the other side with the Prussian and Dutch troops.

The frustration felt by many in the Allied army at the slow response and caution of the Dutch is shown in a letter sent by Adam Cardonnel, the Earl's Private Secretary, to Henry Blaythwayt, the Secretary of State for War at this time, on the same Sunday that the bulletin was published:

> If we had engaged on Wednesday [23 August] in the afternoon, as His Excellency had given positive orders to do, we would not, in all probability, have failed of a glorious victory. The enemy were so harassed and famished, both men and horses for want of provision, that it would have been impossible for them to have made any tolerable resistance.

A couple of weeks later, Marlborough's good friend, Arnold Joost van Keppel, Earl Albemarle, wrote in rueful tones of the likely cost of letting slip such promising opportunities:

> I could almost die for vexation to see we are so little the better here, for our advantage; for when we were, eight or ten days ago, within sight of the enemy, we ought not to have let them escape as we did; and we shall have reason, a long while, to blame ourselves for this neglect.

Albemarle was quite right, as the French commanders would not go on making these mistakes, and what might have been had cheaply in the early campaigns, would cost dear to obtain in later years.

At the end of August the Allied army closed up to Venlo, and invested the town and citadel, but Marlborough was frustrated at the steady and measured pace that the Dutch adopted in preparing for the siege. He wrote to a friend in Holland on 4 September 'The troops have been too long before Venlo this eight days, and they now talk of opening the trenches two days hence. If this be zeal, God preserve me from being so served.' However matters did proceed, albeit at no great speed, and on the last day of the month the place was subject to an assault, and Captain Robert Parker described what was generally held to be an astonishing and sudden success:

> About noon the grenadiers and 300 men of the other three regiments of our brigade, joined us soon after; the Lord Cutts, Brigadier Hamilton,

and several young noblemen came to see the attack made. The Lord Cutts sent for all the officers, and told them, that the design of the attack was only to drive the enemy from the covert-way, that they might not disturb the workmen in making their lodgement; however, if they found them [the French] giving way with precipitation, we were to jump into the covert-way, and pursue them, let the consequences be what it would. We all thought these were very rash orders.

Despite such misgivings about the wisdom of the whole enterprise, the attack went in on time:

About four in the afternoon the signal was given, and according to our orders, we rushed up to the covert-way; the enemy gave us one scattering fire only, and away they ran. We jumped into the covert-way and ran after them; seeing them get into a ravelin, pursued them, got in with them, and put most of them to the sword.

The defence collapsed in complete confusion, and the rest of the French garrison threw down their weapons 'Thus,' Parker goes on, 'were the unaccountable orders of Lord Cutts as unaccountably executed, to the great surprise of the whole army.' Christian Davies, who was still hoping to find her errant husband, had re-enlisted as a dragoon as soon as war was declared. She also told of her part in the siege operations against Venlo:

After several motions [manoeuvres], in which we could never draw the French to a battle, a detachment invested the town and citadel of Venlo, on the 29th of August, in the night. The horse not being employed in, we covered the siege, and were sometimes sent out to forage. The poor peasants fled before us, and leaving their implements in the field, my horse trod on a scythe, and was cut in so dangerous a manner, that despaired of his recovery; though he at length was again fit for service. Six days after the trenches had been opened before the town, we assaulted the citadel, and with such success that after we had carried the covered way, we took it; which obliged the town to capitulate on 23rd of September. Stevensweert and Ruremonde were next invested and bombarded, one after another. The former of these bore our fire but two days, the latter three. The Allies, on the 14th of October 1702, appeared before Liège.

This fortress was well garrisoned and proved to be a tough proposition, although the town was occupied by the Prince of Hesse-Cassell without great delay. The French commander of the citadel, the Marquis de Violaine, when summoned to surrender, coolly replied that 'It would be time enough to think of that six weeks after'; but, after a bombardment of just three days, directed by the Dutch engineer officer, van Coehorn, to open a breach in the defences, the Allied assault went in on the afternoon of 23 October 1702. The fighting was desperate and the garrison put up a gallant defence. Donald McBane wrote of the assault, giving a vivid flavour of this kind of action:

We fired all our guns and mortars; we destroyed a great many of them; about three o'clock in the afternoon the Duke of Marlborough came to the grand battery. He commanded twenty grenadiers of each company through the whole army, and ten battalions of the first [line] troops, to storm the fort sword in hand; our orders were to give no quarter to none in the fort; we made all ready for the attack, every grenadier had three grenades … We came with a loud hurrah, and fired our grenades among them; we continued this for an hour and a half, then we jumped over the palisades, we then made use of our swords and bayonets, and made a sore slaughter among the French, which obliged them to cry for quarter; although it was against our orders, we had mercy.

Kit Davies also remembered the attack:

We soon carried the half-moon, and finding less resistance than we expected, we cleared the palisades, mounted the breach sword in hand, and made a cruel slaughter. The English, in particular, distinguished themselves in this assault; for they mounted at a place called the six-cent-pas, the six hundred steps, for so many there were, and steeper than any pair of steps I ever saw in my life.

Always a great one for booty, Davies tells with some regret that her opportunities were, on this occasion, not as bright as she had hoped they might have been. Apparently, going in as one of the follow-up party in the assault, her pickings were not quite what she expected:

I got but little; for the grenadiers, who were in the place before our dragoons had dismounted and left their horses to the care of every tenth man, which we do when we fight on foot, were very industrious in their search. I got, however, a large silver chalice, and some other pieces of plate, which I afterwards sold.

Marlborough's own announcement of the success gave full credit to Queen Anne's soldiers 'By the extraordinary bravery of the officers and soldiers, the citadel was carried by storm, and for the honour of her Majesty's subjects, the English were the first upon the breach.'

Despite such successes, Marlborough could not find a way to force open battle upon the French, and the year's campaigning season trundled to a close. Life in camp, however, was not without adventure for a roving dragoon, and Kit Davies recounts an incident some short time after the capture of the town, when she was returning from an escort duty, and after a little quiet foraging, found a pig:

I was possessed of it for some time, when one Taylor, a corporal belonging to Brigadier Panton's regiment of horse, attempted to spoil me of my booty; he drew [his sword] and made a stroke at my head, which I warding with my hand, had the sinew of my little finger cut in two; at the same time, with the butt end of my pistol I struck out one of his eyes. When we returned to our quarters, I got the sinew sewed up.

The corporal concerned appears to have continued in his general misfortune, as a couple of years later, Davies goes on to tell us, he lost his company's pay while playing cards, and, rather than face the wrath of his comrades, shot himself through the head in desperation. Foraging was plainly an activity fraught with much risk as well as reward, not only because of the enemy's vigilance or, as in this particular case, the unwelcome attention of your own comrades. The unfortunate locals, driven to despair by the depredations of armies on campaign, could be brutal when they caught soldiers on their own. John Deane, a private soldier in the 1st English Foot Guards, wrote of 'A corporal in the Hannovers being caught by the Boors [peasants] and hung up dead in a tree.'

The 1702 campaign was at a close, but the adventures of the Earl of Marlborough were not yet over that year. Early in November, he and a group of officers were surprised, while travelling to the Hague by way of the Meuse river, by a party of French partisans operating out of Guelders. These drove off the escort and seized the yacht with Marlborough's party on board. By some oversight, all the officers had passes of safe conduct except for Marlborough, but his clerk, Stephen Gell, saved him from being taken prisoner by slipping the Earl a pass (albeit one that was out of date) made out for his younger brother, Charles Churchill. The Irishman commanding the French raiders, a deserter from the Dutch service named Captain Farewell, was satisfied with the pass and Marlborough and his party were able to proceed unmolested. It is also possible that whispered promises were made, for that officer soon absconded from the French service to rejoin the Dutch army, where a lucrative appointment was found for him. Marlborough's own comment on the incident, that could have had such profound consequences for the Allied cause, was 'I thank God they did not know me, but took me for Lieutenant General Churchill.'

Marlborough returned to London at the end of November 1702, and soon afterwards was made a Duke by Queen Anne, in recognition of his successes in the Low Countries. The new Duchess was greatly concerned at the likely cost of maintaining such a dignity, but the Queen made the pair a grant from the revenues of the Post Office to cater for that. Just as when he was a young man, very much favoured at Court, some people thought that the honours and rewards that came the Duke's way were rather too lavish. John Evelyn wrote in his diary on 30 December 1702 (O.S.):

> After the excess of honours conferred by the Queen on the Earl of Marlborough making him a Knight of the Garter and Duke for the success of but one campaign that he should desire £5,000 a year out of the Post Office [funds] to be settled on him was by parliament thought a bold and unadvised request from one who had, besides his own considerable estate, £50,000 at interest. This was taken note of and displeased those who had until now held him in quiet esteem.

Evelyn adds, rather waspishly, that:

Everyone knew by what merit he had become such a favourite, for his sister was a miss[tress] to King James II when Duke of York, and his father had been but a clerk of the Green Cloth, ingrossing all that stirred and was profitable at Court. He is a very handsome person, well spoken and affable, and supports his want of acquired knowledge by keeping good company.

However, it should be remembered that, in the warm afterglow of the triumph at Blenheim, only eighteen months later, the same diarist was not slow to seek the Duke's company, and make himself as agreeable as he possibly could to the returning hero. Fame and fortune were coming Marlborough's way, and many of the rewards were highly deserved, but his only surviving son, the Marquess of Blandford, died of smallpox in February 1703, to the deep grief of the Duke and Duchess. Despite this, Marlborough very soon had to cross to Holland once more, as the time for the new campaign approached.

By the third week of April 1703, the Allied army in the Low Countries was once again in the field, and had closed up to the important French-held town of Bonn, preparing for a siege of the place. Marlborough wrote on 24 April 'Bonn should have been attacked by now … However, all the troops will be there tomorrow.' In case it should be thought that such siege operations were dull, it is worth reading the accounts of the bitter fighting that took place before the town fell to the Allies. The Zell (Celle) troops, supplied by the Electoress Sophia of Hanover for the campaign, proved neither well equipped nor properly trained, and were stood down. Instead, Lieutenant-General von Bulow's Prussian troops manned the trenches, facing a strong outlying fort which guarded the approaches to the town. The list of munitions gathered for the bombardment was impressive, and included four 100lb mortars, each with 500 charges of powder, 7,000 round-shot for smaller pieces, 800 'great grenadoes' (explosive shells) and 10,000 hand grenades for the stormers to use, should they be employed in an assault.

The French governor of Bonn, the Marquis d'Alègre, viewed the impressive Allied preparations with some trepidation, and tried to deflect the fury of Marlborough's attack. There was, he claimed 'An agreement made last year, between the Electors Palatine and of Cologne, that the cities of Dusseldorf and Bonn should not be bombarded, in order to preserve the churches, palaces and public buildings.' The Marquis now requested the performance of this agreement, and went on to declare that, unless the same were observed, the Elector of Bavaria would destroy the city of Nieuburg, belonging to the Elector Palatine. Marlborough's response was sharp, drawing a nice line between how he would conduct his campaigns, and what he expected from an otherwise chivalrous foe, who was plainly attempting to divert him from his duty, with some clumsy attempt at a kind of blackmail. The Duke's reply ran that it was 'Not his custom or inclination to destroy cities or public buildings out of malice or design' provided that the enemy's conduct did not put him to such a stern necessity. That was that.

By 8 May the big guns were in place before the outlying works, and a bombardment of Bonn began. The following day, the gunners having made a breach, 400 Prussian Grenadiers stormed the fort, and at once Marlborough began to place heavy guns there to engage the main defences of the town. However, d'Alègre put in a spirited counter-attack on 10 May, to impede the Allied preparations. This had some success, although the garrison troops were eventually driven back into the town, and a French observer wrote that:

> About two in the afternoon, the Marquis d'Alegre made a sally with 1,200 infantry and 400 horse, at General Dedem's attack. They at first did very considerable damage to the works, and killed all before them; But the Allies having caused a great number of troops to advance, they retired in very good order, having lost about 30 men, a captain of the Royal Grenadiers and an Aid Major of the Crown [Aide de Camp]: Mons. De Polastron, Colonel of the Regiment, with some other officers, being wounded. They nailed up [spiked] ten of the besiegers cannon, and six of their mortars, killed fourscore of their men, wounded 160 and took Colonel Malsbourg, and several other officers, prisoners.

Dealing with so accomplished a soldier as the Marquis d'Alègre, even when penned up inside a second-rate fortress, was plainly a tricky business. However, despite such local French successes in the outer-works, the Allied siege operations were pressed vigorously forward, and on 15 May the French commander beat a parley, and surrendered the town to Marlborough on honourable terms. The Duke wrote on 16 May: 'The Governors of the town at last agreed to what I have offered, and in one hour I shall be in possession of one of the gates ... I shall not stay to see them.'

The capitulation was in good time, as Marshal Boufflers, the commander of the French field army in Flanders, had taken the opportunity offered by Marlborough's attention being on the capture of Bonn, to move out and threaten both Liège and Maastricht. The Duke, understanding that Bonn must soon fall, had already detached Veldt-Marshal Overkirk's Dutch corps to cover Maastricht, and Boufflers's otherwise rather good plan came to nothing. When Marlborough joined Overkirk some days after the fall of Bonn, the French withdrew in considerable haste. Even as competent a commander as Berwick took alarm, prematurely blew up the defences of Tongres on 26 May, and abandoned the place to the approaching Allied soldiers before it was even under real threat. An example of the effect that these reverses had upon at least some of the rank and file of the French regiments is given by Samuel Noyes, chaplain in Orkney's regiment, in a letter he wrote on 7 June 1703, when he said that 'Eight drummers of the Regiment of Picardy deserted to us in a body.'

At about this time Donald McBane got separated from his comrades while on the march, and fell in with a band of French soldiers:

> Up comes a French dragoon seeking plunder and took me prisoner, he took my sword from me sore against my will; he drove me before him, until he came to a wood side where he wanted to ease nature, he alighted and took a pistol with him, commanding me to hold his horse. When his breeches was down I mounted his horse, and rode for it, he cried and fired after me, the bullet came through my hair and cap and grazed on my head. I loosed my

sword that was tied to the saddle, and with it whipped the horse, he cried in French stop the English rogue, a great many wives [camp followers] were before which cast stones at me, which obliged me to ride the faster, until I came to the front where our Royal Regiment was. When my Captain saw me he was amazed, saying he never thought to see me again.

Henry St John, writing to his friend, Lieutenant-General Thomas Erle at this time, told of a daring raid by six squadrons of French cavalry, who tried to surprise the picket at the Allied camp:

They put green boughs in their hats (our signal of battle) and, when challenged by our out-sentinels, answered they were friends, talked English and Dutch, as they saw occasion, and said they had been reconnoitring. This discourse they held with a lieutenant of Danish horse who was upon an advanced post with 30 troopers. Upon this he asked whether they had seen the enemy. They answered yes and if he would ride but a little way off with them they would show him the enemy. He not suspecting anything rode off with them, and when they were at a reasonable distance from his party they seized his pistols and told him he was dead if he stirred, notwithstanding which he broke loose from them, rode back towards his men, had the good fortune to escape all their shot after him, and with his 30 men, without either his own pistol or sword, charged through them.

Such skirmishes and minor, though violent, incidents were the common daily currency of a campaign.

Although Marlborough was gradually able to capture a string of valuable French-held fortresses, he could see that this was not the way to win the war. That could only be done in decisive open battle, but the Dutch remained wary and, on occasions, negligent. As the month of June approached, the Duke prepared a scheme to capture Antwerp. Writing to Sidney Godolphin, he explained what he had in mind:

Before I left Bonn, measures were taken for the embarking of 20 battalions of foot, if it be possible to get boats enough, and 21 squadrons of horse are to march the nearest way to Bergen Op Zoom, where they are to join the 20 battalions that go by water. These troops are to take the most advantageous post near Antwerp, after which there will be care taken to join more troops to them. If this design of Antwerp can be brought to perfection, I hope we shall make it very uneasy for them to protect Brussels and the rest of their great towns.

The value of the use of the great waterways in the region for the rapid transportation of troops is plain. In the same way, the laborious task of moving guns, munitions and supplies along the indifferent roads of that time was rendered easy by making use of the canals and rivers. Many battles, both large and small, expensive in veteran soldiers, were fought to keep open the waterways, and deny their use to an opponent.

Marlborough was also handicapped by a lack of discretion among his generals, and his plans often became common knowledge. During the operations against Bonn, he had written 'I have seen a letter from Paris that the siege of Bonn is but a feint, but that the real design was upon Antwerp.' This, as it happened, was exactly the case, and seemed to have been more than simple intelligent analysis of what he might do next.

In the event, the project against Antwerp miscarried badly, once again largely because of a lack of energy in the Dutch generals involved – Coehorn, Tilly, Dohna, Opdham and Spaar, who plainly had little faith in what was, admittedly, an ambitious and complex undertaking. On 26 June 1703 the Dutch did seize a portion of the French lines, those under Opdham getting off quite lightly, but Spaar's detachment having a hard fight. The report of one of the Dutch field deputies concluded: 'At two this morning the troops commanded by General Opdham broke up, and marched towards Eckeren (which is intended for the head-quarters) with a design to show themselves today, before the Lines of Antwerp.'

These manoeuvrings of the opposing armies towards Antwerp soon led to a bitterly fought battle at that same small town of Eckeren, close to the great port and city. Despite bad weather – 'It is not to be imagined what our poor foot have suffered in these last marches' – Marshal Boufflers had managed to combine his army with that of Isidore Bedmar, and on 30 June 1703 he struck at Opdham's Dutch corps, encamped nearby in Eckeren. With some foresight Marlborough wrote to the Lord Treasurer, Sidney Godolphin, on the day of the battle itself: 'If M. Opdham be not upon his guard, he may be beat before we can help him which will always be the consequence when troops are divided.' The Duke delayed sending the letter and added a postscript 'Since I sealed my letter, we have a report come from Breda that Opdham is beaten.' Meanwhile, the Irish soldier of fortune, Peter Drake, was on the march into battle:

> There was an order for all the grenadiers, and the detachments from the several garrisons in the country, to join the Marechal de Boufflers, who commanded a flying army [column] of 10,000 men. All the forces being arrived, and reviewed by that General the next day we marched, in order to attack Opdham, who commanded much about the like number of Dutch troops, near the little town of Eckeren. The action was pretty sharp.

This brawling engagement at Eckeren, which ruined the Duke's plans against Antwerp beyond hope of recovery, was described by the Count de Merode-Westerloo, a wittily observant Walloon officer with a sometimes acid tongue, at that time serving as a loyal subject of King Philip V of Spain. He wrote that the Dutch:

> Drew close to our lines near Antwerp, and eventually encamped a bare league away at Eckeren. Meanwhile Koehorn and Sparre approached our defences on the opposite bank of the Scheldt. This caused us to run to and fro over the river for some little time, constantly crossing and re-crossing and passing through Antwerp in order to keep them under observation with M. de Bedmar's small army. After carrying on in this fashion for some time, we eventually thought up an enterprise against their camp at Eckeren. We found ourselves three times as strong as the

enemy, and we set out secretly through our lines at three points, making no noise, the time being about five in the morning [30 June 1703].

The Comte, whose small brigade consisted only of his own newly-raised (Westerloo) regiment of Walloons and the French Régiment de Vexin, was joined on the start-line by the German-recruited de Brias Régiment, a welcome addition to his rather meagre bayonet strength. As it grew light the attack went in:

> Our first line then stormed over the dykes on the left, and from the beginning pushed the enemy back. I was sent off with my brigade to attack the enemy from the rear. There they had drawn up the [Dutch] battalions of Fagel and Friesheim and some other detachments under Major-General Dohna. The village cemetery was a good position, and in front of it they had sited four cannon. I moved forward along the dyke, and although the French wanted me to march under cover, I rode along the top, and advanced at a steady pace. When we reached the small sluice near the bend in the dyke which leads away towards Wilmerdoch, I met Countess Tilly who had just been captured in her six-horse coach by our dragoons as she tried to make good her escape. The enemy's musket fire became heavy as I busied myself paying my compliments at her coach door, and this frightened her, with the result that she returned me only a short salutation.

Merode-Westerloo was then summoned from these agreeable gallantries by the Marquis de Guiscard, who brusquely ordered him to assault the village with his brigade. The Comte would have preferred to carry out a proper reconnaissance but, fearing that the French might suspect him of hanging back, he promptly detached his grenadiers to attack along the line of the main road, sent the Régiment de Vexin to attack on the left, and meanwhile led his soldiers and the de Brias Régiment on the right. At first the inexperienced Walloons hung back under the heavy Dutch musketry fire, but they rallied soon enough, and Merode-Westerloo described the storm of the cemetery itself:

> The enemy were trying to get back into the cemetery, where they still had plenty of reserves, and, hot on their heels some ten yards behind, I tripped over the body of a dead man in the passageway between two houses [which ran from the dyke to the church] and fell without being wounded, thus occasioning the rumour that I was slain to run throughout the army. Four or five of my soldiers trod on me one after another, forcing me into the mud as I tried to struggle to my feet. In fact, I was rather fortunate to be flat on my face at this juncture, for the enemy, now safely within the cemetery, were firing hotly at us at point-blank range, killing and wounding plenty of those around and behind me. Getting up at last, I made my way into the cemetery through a small breach that I happened to notice, followed by a confused crowd of about a hundred men. Then, after forcing our way into the very midst of the enemy, the men of my brigade, joined by the Dragoons de Richebourg, who had come on dismounted from the bank of the dykes, charged the enemy on all sides.

> This went so well that the enemy abandoned the cemetery, village and all four cannon, and fell back in dire confusion.

After heavy and bloody fighting, such as was so well described by the Comte, the heavily out-numbered Dutch soldiers, despite their brave stand, fell back to try and recover their order. Merode-Westerloo, who could not resist a sharp comment about his own superiors, remembered that:

> The enemy's only thought was to escape from the cul de sac they had placed themselves in. This however, they could only do through the village I had chased them out of. I would dearly have liked to entrench the place had I possessed picks and shovels. Besides the killed and wounded, the great heat of the day and the fatigues of combat had induced many more to take shelter in the village cellars. Some soldiers were drunk with the excitement. I continued fighting in the cemetery, but eventually it proved necessary to pull out and fall back behind the dyke. An astonishing thing, I never saw a single general officer during all this affair.

The Comte might just as well have been speaking for the Dutch army, as Opdham, the field commander, had gone forward to reconnoitre the French approach early in the day, then got lost and took himself off to report to the States-General that their army had been surprised and destroyed at Eckeren. In fact, after bloody fighting both armies drew off; the battle was an inconclusive draw, although most of the honours lay firmly with the French. The Dutch had been badly mauled, but Robert Parker, serving with the Royal Regiment of Ireland, gave little credit to the French for what was a generally well-handled operation on their part, when he wrote of the action:

> Boufflers had attacked Opdham, and after several repulses, at length broke into that part where Opdham commanded, and cut between him and the rest of his troops. Upon this he concluded everything was lost. Notwithstanding this disadvantage, the Lieutenant-General Slangenberg and Tilly maintained their ground with great obstinacy. The day after the battle our army arrived, and Villeroi being joined by Boufflers, drew out of his lines, declared he would give us battle. The Duke was ready to take him at his word, and the next day advanced within half a league of him, being determined to attack him the following morning; but Villeroi thought better of it, and stole back within his lines, before it was day.

Slangenberg, so obstinate and unhelpful on other occasions, had proved to be a rock for the Dutch infantry, as they struggled to halt the French onslaught. Boufflers's report to Versailles ran: 'There took place a very hard fought and determined combat ... Your Majesty's army brought off all the advantage and all the marks of victory, chasing the enemy from their camp.' The French had suffered some 1,250 casualties, and had inflicted much heavier losses on the Dutch, including many of their guns.

The French took up an advanced position to cover the approaches to Antwerp after the battle. On 23 July Marlborough made a final attempt on the city, marching his own army to combine with Slangenberg's Dutch, in order to attack the French camp at St Job. Marshal Villeroi hastily withdrew his detachment into defensive lines, leaving his tentage and camp stores in flames behind him. The position was too strong to be assaulted and, disappointed, but not entirely surprised, Marlborough turned away.

After the failure of his grand plan to capture Antwerp, and the sharp rebuff delivered by Boufflers to the Dutch army at Eckeren, Marlborough's attention was drawn to the lesser, but still important, fortress of Huy on the Meuse: 'It is very convenient to us to have that place.' Despite the natural strength of the main defences, standing as it did on a rocky hill, the defences crumbled before the Duke's guns, and by 24 August 1703 Samuel Noyes, serving with Orkney's Regiment, was able to watch the outlying forts as they suffered before the Allied attack. Seventy cannon and forty-six mortars were used, and he described the scene with some relish:

> At 4 [4pm] I saw a detachment of grenadiers marching upon the hill to the bottom of the rock, and presently the attack began, and the French appearing on the top of the castle, our cannon and bombs from all the batteries, but especially 10 three-pounders from the English field train which was now planted on Fort Joseph (which overlooked the castle and flanked them), murdered them so cruelly that within less than two hours they cried quarter. Ours at first would not regard them, but fired on very furiously for near a quarter of an hour. They continued calling out, beat a drum and instead of a soldier's neck-cloth or some little flag (the usual white flag in these cases) they held up a regimental colour, lest a small flag should not be seen by reason of the smoke. One poor ensign was to our view plainly shot in two and another immediately took the colour up. At 6 of the clock exactly all firing ceased.

Two days later the chaplain wrote in his journal that:

> The Great Fort, viz; Fort Joseph, had surrendered shamefully the day before without being attacked, [the garrison asking] articling only to go into the castle, but the governor refused it. It seems the commander was a merchant's son who had lately bought his commission to a company, and not being used to these things was frightened out of his wits by cannon and bombs ... The two lesser forts, viz; Fort Picard and Fort Rouge, were quitted that morning, the enemy retiring into the castle.

The citadel of Huy surrendered on 25 August 1703, and the Allied camp bulletin two days later described the circumstances. It ran:

> All the batteries firing incessantly the whole afternoon in less than two hours killed them upwards of forty men; our troops advancing in the mean time, and having, under the cover of our fire, placed several ladders at the foot of the castle, though we intended only a feint, the enemy thought we were coming to the assault, and thereupon, about six in the afternoon, beat a parley, and offered to surrender upon condition to march out to Namur with the usual signs of honour; but my Lord Duke of Marlborough having

sent a message to M. Millon, the governor, that if the garrison would surrender as prisoners of war, all the officers and soldiers should retain whatever belonged to them, and be exchanged for a like number of ours when the Marechal de Villeroi should desire it, and that they were to expect no other terms – these proposals were at first rejected by the governor, and orders were thereupon given for beginning the attack again yesterday morning [26th August], which the governor perceiving, he accepted the terms offered him, and a detachment of our troops took possession of the castle. In the evening the garrison marched out into the town, from whence they will be conducted to Liege or Maastricht, till the exchange be settled. The whole garrison (including that of Fort St Joseph, which the governor would not receive) consisted of about nine hundred men, commanded by two brigadiers. We found in the place a considerable quantity of ammunition and provision, sufficient to subsist the garrison for more than a fortnight; but the governor alleges his men would hold out no longer, and obliged him to surrender. We have had in the whole siege but eighteen men killed, and thirty-five men, besides some officers, wounded.

The performance of the garrison of Huy was generally felt to have been feeble, shown by Marlborough's dismissive treatment of the Governor's request to be allowed to yield on honourable terms. Prisoners of war could be used to get back your own people from enemy hands by exchange, and they had a considerable value as a result, even though they had to be fed and, to a degree, housed in the meantime. Those yielding a fortified place on agreed terms by virtue of their stout resistance, on the other hand, had no such value, as they just slipped off to rejoin their own army, usually with their arms, colours and baggage intact. As it happened two battalions of Allied infantry, surprised and captured earlier in the year, were soon exchanged for the garrison of Huy.

With Huy safely in his hands, Marlborough then hoped to move smartly out to attack the French field army. This had cautiously approached from the west, hoping to impede the operations against the town, and the French were now trailing their coats in the area of defensive lines constructed the previous year near to Ramillies. Once again the Dutch were reluctant to engage in open battle and pressed the Duke to instead move to besiege Limburg. He agreed to do so, but wrote to Hiensius, the Grand Pensionary of Holland, on 10 September: 'We should have taken their lines with very little loss. But the discord in our camp will encourage the enemy who knows everything that goes on among us.' Despite the difficult ground on the approaches to Limburg, a 300-strong storming party soon seized the lower town there. The fortress and upper town, subjected to a severe artillery bombardment, fell on 27 September. Kit Davies remembered that: 'The Governor seeing part of the rampart demolished, beat the chamade, and surrendered prisoners of war. However, all the officers were handsomely treated and nothing taken from them.' Marlborough wrote that day to the States-General in the Hague: 'I send congratulations to Your High Mightinesses on the capture of the town and fortress of Limburg, where the garrison have been obliged to give themselves up prisoners of war.'

Guelders was then invested and bombarded by Count Lottum. Its garrison capitulated in December, and the campaign drew to a close. The whole of Guelderland and the Bishopric of Liège had now been secured for the Allies but, despite these successes, many of Marlborough's soldiers were left with the distinct sense that they were wasting their time in the campaign. Lieutenant Richard Pope, serving with Schomberg's Horse, wrote to a friend that 'I have not before given you the trouble of a letter we having done nothing in this campaign but march and counter-march, to very little purpose as I conclude.'

Plans the Duke had prepared for a new autumn campaign in the Moselle valley were put into disarray in the meantime, when Marshal Villars and the Elector of Bavaria defeated Count Styrum, the Imperial field commander in the Danube valley, at the battle of Höchstädt late in September 1703. Worse still, the Duc de Tallard, until recently the French Ambassador in London, had captured Landau after defeating an Imperial force at Spyr (Speyerbach), and the passes through the Black Forest, necessary for the reinforcement of France's ally, the Elector of Bavaria, were now free to use. The pressure on the third party in the Grand Alliance, Imperial Austria, was growing, and the Emperor also had to contend with a rebellion in Hungary. With the end of the campaign season for 1703 Marlborough made ready to return to London, but he was considering how a suggestion made by Prince Eugene of Savoy, the President of the Imperial War Council, that he should go and campaign in southern Germany, could be put into actual effect.

As was the custom at this time, general officers on both sides would often obtain passes of safe-conduct from their opponents, so that they could move about the theatre of war fairly easily, as could their bulky retinue and campaign equipment, without the burdensome necessity of having to provide large armed escorts for their security. Such courtesies did not always proceed smoothly, as on the occasion the previous year when Marlborough was almost taken prisoner by Farewell's patrol, having neglected to procure a pass for himself. On 9 October 1703, Marlborough wrote to the Duke of Berwick from the Allied camp at St Tron:

> I am going in a few days to Dusseldorf, and though I return hence to the army, yet I would willingly, in the mean time, send away to Holland part of my equipage, and being loathe to trouble the Marechal de Villeroi myself in this subject, I entreat your Grace to procure me his pass and send it to me at your leisure. I have dispatched the passes your Grace desires for yourself and equipage.

Plainly it was felt that one good turn deserved another. However, presumably due to pressure of work on Marlborough's small staff, Berwick had to remind Marlborough over the matter, and the Duke wrote to him again on 23 October, taking, in the process, the opportunity to solicit another favour:

> I am very sorry that the omission of my secretary should occasion your Grace a second trouble. However I take this opportunity of returning the pass, to repeat my wishes for your good journey, and should be glad in the

mean time, if you think it proper, and not otherwise, that you would desire the Marechal de Villeroi to give me a pass for twenty pieces [casks] of burgundy or champagne to come to Huy or Liege.

Meanwhile the trials of going on campaign, particularly when having to take ship and cross the sea to the war, are shown clearly in the letters of cavalry officer, Richard Pope:

After having met with a storm (for of late years I can never go to sea with horses without finding some such thing), in which we had our sails blown away, and sprung a leak, which kept us to the exercise of continual pumping, and one of our guns broke loose, and had been likely to overset the ship, for they were in a condition to do nobody any harm but ourselves, and with the loss of 18 horses of the regiment, we arrived at Williamstadt, having run more dangers than a man may need do in the horse service in several campaigns.

In the same way, an anonymous English soldier, serving with Raby's Dragoons, found that his unit was detailed to leave the Low Countries late in 1703, as part of a general reinforcement of the Allied armies gathering in Spain. In his memoirs, he remembered the extraordinary privation of the journey across the sea:

Now about the middle of September we had orders to leave the camp [near Huy] in order to go to Portugal, so on the 30 of September 1703 we came to Gursum where our regiment was quartered the winter before, where our horses was now sold. On Saturday the 30 of August 1703 we went on board the *Samuel*, a transport, in order for our intended voyage and the wind was very fair for us, but our forces being not all ready we lay riding at Williamstadt and thereabouts until the 27 of November 1703.

Bad weather then struck and much of the slowly gathering fleet was thrown about the Narrow Seas and badly damaged, with lost spars, damaged rigging and dragged anchors. The dragoon goes on:

The fleet is forced to stay until it is repaired, and it was February before it was fit to sail; so we came to Spithead and lay there until the 20 of February and then set sail, and with the blessing of God we got into Lisbon Harbour on the 2 of March 1703[4] and lay in the harbour until the 13 of the same month. On the 13 of March we landed at Beliles [Belem], about a league from Lisbon but such weather was not known by the age of man, with rain and winds we could no keep a tent standing, and so it was all the month of March.

For two years the campaigns of the Grand Alliance against Louis XIV had languished, while the French steadily made ground against Imperial Austria in northern Italy and the Danube valley. The Alliance was losing the war, and it remained to be seen whether a new, daring and dangerous Allied project in 1704, an enterprise of the most novel and adventurous kind, promising high reward but running terrible risk, would come to fruition.

Chapter Four

So Glorious a Victory – The Campaign in the Danube Valley, 1704

While the Duke of Marlborough's efforts at a decisive campaign in the Low Countries dragged on under the deadening hand of the Dutch field deputies, the third partner in the Grand Alliance, Imperial Austria, was in some peril. Maximilian Emmanuel Wittelsbach, the Elector of Bavaria, although owing allegiance to the Austrian Emperor, had concluded a treaty with Louis XIV and attacked Imperial forces in the Tyrol; he had then gone on to occupy the Imperial free city of Ulm. Early in 1704 Austria was under attack by a combined French and Bavarian army in the Danube valley, while at the same time Hungary was in violent revolt. If, as seemed possible, the Elector and his French allies moved on to Vienna, and the city fell, even for just a short time, Austria could well be driven out of the war and the Grand Alliance would almost certainly collapse. Courtesy of the Elector's duplicity, this was Louis XIV's grand strategic thrust in 1704.

Marlborough recognised Vienna's apparent peril as an opportunity to free himself of Dutch interference. Prince Eugene of Savoy, the President of the Imperial War Council, had prepared a plan and, after a certain amount of plotting with the Imperial Ambassador in London, Count Wratislaw, Queen Anne sent Marlborough back to his armies in March 1704, with an instruction to go to the aid of Austria, if he saw fit. This was a wide-ranging licence to take almost whatever action he thought necessary. The Dutch, understandably concerned for their own security, were reluctantly persuaded to agree that those troops in the pay of England should be permitted to march south, while those in Dutch service would remain to defend their border against any fresh French threat. Marlborough assured the States-General that should this occur, he would return to the Low Countries in good time; in the event, this promise was never put to the test.

After the most careful preparations, Marlborough's army began its march from Bedburg on 19 May 1704, heading up western bank of the Rhine, towards the Moselle and Alsace (either of which, for all the French knew, might be his intended targets) and the Danube valley. Strict march discipline was enforced, and the soldiers proceeded by easy stages; exhausted troops would be of no value when they got to their destination. Captain Robert Parker of the Royal Irish Regiment wrote of the journey:

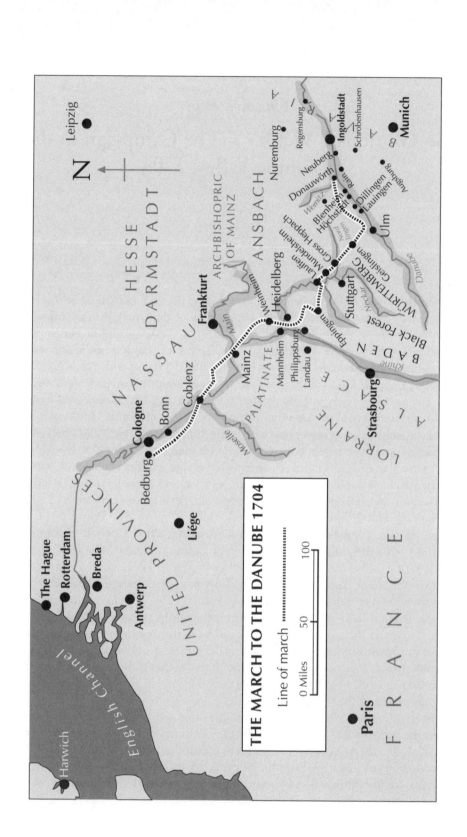

THE MARCH TO THE DANUBE 1704

Line of march ......

0 Miles   50   100

We frequently marched three, sometimes four days, successively, and halted a day. We generally began our march about three in the morning, proceeded about four leagues, or four and a half each day, and reached our [camp] ground about nine [am]. As we marched through the countries of our Allies, commissaries were appointed to furnish us with all manner of necessaries for man and horse; these were brought to the ground before we arrived, and the soldiers had nothing to do, but to pitch their tents, boil their kettles, and lie down to rest. Surely was never a march carried on with more order and regularity, and with less fatigue to both man and horse.

This apparently inexplicable movement by the Duke's army away from the Low Countries puzzled the French. Such a venture, drastically reducing the strength of the Anglo–Dutch armies in the region, seemed to leave the frontier of Holland wide open to attack. However, the progress of the marching army could not be ignored, as an attack on the Marquis de Bedmar in the Moselle valley would outflank the whole French strategic posture in northern Europe, as would an advance into Alsace. So Marshal Villeroi, the French commander in the Spanish Netherlands, found that he was obliged to march south too, away from the Dutch frontier, trying to keep pace with Marlborough and his bewildering campaign. Parker wrote that 'This made the Dutch easy, for they were apprehensive that, on the Duke's marching from them, the French would over-run their whole country.' On 26 May Marlborough reached Coblenz, at the confluence of the Rhine and the Moselle, but, instead of turning to the west to attack Bedmar, his army marched onwards, crossing to the eastern bank of the Rhine, and gaining strength from reinforcements that had been arranged to rendezvous with him there. Villeroi wrote to Louis XIV at the end of May 'There will be no campaign on the Moselle this year, the English have all gone up into Germany.'

The success of Marlborough's march, with the flank of his columns potentially exposed to French attack for long periods, depended upon his opponents being kept in doubt as to his intentions. The French could see that the Allied army might well go to the Danube valley, and that the French forces already there, under the command of Marshal Marsin, would as a result be in danger. Marshal Tallard (as he now was) had moved through the Black Forest with reinforcements for Marsin in May, but until, and if, Marlborough began to cross the Swabian Jura hills, using the narrow Geiselingen pass, the French could not be sure that an Allied attack in Alsace would not still take place. Accordingly, for the time being, they had to concentrate their available forces there, and not commit further troops to the Danube.

The conditions for the march of the Allied army deteriorated soon afterwards, as the weather was poor and the roads began to turn to mud in the rain. The Duke's concern for his soldiers is plainly shown in a letter he sent to Henry St John in London, on 2 June:

I am pursuing my march with the horse towards the rendezvous [with Goor's Dutch corps] near Philippsburg, but the ill-weather with the badness of the roads for the artillery will keep the foot back for three or four days longer than

I expected. We have nothing new from Prince Louis of Baden [the Imperial field commander in Swabia], nor of the march of M. de Villeroi.

Despite the bad weather, Donald McBane remembered the march cheerfully: 'We set out for Germany and had seven weeks march, but had plenty of good bread and wine, and the people were very kind to us along the Rhine.' The ability of Marlborough's quartermasters to pay hard cash for the supplies they needed ensured that they found a ready welcome in the lands through which the Allied army marched. Kit Davies, with Hay's Dragoons, wrote approvingly of the Duke's compassion for his soldiers: 'I cannot help taking notice of the Duke of Marlborough's great humanity, who seeing some of our foot drop, took them into his own coach.' At the beginning of June, the Duke wrote to Charles Churchill, his younger brother and General of Infantry, with advice concerning the best road to be taken with the infantry and guns:

> I send by this express on purpose to be informed of the condition you are in both as to the troops and the artillery, and to advise you to take your march with the whole directly to Heidelberg, since the route we have taken by Ladenburg [with the cavalry] will be too difficult for you. Pray send back the messenger immediately, and let me know by him where you design to camp each night, and what day you propose to be at Heidelberg, that I may take my measures accordingly.

Meanwhile, news came in of the movements of the French; the camp bulletin, issued from Ladenburg on 4 June, reads:

> We have this morning received advice from the Comte de Vehlen, General of the Palatine horse, who commands the forces in the lines of Stollhofen, that M. de Tallard repassed the Rhine on Monday the 2nd inst. at Altenheim, and was marching towards Landau, in order, it is supposed, to join the Maréchal de Villeroi, or to oppose our passage of the Rhine, the bridge which the Governor of Philippsburg is making there giving them a jealousy that we are coming that way.

Tallard, in fact, was returning from his audacious operation to resupply Marsin. Still, the Duke, playing on such French apprehensions, had ordered pontoon bridges to be laid at Philippsburg, as if the intention was really to invade Alsace after all. In this way, the eyes of the French would be kept away from his true intentions for a while; the delay was important to Marlborough, as his army was becoming strung out with the exertions of the march. That same day he wrote to Charles Hedges:

> I am halting here [Ladenburg] to-day and to-morrow to give an opportunity to the foot which passes the Main [river] this day to come nearer to us, and to the horse that are here to recover a little their tedious march ... I now expect to be in ten days upon the Danube, near the Elector of Bavaria, who, if he finds himself pressed, I am apt to think may offer to make his accommodation [with us].

Adding that it would be useful to have the plenipotentiary power (as Wratislaw had) to negotiate terms with the Elector, Marlborough went on:

> I take him to be a very fickle Prince, you will please to know the Queen's pleasure, whether her Majesty may not think it fit to give me the like powers, that if he should be willing to comply, and come over to us upon reasonable terms, I may conclude a treaty with him, without giving him time to fly off again.

These powers were duly granted to the Duke, although, as it would turn out, he never had the chance to use them to bring about a successful conclusion. The Duke remained concerned at the deteriorating pace of the army's progress, although the skies began to clear soon afterwards, and he did not forget that his men needed supplies. In a letter dated 8 June, to Charles Churchill, Marlborough shows how the smaller details of campaign life did not escape his keen attention:

> By a letter I have seen from Colonel Rowe, he writes that the foot may soon be in want of shoes; that they are to be had at Franckfort at reasonable rates, and that the contractors will send them forward to Nuremberg; therefore I desire you will call the commanding officers together that you may know the number they will want, and thereupon order Colonel Rowe to write to Franckfort that they may be hastened to Nuremberg, where we can send for them or order them to come forward to us.

Nor did he forget the comfort of the marching soldiers as they tramped along, adding to the letter 'I hope [that with] this warm weather you take care to march as early as to be in your camp before the heat of the day.' As the army progressed southwards Marlborough was anxious over the growing French concentration in Alsace, where Marshal Villeroi had now joined forces with Tallard, and urged that his Imperial allies take steps to counter the potential threat. He wrote to Sidney Godolphin at this time:

> Having received intelligence yesterday that in three or four days the duke of Villeroy, with his army, would join that of the marshal de Tallard about Landau, in order to force the passage of the Rhine, I prevailed with Count Wratislaw to make all the haste he could to prince Louis of Baden's army, where he will be this night, that he might make him sensible of the great consequences it is to hinder the French from passing that river, while we are acting against the elector of Bavaria. I have also desired him to press, and not to be refused, that either Prince Louis or Prince Eugene go immediately to the Rhine.

The Duke was plainly also aware of the danger of the French and Bavarians being able to deploy superior numbers in the Danube valley. He was by this point growing less concerned at the potential French threat to strike at his marching columns; he was moving his army out of their reach, and his lines of communication and supply were shifting to central Germany. The time for his opponents to attack him on the march was almost over, although he still had to get his troops over the Swabian Jura hills in order to confront the Elector of Bavaria.

At Mundelheim, on 10 June, Marlborough met for the first time the President of the Imperial War Council, 37 year-old Prince Eugene of Savoy. The Prince reviewed the Duke's cavalry and commented approvingly that 'He had heard much of the English cavalry and found it to be the best appointed and the finest he had ever seen.' The two men quickly became close friends and confidantes, but relations with the Imperial field commander, Louis-Guillaume, Margrave of Baden, were less rosy. Baden was brave enough, but was pompous and jealous of the friendship of the Duke and the Prince. Working with him was not an easy matter, particularly as it was suspected that he was in indiscreet correspondence with his old comrade, the renegade Elector of Bavaria. There was also a period of wasteful marching to and fro while the Margrave got his forces, which had been gathering forage and supplies, properly into position, ready to cover Marlborough's move into the Danube valley.

Meanwhile, the French commanders in Alsace remained in uncertainty. Marlborough could strike at them still, or move to the Danube. On 12 June the French War Minister, Michel de Chamillart, wrote to Tallard: 'Nobody knows the country better than you, and as Marshal Villeroi is very well informed about it, His Majesty knows no better than to put to you two again, the choice as to what to do.' It was a key question for the two field commanders, who were asked to submit plans to foil Marlborough's campaign. However, both men were consumed with doubt, Tallard writing: 'In view of the superiority of the enemy forces between the Rhine and the Danube, assistance to Bavaria is so difficult as to appear almost an impossibility.' In this he was right; the Allies could muster at this time more troops in the centre ground than either of the two widely separated French and Bavarian armies. General Legalle was sent to Versailles to explain the problems, but Louis XIV decided that Tallard should, once again, move though the Black Forest and link up with Marshal Marsin, while Villeroi fixed the Imperial forces on the Rhine, and so prevented their use on the Danube.

The armies of Marlborough and Baden at last combined on 22 June, on a day foul with rain and wind. With 60,000 troops, they now outnumbered the armies of Marshal Marsin and the Elector, who had about 40,000 men between them, and were obliged to go into the shelter of an entrenched defensive camp at Dillingen on the north bank of the Danube.

One of the Elector's regimental commanders was Colonel Jean-Martin De La Colonie. His unit, the Grenadiers Rouge, was composed of French and Italian deserters and other miscreants who were permitted to volunteer for further service rather than face court martial. They were a rather motley bunch, almost a penal battalion, and the Colonel was having a lot of problems with them at this time. He wrote of the measures necessary to instil discipline in them, after a rash of incidents, which aroused the fury of citizens of the town in which they were quartered:

> I did my best to suppress their thieving ways and brigandage which
> obtained with these men and rendered them unbearable. The best of them

deserved hanging ten times over, and it was almost impossible to put a stop to the bad habits they had contracted. The burghers of Straubing never ceased to complain of them the whole winter long, and the quarrelling and fighting that went on between the grenadiers themselves took up nearly my entire attention. Finally, after exhausting all the ordinary measures of maintaining discipline, I was compelled to ask for power to flog them at my own discretion, without convening a court-martial. This was granted me, and in order to get clear evidence as to the guilty parties, whom I found it perpetually necessary to chastise in this severe fashion I organised a series of patrols, night and day, in all the streets of the town. In this way I put a stop to a greater portion of the evil under which the citizens suffered.

Although the Grenadiers Rouge were apparently of rather dubious quality, experience would show that they became good campaigners and stout fighters in time.

Marlborough had cast loose his exposed lines of supply and communication along the Rhine, as he passed through the Swabian hills. Despite this, the Duke was continually worried at the state of his marching troops, and the wear and tear on his army. When they got to Bavaria they would have to be in good condition if the Elector and Marsin were to be confronted with any chance of success. He wrote from Sinsein on 18 June to his brother, Charles Churchill:

In my last I desired you not to press your march so as to prejudice your men or horses, for that if you came a day later than the route appoints, it would not be material. Pray acquaint Colonel [Holcroft] Blood that he should spare the contractor's horses as much as may be, and make use of as many others for the train as the country can afford even one march beyond Gieslingen, after which he can expect no more assistance from the country, but must depend entirely on his own horses.

Marlborough's thinking is clear. Once past the Gieslingen gap in the Jura hills, the Allied army would be operating in a country no longer lush with supplies and willing assistance, but potentially hostile and swept clean by the Elector's hungry troops. Another letter to his brother, sent two days later, indicates that the pace of the campaign was quickening, the army moving from line of march to combat readiness and dispositions. The Duke concluded his note: 'One day's march on the other side of Gieslingen you just give notice that all the officers must take care of their own baggage from thence [onwards].' A week or so earlier, Prince Eugene had gone to command the Imperial troops at the Lines of Stollhofen, holding the line of the River Rhine against any new French incursion into southern Germany. If he could achieve this, then the armies of Marsin and the Elector would be firmly isolated in the Danube valley, and exposed to the full fury of the onslaught of Marlborough and Baden. However, on 27 June, Louis XIV's fresh instructions to his two Marshals for the future of the campaign were received; Villeroi was to fix Eugene on the Rhine while Tallard took his army as reinforcement to the Danube.

At the beginning of July, news came in to the Allied camp at Amerdingen that Eugene had failed in his task to hold the line against the French. Tallard had out-manoeuvred the Prince, and was coming forward through the Black Forest with a fresh army, although the Marshal spent several unproductive days trying to take Villingen, which lay inconveniently on his line of march. Eugene had been given a formidable task, with insufficient strength, even after reinforcement with Danish infantry. He was now in pursuit of Tallard, but with his relative lack of numbers, only some 18,000 troops, the Prince was unable to intercept the Marshal's progress. At the same time, in the Danube valley, Marlborough was concerned that, even as he moved forward to grapple with the French and Bavarian armies, his own order of battle was still incomplete. The original plan, for the Duke and the Margrave to operate independently, had not been possible due to delays in the arrival of the Danish contingent under the Duke of Württemberg. This left Marlborough with too few troops to operate without the close support of Baden. As it was, three days earlier he had written to Sir Charles Hedges:

> We are now within two leagues of the Elector who is retired with his army into his lines between Dillingen and Lavingen; but we shall not be able to press him so as it were to be wished until the Danish horse come up, which will not be, I fear, these five or six days; though if the Duke of Wurttemberg had hastened his march according to the repeated orders I sent, he might have been here by this time.

As the Duke well knew, Count Scholten, commanding the Danish infantry, had, a couple of weeks before, been sent to reinforce Eugene at the lines of Stollhofen, and their cavalry had been engaged in covering this movement. It seems that Marlborough, when it suited him, could engage his memory quite selectively, a common trait among commanding generals. Tallard's approach, however, inevitably increased the pace of operations on the Danube; with a fresh French army on the scene, if Marlborough did not force the line of the river now, he might never do so.

The Duke's forward supply depots, established at Nordlingen, would be too far away once the line of the Danube was crossed, and the Allied army was operating deep in Bavaria. So the Duke looked to secure a good place to both bridge the river and establish a forward base. The ideal location appeared to the small town of Donauwörth, where the Wörnitz river met the Danube. The Elector, from the snug security of his entrenched camp at Dillingen, had also seen this possibility, and sent a strong corps, under Comte Jean d'Arco, to hold the town and the heights that dominated the crossing place; a hill known as the Schellenberg. D'Arco had under command veteran French and Bavarian infantry, together with dismounted dragoons, and two batteries of guns. In addition, Bavarian militia and a French battalion garrisoned the town under command of Colonel Du Bordet. Francis Hare remembered that 'Thirteen thousand of the enemy were encamped upon the Schellenberg and they were busy in fortifying and entrenching themselves.'

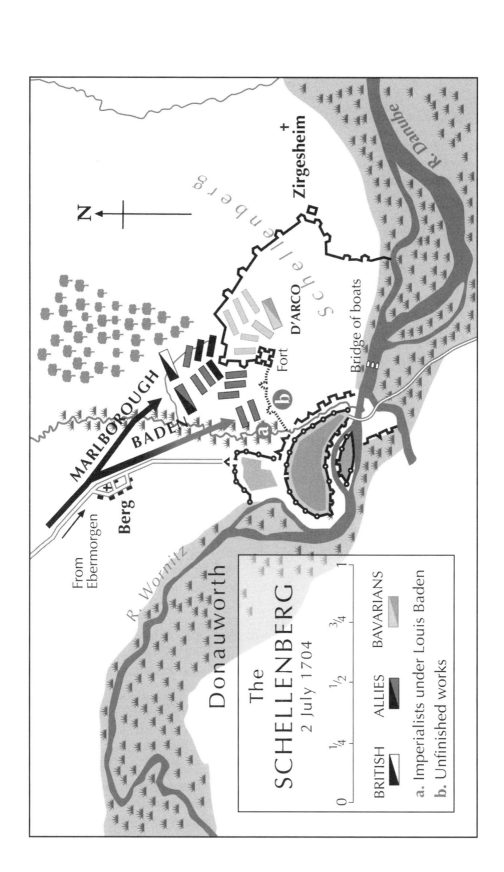

The
SCHELLENBERG
2 July 1704

BRITISH   ALLIES   BAVARIANS

a. Imperialists under Louis Baden
b. Unfinished works

Donauworth

R. Wornitz

From Ebermorgen

Berg

MARLBOROUGH

BADEN

Schellenberg

D'ARCO

Fort

Zirgesheim

R. Danube

Bridge of boats

Colonel De La Colonie described the hurried efforts of D'Arco's French and Bavarian corps to improve and complete the rather sketchy defensive works that existed on the Schellenberg:

> The time left to us was too short to complete this satisfactorily; we could only place fascines one on the other, sparsely covered with earth, so as to form something of the nature of a parapet, which, moreover, was neither high enough nor wide enough to be of much use. As to the ditch on the enemy's side, from which works of this sort derive their chief strength, the Imperial force gave us no time even to begin it.

He then comments on the thinly defended stretch of slope between the hill and the old walls of the town, a potentially fatal weak spot in the defensive arrangements:

> No attention had been paid hitherto to this flank because the town of Donauworth protected this side more than the other; its glacis so commanded the line of approach to it that a column would have to defile along the edge of the wood to avoid the fire of the fortifications, which thus ought to have formed one of our principal defences.

The Colonel was right, unless of course a commander was on the scene who was determined enough to accept the heavy casualties dictated by the narrow angle of approach, necessary to avoid fire from the town. All defences can be overcome if enough effort is made to do so.

The Margrave of Baden protested at the likely cost of a frontal assault on Donauwörth and the Schellenberg – he quite rightly feared heavy losses – but Marlborough overruled him. D'Arco could not easily be manoeuvred out of his position on the hill, and time was pressing as Tallard was now moving forward. The Duke's Wing of the army was leading the march and was closer to the town; it would provide the troops for the main assault, led by 5,750 stormers, drawn from the grenadier companies and volunteers from every battalion in the Allied army. Baden at length agreed to bring forward a brigade of Imperial grenadiers to support the attack. Leaving their camp at 3am on 2 July 1704, the Allied columns steadily approached Donauwörth over muddy roads, After crossing the Wörnitz river at Ebermorgen in the early afternoon, the leading Allied troops came in sight of the Schellenberg, on whose slopes the Bavarian and French soldiers could be seen labouring to improve the dilapidated defences. Kit Davies remembered that:

> Our vanguard did not come in sight of the enemy's entrenchments till the afternoon: however, not to give the Bavarians time to make themselves yet stronger, the duke ordered the Dutch General Goor, who commanded the right wing, composed of English and Dutch, with some auxiliary troops, to attack, as soon as possible: thus we did not stay for the coming up of the imperialists.

Colonel Holcroft Blood (whose father had famously attempted to steal the Crown Jewels during Charles II's reign) got a battery into place between the outlying village of Berg and the foot of the Schellenberg, where the Kaiback stream made the ground boggy. An Imperial battery, sent forward by Baden, soon joined them. The elevation of the field pieces, necessary to reach the defenders on the slopes above, meant that the projectiles skimmed the breastwork and left the Bavarians almost unscathed, but then ploughed through the ranks of the French battalions standing on the higher slopes behind them. Colonel De La Colonie was at that moment giving his men a few words of advice to encourage them for the coming fight:

> I had scarcely finished speaking when the enemy's battery opened fire on us, and raked us through and through. They concentrated this fire on us, and with their first discharge carried off Count de la Bastide, the lieutenant of my own company with whom at the moment I was speaking, and twelve grenadiers, who fell side by side in the ranks, so that my coat was covered in brains and blood. So accurate was the fire that each discharge of the cannons stretched some of my men on the ground. I suffered agonies at seeing these brave fellows perish without a chance of defending themselves but it was absolutely necessary that they should not move from their post.

At about 6pm watchers standing in comparative safety on the smaller hill near to Berg saw the attackers go in. Marlborough's chaplain, Francis Hare, was among their number and noted the time. He wrote that:

> The detachment moved in six lines (viz. four of foot and two of horse) up the rising ground, the English being on the left of all, and close by the wood. The fascines being brought from thence by the horse, every officer and soldier took one, and they were ordered to carry them till they could throw them down in the enemy's entrenchments, and to move on closely and slowly, forbearing to fire till they came thither. They now proceeded upon the attack, Brigadier Ferguson leading up the first line of foot, Count Horn and the other generals bringing up the rest. Lieut-Gen. Goor commanding the whole.

Lord John Mordaunt (who had once aspired, without success, to the hand of one of Marlborough's daughters) led the attack with a forlorn hope of eighty men from the 1st English Foot Guards. This party led the way at a smart pace, the troops shouting and cheering with all their might, but the fascine bundles they carried were wastefully thrown into a sunken lane at the bottom of the hill. De La Colonie wrote of the tense wait on the hill for the attackers to show themselves as they came out of the low ground onto the slopes:

> The English infantry led this attack with the greatest intrepidity, right up to our parapet, but there they were opposed with a courage at least equal to their own. The little parapet which separated the two forces became the scene of the bloodiest struggle that could be conceived.

The approaching ranks of Allied stormers had been riven by the ferocious Bavarian musketry and discharges of canister-shot from the battery in the hill.

The general commanding the assault, Johan Wigand van Goor, was shot in the eye and killed, and the soldiers fell back from the breastwork to recover their order. Donald McBane, who stood in the firing line as one of the stormers, remembered that the attackers soon 'Filled up their trenches with dead men.' Exultantly, Bavarian grenadiers vaulted the parapet to pursue them down the slope, but solid volleys from the English Foot Guards and Orkney's Regiment, just then labouring up the hill into position to support the attack, stopped them soon enough, and drove the defenders back into shelter.

As the assault on the stout defences was renewed, it became apparent that a line of gabions (wicker baskets filled with stones) linking the walls of the town with the defences on the Schellenberg was now unoccupied. The French troops assigned to hold the line there, drawn from the Régiment de Nectancourt, had been directed elsewhere in the battle, and D'Arco's position was dangerously exposed on his left as a result. De La Colonie remembered:

> The town commandant [du Bordet] instead of lining the covered way with his best troops, had withdrawn them all into his main works; he seemed to assume that the best way of ensuring the safety of this place was to shut up his troops and lock the gates.

The Margrave of Baden, standing with his Imperial grenadiers beside the Kaiback stream at the foot of the hill, soon learned of the abandoned works. He hurried his troops along the line of the muddy stream, just out of musket-shot of the walls of Donauwörth. At the line of deserted gabions he formed his troops facing up the hill to where the open flank of D'Arco's position lay, and steadily they began the breathless climb up grass slopes now being made slippery with light rain. Dr Hare, still an avid observer of the action from the hill at Berg, wrote of this flanking movement by the Imperial Grenadiers:

> The Imperial foot, which had gained the trenches [line of gabions] immediately inclined to the left, and took the enemy in the flank to favour and facilitate the attack of the English and Dutch. But for all that the enemy continued to oppose their entrance, and disputed it so obstinately that Lieutenant-General Lumley ordered Lord John Hay's regiment of dragoons to dismount and charge the enemy on foot.

The remorseless pressure on D'Arco's troops, both in front and to their left, finally told. Francis Hare goes on: 'This order was forthwith obeyed by that noble Lord, who dismounted and put himself at the head of his regiment, and was marching up bravely to attack on foot just as the enemy began to give way and our men had entered the trenches.'

De La Colonie was among those in the defences who saw the Imperial troops clambering up the hill to their left, and assumed they were reinforcements sent from the town. Soon the mistake was realised, as Baden's grenadiers poured heavy volleys of musketry into the flank of the French and Bavarians, who could fairly complain that they did not know which way to turn. All rapidly became confusion, and the Colonel was struck on the jaw by a musket ball and temporarily stunned. The defence fell to pieces as the Allied troops crowded onto the Schellenberg. D'Arco's army was fleeing towards the rear of the hill and the pontoon bridges over the Danube that offered the elusive chance of escape. Kit Davies, although wounded and unable to participate in the pursuit, remembered that:

> A cruel slaughter was made of them, and the bridge over the Danube breaking down, a great number were drowned, or taken prisoners. In the second attack, I received a ball in my hip, which is so lodged between the bones that it can never be extracted. Captain Young who, poor gentleman, was soon after killed, desired me to get off; but, upon my refusal, he ordered two of my comrades to take me up, and they set me at the foot of a tree … We lost, of my acquaintance, Captain Young, Captain Douglas, and Lieutenant Maltary, besides a number of private men. I was carried to the hospital [presumably a rudimentary regimental dressing station] near Schellenberg and put under the care of three surgeons, Mr Wilson, Mr Laurence and Mr Sea, and narrowly escaped being discovered.

The French and Bavarians, outnumbered, out-gunned and outflanked, had broken and were running for their lives. De La Colonie, now back on his feet and not feeling at all well, tried to rally his men, but they were in full flight:

> They disappeared like a flash of lightning without ever looking back. I looked on all sides for my drummer, but he had evidently thought fit to look after himself, with the result that I found myself at the mercy of the enemy and my own sad thoughts.

Discretion being the better part of valour, the Colonel looked to get out of peril himself, and took off towards the rear of the hill:

> The plain [crest of the Schellenberg] was too wide for me to traverse in my big boots at the necessary speed, and to crown my misfortunes was covered with cornfields. So far, the enemy's cavalry had not appeared on the plain, but there was every reason to believe that they would not long delay their arrival.

Marlborough had now let loose his cavalry, together with the remounted squadrons of dragoons, in a ruthless pursuit of the broken defenders. Such techniques were commonplace after a defeat at the time, with the fugitives chased, harried and cut down without mercy, the blades flicking and slashing among the imploring upturned hands. De La Colonie takes up the story:

> I found a convenient path along the bank of the river [Danube], but this was not of much avail to me for, owing to my efforts and struggles to reach it through several fields of standing corn, I was quite blown and exhausted. On my way I met the wife of a Bavarian soldier, so distracted with weeping that she travelled no faster than I did. I made her take off my boots, which fitted so tightly about the legs that it was absolutely impossible to do this for myself.

The French colonel plunged into the wide waters of the river and struck out for the far side: 'I knew how to swim, although the risk here was very great owing to the breadth and rapidity of the Danube. I threw myself upon the mercy of the stream. Finally, after a very long and hard swim, I was lucky enough to reach the other bank.' Some Dutch dragoons took shots at him with their carbines, but were more interested in plundering his coat and kit left lying at the river's edge.

Others were less fortunate and many fugitives were denied quarter, to be cut down by the Allied horsemen, while at least one of the pontoon bridges over the river collapsed, throwing scores of men into the Danube to struggle and drown. It is to be hoped that the Bavarian woman got safely away. Comte D'Arco hurried to Donauwörth town where the garrison commander was, after some delay, induced to admit him and a number of others. The Comte then went off to find the Elector of Bavaria to make his sorry report of the utter destruction of his corps. Colonel Du Bordet attempted to lay waste to Donauwörth that night, to reduce its usefulness as a base for the Allies. Kit Davies recalled that:

> That evening having received orders from the elector to burn the town and provisions, to blow up the ammunition, break down the bridges, and to retreat to Augsburg, they [the French] clapped straw into the houses, to which they began to set fire; but had not time to perfect their design, for fear of their retreat being cut off, the allies being got into the suburbs, and laying [pontoon] bridges over the river, which compelled them to withdraw at four o'clock in the morning.

The Allied soldiers helped the citizens to put out the fires started by the retreating garrison. Among the booty taken were nineteen guns (including three found in the town), twelve pontoon bridges, 20,000 pounds of gunpowder, 3,000 sacks of flour and oats, thirteen standards and colours, and all the tentage and camp gear of the defeated army. As Kit Davies commented:

> These were the fruits of our victory, which, however, we purchased by the loss of three thousand brave fellows killed and wounded, and, among several other general officers of distinction, General Goor received a musket-ball in the eye, and instantly expired.

De La Colonie had reached the safety of the far bank of the Danube, and, exhausted by his efforts, was luckily able to enlist the aid of some soldiers there:

> I found to my relief on the river-bank a quarter-master and a dragoon of the regiment of Fonboiser, who, on their way back from some duty, had stopped there in order to satisfy their curiosity as to what was passing on the other side of the Danube. I landed nearly at their feet, and the quarter-master, who gathered from my waistcoat and linen that I was an officer, came forward most politely to ask who I was and what he could do for me. As soon as he had learned that I was the lieutenant-colonel of the French grenadiers, he immediately dismounted and searched the dragoon's valise, producing a cap and a shirt, which he made me put on,

together with a cloak over-all, and he insisted that I should mount his horse, while he rode that of the dragoon, whom he took up behind him.

The exhausted colonel was taken to the small town of Rain, a few miles away, and learned there that almost all the baggage of the army had been lost in the flight from the hill, either seized by the Allies or tipped into Danube when the bridge broke down. Still, after an uneasy night's sleep:

> I was still in bed when I thought I heard the voice of my valet. I sprang in one jump from my bed to the window to see if I was not mistaken, and sure enough I saw him below me, fussing about to get some miserable carts out of the way in order to let my carriage by.

By this good fortune De La Colonie was one of the few officers from D'Arco's corps to save his baggage. The Comte himself was not so fortunate, as all his campaign equipment, including his silver dinner service, was seized by the victors of the battle. Captain John Blackader, present with Fergusson's Cameronian Regiment, walked over the hill that night in the drizzle. The place was a shambles with the dead and wounded lying thickly around on every side: 'The carcasses were very thick strewed upon the ground, naked and corrupting; yet all this works no impression or reformation upon us, seeing the bodies of our comrades and friends lying as dung upon the face of the earth.' The grim Scottish soldier constantly despaired of the licentious conduct, as he saw it, of the troops in Marlborough's army, and now seemed to feel that on those reeking slopes some, at least, had paid in full for their past misdeeds. The Duke of Marlborough wrote to Queen Anne with news of the battle:

> I must humbly presume to inform your majesty, that the success of our first attack of the enemy has been equal to the justice of the cause your majesty has so graciously espoused. Mr Secretary Harley will have the honour to lay the relation of yesterday's action before you. To which I shall crave leave to add, that our success is in great measure owing to the particular blessing of God, and the unparalleled bravery of your troops.

Vienna was soon alive with delight at the outcome. Emperor Leopold wrote a letter to Marlborough in his own hand (a most unusual honour), with congratulation at news of the victory:

> Illustrious, Sincerely Beloved. Your deserts towards me, my house, and the common cause, are great and many, and the singular application, care and diligence, which you have expressed, in bringing up and hastening the powerful succours, which the most serene and potent Queen of Great Britain, and the States-General of the United Netherlands, have sent me to the Danube, are not to be ranked in the last place; but nothing can be more glorious than what you have done, after the conjunction of your army with mine, in the most speedy and vigorous attack and forcing of the enemy's camp at Donawert, the second of this month; since my generals themselves, and ministers, declare that the success of that enterprise (which is more

acceptable and advantageous to me, in this present time, than almost any thing else that could befall me) is chiefly owing to your councils, prudence, and execution, and the wonderful bravery and constancy of the troops, who fought under your command. This will be an eternal trophy to your most serene Queen in Upper Germany, whither the victorious arms of the English nation have never penetrated since the memory of man.

The Allied armies now stood between Vienna and the French and Bavarians, and they could deploy greater numbers at any given point than their opponents, for the time being at least. However, many were made sombre by the scale of the casualties sustained in the assault, over 5,400 Allied soldiers having been killed or wounded, a quarter of those taking part. On the other hand, D'Arco's corps was shattered and only about 3,000 of his men escaped to ever rally to the colours. One facetious critic in London asked 'Are there not many hills in Germany, and must we fight such a battle for each one?' The objections raised by the Margrave to the attack were well known, and the Dutch minted a coin in commemoration of the event; but it featured Baden (who had sustained a serious wound to the foot in the fighting) and not Marlborough, whose plan was put into execution and whose victory it truly was. Queen Anne wrote to the Archduke Charles with word of the victory on 14 July:

> I received yesterday by an express from the Duke of Marlborough that the Allies have gained a signal victory over the French and Bavarians, who occupied a position near Donauwert. They entirely defeated them and took that village. I think this news will be no less pleasing to you, on the account of the effect such a fine victory must have on Vienna, than it is to me, in giving me joy as much on behalf of the common cause, as because of the part taken by troops in this glorious action, under the command of the said Duke of Marlborough.

With Donauwörth and the Schellenberg safely in Allied hands, Marlborough had his forward base and crossing point over the Danube. The Elector of Bavaria had no choice but to abandon the line of the river. With a numerically inferior army, now weakened by their losses in the battle, he was obliged to leave the strong camp at Dillingen and fall back southwards to Augsburg, where he would have the protection of the Lech river. This was another good barrier, difficult to cross even with the pontoon bridging train that Marlborough had dragged along from the Low Countries, and would offer some measure of security.

Marlborough appeared to exaggerate the strategic effect of the victory over D'Arco's corps on the slopes above Donauwörth. The Duke was also over-optimistic concerning Eugene's ability to impede Tallard's progress on the march from the Rhine, and he wrote to Godolphin on 9 July:

> We have heard nothing of Prince Eugene since the 5th, so that we take it for granted that the Marshal de Tallard has not pursued his march, which he began on 2nd of this month [actually the date that Marlborough heard

of Tallard's movement forwards]; and I cannot but be of the opinion that if he has had a true account of what has passed at the Schellenberg, he will be desirous of having fresh orders sent before he advances further.

The Marshal had interrupted his progress, but this was to lay siege to the relatively unimportant town of Villingen; an enterprise he abandoned after four days on the approach of Prince Eugene. Tallard was now pressing on towards Ulm and the vital junction with the beleaguered forces of Marsin and the Elector. The Comte de Merode-Westerloo, whose Walloon cavalry brigade was with Tallard's army, wrote of the march through the Black Forest:

> We reached Hornberg at the same time as the rest of the army, to find the fine chateau abandoned, and the small town sacked by our marauders before we arrived. There we camped and rested the space of one day, to await the arrival of the head of our large convoy. Moving on, we next deployed on to the heights above Villingen, and duly invested the town next morning [in all likelihood this was 16 July 1704], as we wished to seize the place and use it for a forward-base. In the meantime the convoy crawled out of the Black Forest passes. In spite of our opening trenches and mounting mortar and cannon batteries, we were eventually forced to abandon the siege [on the approach of Eugene's army], after wasting much valuable time and material; for the townsfolk and the small garrison defended the place so well, even though it had only a single ancient wall, that we had no choice but to move on and join the Elector of Bavaria.

While Tallard made his way through the wooded passes, Marlborough's own campaign dragged a little. He had not been able to bring the heavy guns of his siege train on the march up the Rhine; the ordnance had to take a longer and far slower route, away from possible French interference. Baden had assured him that a siege train would be provided, once he got to Bavaria, but this proved not to be the case. Because of such deficiencies, it took the Duke a time-wasting four days to prepare to take the small town of Rain, just to the south of Donauwörth and well garrisoned by French and Bavarian troops. Having written to the Secretary of State, Robert Harley, that the guns were awaited before siege operations could begin, the Duke was still having to employ patience four days later, on 13 July, when he wrote to an acquaintance from the camp at Burkheim:

> Now we have met with a disappointment in the want of our artillery from Nuremburg for attacking Rain, wherein the enemy have a garrison of about a thousand men, which we were unwilling to leave behind; but what we expected being now come, or within reach, we shall open the trenches this night and I hope soon make ourselves masters of the place.

Jean-Martin De La Colonie had managed to gather together most of his grenadiers, those that got away from the disaster on the Schellenberg hill, and now found that the onerous task of organising the defence of Rain fell to him. Comte D'Arco wrote from the Elector's camp near Augsburg with congratulations on his escape, but also:

Having complimented me on the retreat from Schellenberg, he pointed out that His Highness [the Elector] hoped I should show no less zeal in the defence of Rain, which he now placed in my hands, and as the enemy would doubtless attack it, he had ordered a detachment of six hundred men, some cannon, and stores, to join me, which were already on their way. By this time I had about four hundred grenadiers who had managed to save themselves and the colours.

Rain was not properly fortified or really defensible for long, despite the rather meagre reinforcement sent by the Elector to assist De La Colonie. After some stiff fighting, and with the Allied heavy guns at last getting into place, the Colonel was summoned to surrender, but he requested:

A capitulation with all the honours of war, without which I assured them, I would sustain any assault that they might make. They tried cajoling, then threats, but finally, seeing that I refused the bait, granted what I asked ... I here had proof how essential it is in all military matters to maintain a firm attitude.

De La Colonie's garrison was permitted to march away to Munich. Marlborough, having at last got possession of the town, which would otherwise have sat inconveniently on his lines of supply, could turn his full attention to the main French and Bavarian army.

Prince Eugene, it must be said, was not impressed by the pace of the campaign being undertaken by Marlborough and Baden: 'They amuse themselves laying siege to Rain and burning a few villages instead, according to my opinion, which I have made known to them clearly enough, of advancing directly upon the enemy.' The Prince's critical comments must be seen in the light of his own failure to block the French advance from the Rhine, having been decoyed by a clever ruse, so allowing Tallard and his army to slip past on the road to the Danube valley. Eugene had then been obliged to divide his own army; leaving a substantial force behind on the Rhine to hold Villeroi in place, he marched in Tallard's wake, with troops too few in number, even after reinforcement with Danish troops sent by Marlborough, to seriously impede, much less confront, the Marshal. At this point, not one of the Allied commanders was performing particularly successfully. Their opponents, despite even so serious a reverse as the Schellenberg defeat, could apparently wait for events to unfold as autumn came on; the onset of winter would kill off Marlborough's campaign soon enough.

The Elector of Bavaria, in the meantime, was made anxious by the unexpected ferocity of Marlborough's campaign. He had watched the destruction of D'Arco's corps on the Schellenberg hill from the far side of the Danube, and attempted now to deflect the worst effects of his own duplicity by some sly negotiation with his opponent. As it turned out, despite hints to Marlborough that he would return to his allegiance to the Emperor and break with Louis XIV, it soon became apparent that the Elector was just playing for time, while the fresh French army under Tallard drew near. The Duke wrote to Secretary of State, Charles Hedges, on 16 July:

I was in some hopes that I might by this post have given you an account of the Elector of Bavaria's having embraced the interest of the Allies, matters being brought so far that he had appointed to meet Count Wratislaw yesterday in order to sign the Articles that had been agreed upon. But instead of complying with his promises, he sent his secretary to acquaint him [Wratislaw] that being informed Comte Tallard was marching with an army of 35,000 men to his relief it was not in his power or consistent with his honour to quit the French interest. While this has been in agitation we have been attacking the town of Rain, which has been obliged this day to capitulate.

Marlborough, frustrated at the prevarication of the Elector, concerned at reports of Tallard's approach, and apprehensive of valuable time passing unproductively while summer sped by, now opened a new and controversial campaign. In the same letter to Hedges he wrote: 'We are going to burn and destroy the Elector's country to oblige him to hearken to terms.'

The horrors of the religious wars of the early and mid-seventeenth century had brought a supposedly more civilised approach to warfare in Europe (despite the enthusiastic French devastation of the Palatinate in the 1680s), and the Duke's decision to lay waste to Bavaria aroused protest and criticism. Baden refused to take part, until bluntly ordered to do so, and Marlborough wrote rather defensively to the Duchess at this time that the English troops took no part in the burnings. Whatever the truth of this, the soldiers themselves had little, if any, objection to the work, and it did reduce the Elector's ability to use his own lands as a base for future operations, however ruthless the devastation may have seemed to those far away. Also, the Bavarian army was dispersed to protect the Elector's estates from attack, and this significantly reduced the strength of Marlborough's opponents on the field of battle when the crucial moment came. Private John Deane commented in his journal that the district was 'Still burning all round by the Emperor's orders', while Adam Cardonnel wrote of the campaign that: 'Our last march was all in fire and smoke. I wish to God it were all over that I may get safe out of this country.' Kit Davies, though, was in typically robust mood after recovering from her Schellenberg wound, and made no complaint about being employed in the raiding forays across Bavaria: 'The allies sent parties on every hand to ravage the country, who pillaged above fifty villages, burnt the houses of peasants and gentlemen, and forced the inhabitants, with what few cattle had escaped, to seek refuge in the woods.'

Colonel De La Colonie, whose own remustered regiment was now near Munich, wrote that his troops were sent out to feel for the Allied raiders, and to assess the level of destruction being caused:

I followed a route through several villages said to have been reduced to cinders, and although I certainly found a few burnt houses, still the damage was as nothing compared with the reports current throughout the country. By means of the woods I was able to push on from village to village in the direction of the enemy's army, and found there even less evidence of damage; the villages seemed practically entire, and it was only on entering them that it was possible to see any trace of burning in a house here and there.

He added a comment that vividly shows the severity of this kind of warfare: 'We came across marauders on our road, who were promptly shot.' The Colonel then recounts an incident when the Grenadiers Rouge became engaged in a vicious running battle with the Imperial Schvein Regiment, illustrating very well that warfare in the early eighteenth century was nowhere near as formal and rigid as is often thought:

> I started in pursuit with the first half of the regiment that had passed over [a river], and left an order for the rest to follow us. We were now in hard chase of the enemy's rearguard, and came up with it a good quarter of a league from the village, owing to their march having been hindered by the woods and my extreme diligence in pursuit. I first caught sight of them retiring over the brow of a wooded ridge, when I gave my grenadiers orders to fix bayonets and not to fire without permission from me. We then hastened our pace, and the enemy seeing us on the point of falling upon them, halted, turned about, and opened fire upon us, with the result that a number of my men were killed on either side of my horse without, strange to say, even wounding him.

De La Colonie's mount became so agitated and unmanageable by the musketry that the Colonel was forced to dismount and lead his men forward on foot:

> After delivering this volley, the enemy continued their retirement with even more precipitation than before, and without reloading. Here, then, was our turn in the game. We let ourselves go headlong upon them, and every one of our shots told … My grenadiers followed eagerly, slaying them with bayonet thrust and gunshot, giving no quarter, so as not to delay the advance.

The Grenadiers Rouge were soon be sent to Ingolstadt to bolster the garrison there, but De La Colonie was exasperated at the lack of wisdom of the Elector's chosen course, dispersing his army widely to counter the Allied raiding parties:

> What astonished me, and what no one has been able to explain to me, was that on leaving his entrenchments [at Augsburg] he did not recall at least fifteen thousand men from the Bavarian army, including our own detachment. Such a considerable reinforcement might well have given us victory, for the valour of these troops was beyond question.

Marlborough, of course, would be well aware of the pressure his campaign of destruction put upon his opponent, and must have viewed the continued dispersion of the Bavarian army with satisfaction. At this time, he received a letter from Comte D'Arco, who was making some attempt to rebuild the strength of the Bavarian army after the disaster at the Schellenberg, and his reply was dated 23 July 1704:

I have received the honour of your letter regarding the exchange of prisoners of war ... Have the goodness to send me the lists of those who you have of ours who are taken since I arrived in this country, we will send a similar number for exchange, man for man, according to their rank .. If you want to have a list of those [French and Bavarian] wounded at Donauwörth, you do not have to send a list of equal size, they can be returned at your request.

The Duke then shifted tack a little, perhaps becoming reluctant to help the Bavarians in restoring their capability. Three days later he was writing again to D'Arco:

I have received the honour of your letter with the lists of our prisoners which you have with your army, which I have sent to the Prince [Margrave] of Baden; we are ready to send you in exchange the same numbers from your wounded at Donauwörth.

Marlborough relented later in the week, plainly wanting to have the care of the enemy wounded off his hands if he could, writing to D'Arco 'I have sent a letter to the commander in Donauwörth, concerning one of your wounded officers who, if you desire, will leave with the soldiers there under his parole.'

By 29 July the Duke's campaign to batter the Elector into submission was in full brutal flow. He wrote to London:

Since the advance of M. Tallard he [the Elector] would not hear of any accommodation, though I have not been wanting on my part, and am sorry he has at last obliged us to extremities, the Comte de la Tour [the Imperial cavalry commander] being gone out this morning with strong detachment of horse and dragoons to destroy and burn the country about Munich, as I fear we shall be forced to do in other parts, to deprive the enemy as well of present subsistence as future support on this side.

Those Allied soldiers not thus engaged were kept in good fettle with parades and reviews. The camp bulletin the following day ran 'On Monday my Lord Duke of Marlborough reviewed all the troops of the left Wing of the army, which appeared in very good order.'

On 6 August 1704, Marshal Tallard, having delivered his precious supply convoy to the hungry, empty, depots in Ulm, moved to combine his army with that of the Elector and Marsin, near to Augsburg. Eugene reached the area of Höchstädt, north of the Danube, at about the same time, and the Prince rode to confer with Marlborough and Baden near to Rain. The Allies still had a superiority in numbers, although Eugene's force was rather exposed as it stood to the west of the main Allied army. The Margrave, feeling eclipsed by the closeness of his two colleagues, suggested that he should take his own army and besiege the important crossing place over the Danube at Ingolstadt, twenty miles downstream from Donauwörth. This move had been considered earlier in the campaign, but shelved as insufficient troops had been available. The suggestion was promptly approved by Marlborough, who was not reluctant to get the obstructive, and possibly unreliable, Imperial general out of the way, even though it meant giving up his numerical advantage over his opponents. On 9 August Baden marched eastwards with 15,000 troops to begin the siege, and the Duke and Eugene could begin their moves against the Elector of Bavaria and his French colleagues in earnest.

In the opposing camp, meanwhile, it was rumoured but not yet known for certain that Baden had gone to Ingolstadt. Tallard appears to have preferred to bide his time, and wait for the Allied campaign to wither away in the mists of autumn. He was concerned, as was Marshal Marsin, at the continued wasteful dispersion of the Bavarian army, and urged the Elector, in vain, to concentrate his army's strength without further delay. Tallard later wrote to the French War Minister that 'There was a total ignorance of the enemy's strength, and M. de Bavière [the Elector] having all his troops, except five battalions and about twenty-three squadrons, spread about the country.' The commanders on neither side had an exact figure of their opponents' strength, as the numbers present in individual battalions and squadrons would vary quite considerably. In any case, the superiority in numbers now enjoyed by the Elector and his French colleagues was not sufficient to ensure that they could simply overwhelm Marlborough and Eugene if they were in a good defensive position. Marsin and the Elector, however, wanted to act decisively and without delay. They saw, correctly, that Eugene's small army, still north of the Danube, was a tempting target, rather isolated, while Marlborough was several days' march away to the south of the river. Accordingly, on 10 August the French and Bavarian armies closed up to the Danube and began crossing to the north bank on pontoon bridges laid at the derelict camp near Dillingen.

Eugene was alerted to the French and Bavarian advance almost immediately, as his forward posts were being overrun. He plainly had insufficient strength to maintain his exposed position, and wrote urgently to Marlborough:

> The enemy have marched. It is almost certain that the whole army is passing the Danube at Lauingen. They have pushed a Lieutenant-Colonel that I sent to reconnoitre back to Höchstädt. The plain of Dillingen is crowded with troops. I have held on here all day; but with 18 battalions I dare not risk staying the night. I quit however, with much regret [the position] being good and if he takes it, it will cost us much to get it back. I am therefore marching the infantry and part of the cavalry this night to a camp I have marked out before Donauwörth. I shall stay here as long as I can … Everything, Milord, consists in speed and that you put yourself forthwith in movement to join me to-morrow, without which I fear it will be too late.

The Duke moved smartly to his friend's support, and despatched that very night twenty-seven squadrons of Imperial cavalry, under command of the Duke of Württemberg. They were followed closely by Charles Churchill, with twenty battalions of infantry, to march westwards and effect a junction with Eugene's army. This was successfully achieved near to Münster, just to the west of Donauwörth, on 11 August, as the remainder of Marlborough's army and the train of artillery moved to the north bank of the Danube. In this way, nearly a week after the French and Bavarian armies combined, their opponents did the same. An anxious period for Marlborough, when his opponents had a fleeting chance to overwhelm one of the detachments of his army, had passed.

The French Marshals and the Elector, in the meantime, were becoming careless. Their confident approach, even though they had not caught Eugene, brought them to the plain of Höchstädt, which seemed a perfect spot to encamp, certainly better than the boggy ground of the Pulver and Brunnen streams near the town of Höchstädt itself. Some four miles wide, from the Danube in the south to the Swabian Jura hills to the north, the whole area was open and even, thick with the still ungathered harvest of late summer. The flanks of the army were secured by the river and the hills, while the whole frontage was protected by the normally marshy Nebel stream; however, this was, according to the Marquis de Montigny-Langost who served with Tallard, rather meagre on account of the recent warm weather, and far less of an obstacle than it appeared to be: 'Only a stream of two feet in width, which formed a small marsh very dried up because of the warm weather, which greatly deceived our generals, who believed it very difficult. This stream comprised the only obstacle.' Marshal Marsin's comment on this stream, on the other hand, was that is was 'A morass, which our engineers thought impassable.' Anyway, in the course of 12 August, the French and Bavarian armies set up their tents, dug latrines, arranged their horse lines, and sent out foragers. The senior officers made themselves comfortable in the barns and cottages of the small villages which dotted the plain, little suspecting that they might soon have to fight a battle on that very same ground.

The combined armies of Marlborough and Eugene had now begun moving towards the west, rapidly closing the gap between themselves and the plain of Höchstädt. In the afternoon of 12 August, the two Allied commanders were able to complete their own close reconnaissance by climbing the tower of Tapfheim church, from where they were able to clearly see their opponents' camp. While this was going on, the Marshals and the Elector of Bavaria, all experienced commanders with worthy records, remained in blissful ignorance of their intentions. Marsin wrote afterwards that 'On the twelve [August] we called a Council of War, to consider whether we should stay for the enemy, who was marching towards us, and resolved we should.' If this really were so, their lack of awareness that they might actually be attacked, and the failure to prepare for the following morning, is simply astonishing.

As the Allied army marched, Marlborough found it necessary to have his pioneers improve the tracks through the woods alongside the road. This noisy activity did not fail to attract the attention of the French, and cavalry patrols under the Marquis de Silly came forward to see what was going on. Some stiff outpost fighting took place before the troopers were driven off, but the French and Bavarian commanders felt no real concern at these developments. The Comte de Merode-Westerloo tried to take part in this skirmishing action, and remembered that: 'I rode out beyond Blindheim village into the corn-filled plain – taking care not to stray too far away from my escort which I might well

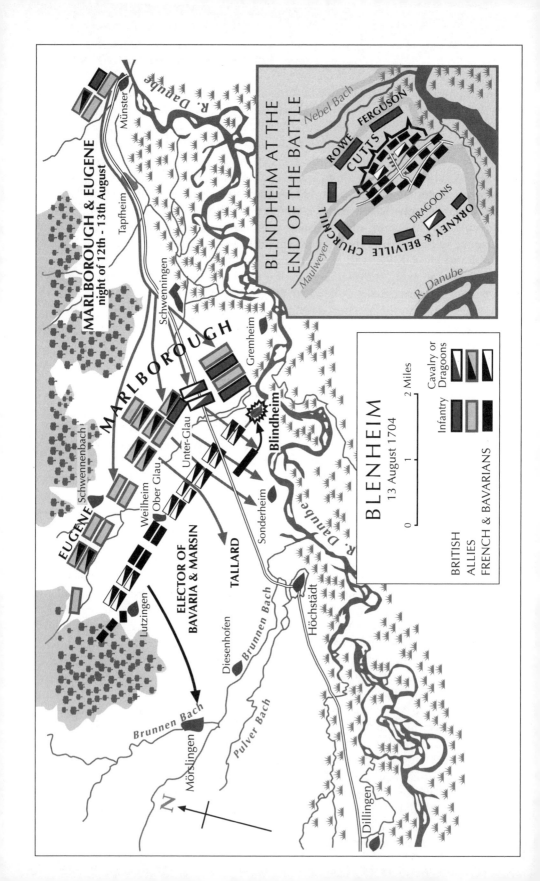

BLINDHEIM AT THE
END OF THE BATTLE

Nebel Bach

ROWE FERGUSON

CUTTS

ORKNEY & BELVILLE DRAGOONS

CHURCH HILL

Maulweyer Bach

R. Danube

MARLBOROUGH & EUGENE
night of 12th - 13th August

R. Danube

Münster

Tapfheim

Schwenningen

MARLBOROUGH

Gremheim

Blindheim

Schwennenbach

EUGENE

Weilheim

Ober Glau

Unter-Glau

Sonderheim

ELECTOR OF
BAVARIA & MARSIN

TALLARD

Lutzingen

Diesenhofen

Brunnen Bach

Höchstädt

R. Danube

Brunnen Bach

Mörslingen

Pulver Bach

Dillingen

BLENHEIM
13 August 1704

2 Miles

Cavalry or
Dragoons

Infantry

0   1

BRITISH
ALLIES
FRENCH & BAVARIANS

N

have needed. When I saw our troops falling back, I also returned to camp.' No alarm was taken, the fine evening passed, and the French and their allies settled comfortably into their tents for the night.

On rising the following morning. Marshall Tallard dictated a letter to Louis XIV, which gives a hint of how profoundly he had misunderstood the intentions of Marlborough and Eugene. After commenting on the mist that lay over the plain, he went on 'The enemy beat the generall at two o'clock, and assembled at three. On sending scouts to view their camp it seems that they will march today. The talk of the countryside is that they will go to Nordlingen.'

Francis Hare left a detailed account of the onset of the battle that morning, Wednesday 13 August 1704, when the leading Allied soldiers:

> Discovered the advanced parties of the enemy [actually foragers] before six o'clock in the morning, and these, as our squadrons came up, retired by degrees towards their encampment. About seven our generals halted and took a full view of the enemy's camp from a rising ground over against it, and found the situation of it to be as follows: their right was on the Danube, having the village of Blenheim (where was Marshal Tallard's quarters) in front; and their left extended to a wood which covered the village of Lutzingen, where were the quarters of the Elector of Bavaria. All along this front there ran a rivulet [the Nebel stream] twelve feet broad in most places and very difficult to pass, and in several parts the ground near it was very marshy. About the centre was the village of Oberglau (the quarters of Marshal Marsin), situated upon the side of the hill about musket-shot from the rivulet. The enemy were encamped upon this hill, which reached from the Danube to the wood, being of a very easy ascent, and having a command of the whole plain ... While viewing these features of the enemy's position at a short distance, his Grace was also more particularly informed of the nature of them by Major-General Natzmer, of the King of Prussia's troops, who had been wounded the year before in the defeat at this place of Count Stirum by the Elector of Bavaria and M. d'Usson.

Hare noticed in particular the curious lack of activity in the opposing camp, as the Allied army poured out past the narrow defile at the village of Schwenningen onto the plain of Höchstädt:

> All this while, the morning being a little hazy, the enemy might suppose that we had only small parties abroad, and might not be aware that the whole army was in motion. However this may have been, they remained quietly in their camp during this early part of the morning. Our columns began to appear a little after seven, both officers and soldiers advancing cheerfully and showing a firm and glad countenance, and seeming to be confident to themselves of a victorious day.

The Comte de Merode-Westerloo, on the other side of the stream, was among those few in the French and Bavarian camp who seemed to be alarmed at the Allied advance:

> I slept deeply until six in the morning when I was abruptly awoken by one
> of my old retainers who rushed into the barn all out of breath ... This
> fellow, LeFranc, shook me awake and blurted out that the enemy was
> there. Thinking to mock him I said 'Where? There?' and he at once
> replied 'Yes-there-there!' Flinging wide as he spoke the door of the barn
> and drawing my bed-curtains – the whole area appeared to be covered by
> enemy squadrons ... I rubbed my eyes in disbelief, and then coolly
> remarked that the enemy must at least give me time to take my morning
> cup of chocolate. While I was hurriedly drinking this and getting dressed,
> my horses were saddled and harnessed.

Soon the Comte was getting his men to their feet and their horses ready. He
also astutely instructed his servants to take his camp baggage to the rear. 'There
was not a soul stirring as I clattered out of the village, nothing might have been
happening,' he recalled. Tallard hurried past, and called out his congratulation
that Merode-Westerloo was so promptly responding to the sudden and
alarming development. Observing all this from the far side of the field, Francis
Hare tells us that:

> The enemy now beat to arms, and fired the signal for their foragers to
> come in. They also set fire to the villages of Berghausen, Weilheim [farm]
> and Unterglau, and to the two mills and some other houses near the
> rivulet, with a view to prevent our passage.

Taken very much by surprise, for all Marsin's specious claims, the French and
Bavarian commanders found that the order in which they had gone into camp
was not an ideal disposition from which to prepare for battle. One of
Marlborough's soldiers wrote that 'We saw all their camp in a motion, their
generals and aides de camp galloping to and fro.' Having viewed the Allied
approach from the church tower in Blindheim village, Tallard, Marsin and the
Elector made a competent enough appreciation of what best to do; drawing up
their cavalry in the cornfields on the open plain, and preparing the villages of
Lutzingen, Oberglau and Blindheim for defence with strong garrisons of
infantry and dismounted dragoons. The ungathered crops hampered
observation, but their batteries were sighted as well as could be, and these soon
began to fire on the advancing Allied columns. The Marquis de Montigny-
Langost wrote that: 'The whole great plain was black with troops, and at seven
o'clock and three quarters that morning [7.45am, although Marsin thought it
was about 9am], the cannonade began very vigorously.' A soldier in the Royal
Irish Regiment became the first Allied casualty that day, when a round-shot
knocked him flying.

Marshal Tallard had decided that it was best to allow his opponents to come
across the Nebel stream without real interference, intending then to use his
powerful cavalry to drive the Allied troops to destruction in the boggy water
obstacle at their back. Marsin, however, decided to fight for every yard of
ground, and his infantry were formed up at the water's edge. Neither Marshal
was necessarily wrong in the tactical choice they made, but Marlborough's plan

depended upon getting his cavalry across the Nebel in good order, and Tallard's dispositions allowed him to do so without great difficulty. Frances Hare again:

> About eight o'clock, the enemy began to cannonade our army as it advanced. Upon which his Grace ordered Colonel Blood to plant several counter batteries upon the most advantageous parts of the ground, and his Grace visited each battery, and stood by to observe the range of the guns and the effect of their fire.

Marlborough's Wing of the army could draw up fairly easily on the firm ground near to Blindheim on the left, but Eugene's Wing was struggling across more difficult country to get into place at the foot of the Waldberg, ready to attack the Bavarians in and around Lutzingen:

> The Imperialists had been in march to take their post on the right, and his Grace, in taking leave of Prince Eugene, desired his Highness to give him notice when the right wing was formed, that they might begin the general attack together. But the ground upon the right being found less practicable than it had been represented to be, Prince Eugene was forced on that account to make a greater circuit through the woods upon his right, and had to extend his wing further than had been anticipated. This took up much time.

Donald McBane remembered that: 'We marched up within shot of the enemy, and halted there upon our arms, until Prince Eugene came through the woods.' Tallard's artillery commander, the highly proficient Marquis de la Frequelière, wrote that his guns were soon in action all along the line: 'One was excited by the extraordinary effect it produced, every shot cutting through their battalions, some of them raking obliquely; and from the very way in which the enemy was deployed, not a round was wasted.' At this time, a round-shot almost finished the Duke's career, striking the ground beneath his horse: 'A large cannon-ball grazed upon the plowed land, close by his horse's side, and almost covered him with dust'. Marlborough remained unruffled, but he was anxious at the delay in beginning the attack as the hot morning wore on; his opponents might have time to recover their poise, and all the advantage gained by the daring advance the previous day would be lost. The Duke, having seen that Divine Service was held by the regimental chaplains, had his infantry lie down to shelter both from the sun and the French fire. Francis Hare wrote of the artillery duel:

> All this while both armies continued to cannonade each other very briskly, but the fire of the enemy's artillery was not so well answered by the cannon with Prince Eugene as it was by that in the left wing [Marlborough's]; for his Highness was obliged to sustain the fire of the enemy's artillery all the while he was drawing up his troops but could not bring his own field-pieces to bear against them on account of the many ditches and other impediments from one extremity of his wing to the other.

Eugene would not get his guns into action until his troops were already heavily involved in their attacks on the Bavarians in Lutzingen and Marsin's French cavalry near Oberglau. However, the chaplain goes on:

> These difficulties being at length overcome, his Highness sent an aide de camp about half an hour past twelve to let the Duke of Marlborough know that he was ready. Upon this his Grace called for his horse, and sent the young Prince of Hesse [who would one day, upon his marriage, become King of Sweden] with orders to Lord Cutts to begin the attack upon Blindheim.

Marlborough's plan was that heavy infantry attacks would be thrown upon the fortified villages on either flank of the French and Bavarian position. While these were in progress, his cavalry, amply supported by infantry, would cross the Nebel stream to confront the cavalry of Marshal Tallard, drawn up in the cornfields across the plain between Blindheim and Oberglau. Eugene's role, with the much smaller Wing of the army, was to tie down Marsin and the Elector of Bavaria between Oberglau and Lutzingen, next to the wooded hills, to prevent any assistance being sent across to Tallard in his crucial battle with Marlborough.

Lord John Cutts (as brave and brainless as the sword at his side in the opinion of Jonathan Swift) had command of a column of twenty British and German battalions on the left of the Allied line. They had driven off de Silly's cavalry and secured Schwenningen village the previous evening, and these troops now went into action against Blindheim, scrambling across the Nebel stream to get into place. At the same time, Marlborough's main body of infantry, commanded by Charles Churchill, began to make their way across the stream near Unterglau. Makeshift bridges, made from fascines and wood torn from the smouldering cottages, were used to manhandle artillery pieces forward to support them.

As Cutts's leading battalions cleared the stream and approached the edge of Blindheim, a blast of French musketry ravaged their ranks. Hare wrote:

> It was near one o'clock when Lord Cutts made the first attack upon Blenheim. Brigadier-General Rowe, on foot, led up his brigade which formed the first line, and which was sustained in the second line by a brigade of Hessians [under Wilkes]. Brigadier Rowe had proceeded within thirty paces of the pales [breastwork] about Blenheim before the enemy gave their first fire, by which a great many brave officers and soldiers fell, but that did not discourage their gallant commander from marching directly up to the pales, on which he struck his sword.

The commander of Cutts's right-hand brigade, Archibald Rowe, was shot down, as were the commanding officer and second-in-command of his own regiment. At the same time Fergusson's brigade tried to work their way between Blindheim and the waters of the Danube, but were equally robustly repulsed by the squadrons of dismounted French dragoons posted in an orchard there. Colonel Dormer of the 1st English Foot Guards was killed in the attempt. Hare recalled a well-handled French counter-attack that threatened, briefly, to overwhelm Cutts's column:

> While this was doing, some squadrons of the French gens-d'armes fell upon the right flank of Rowe's brigade, put it partially in disorder, and took one of the colours of Rowe's Regiment; but the Hessians in the second line, facing to the right, charged these squadrons so briskly that they repulsed them and retook the colour.

The honour of Rowe's Regiment was restored by these stalwart German troops, but a little later, as Cutts renewed his bloody attacks on the village, his flank was again threatened by an advance of Tallard's front-line squadrons. The British cavalry and dragoons had already been detached to rejoin the main body near Unterglau, as had two brigades of infantry (one British and one Hanoverian), and their commander, Henry Lumley, now moved smartly to deflect the cavalry thrust against Cutts's troops. Hare wrote:

> Lord Cutts, seeing fresh cavalry of the enemy coming down upon him, sent his aide-de-camp to desire that some of our squadrons should be sent to cover his flank. Lieutenant-General Lumley accordingly ordered Colonel Palmer [actually Palmes] to march over the rivulet with the three squadrons which were nearest the pass, and these were followed by Colonel Leybourg [Sybourg] with two more, all which had no sooner drawn up than eight of the enemy's squadrons moved down upon them, and ours advanced to meet them. Those of the enemy gave their fire at a little distance, but the English squadrons charged up to them sword in hand, and broke and put them to flight. But being overpowered by fresh squadrons, and galled by the fire of the enemy's infantry posted about Blenheim, our squadrons were repulsed in their turn and forced to retire.

The British troopers had gone too far and were pretty well cut up. One of their squadron commanders, Major Oldfield, was thrown from his horse and trampled 'by two or three squadrons', while another, Richard Creed, was killed. Once again, the brigade of Hessian infantry came forward to help, driving off the French squadrons with their deadly volleys. Three days later, John Creed wrote home to his mother to tell of his older brother's death:

> The enemy forced us to retire and I missing my dearest brother in the retreat I advanced in haste towards the enemy's squadrons with endeavour to rescue him but, a dismal sight, found him struggling on the ground, and one of the enemy over him with his sword in his hand. I shot the enemy and dismounted and lifted up my brother and brought him off but he never spoke more; he had several wounds, but was at last killed by a shot in the head …. Thank God I escaped unwounded.

The French horsemen were elite Gens d'Armes, and this second repulse caused some consternation in the ranks of the French and Bavarian armies.

The adjutant of the Gendarmerie felt compelled by the criticism to write to the War Minister, Michel de Chamillart, in Paris, after the action:

> I shall begin by acquainting you with the despair of all the officers, upon the news they receive from Paris, wherein they find that Monsieur de Silly spreads injurious and malicious reports against them. Is it possible, my Lord, that the reputation of a body so well established everywhere, by so many different actions, can depend on the caprice or malice of a private man, without experience. And is it just to believe him, if he has a mind to disgrace so many brave men, who, in the sight, both of friends and enemies have done all that could be expected from men of courage.

The Marquis de Silly, whose brigade had pushed Marlborough's scouts and pioneers so hard the previous day as they approached the plain of Höchstädt, could hardly, in fairness, be said to be 'a man without experience'.

On hearing of the repulse of the Gendarmerie the Elector of Bavaria, embroiled in a hectic battle against Eugene's Imperial cavalry near to Lutzingen, sent the Marquis de Montigny-Langost to stiffen their resolve with the stirring words 'Go, rally them, tell them I am here in person. Lead them to the charge once again'. The Marquis was wounded before he could reach the Gendarmerie, and taken prisoner soon afterwards; his captor, who had taken charge of the young man's purse, was then in turn wounded by a stray musket-ball, and so Montigny-Langost got away.

The Allied infantry attacks, both against Lutzingen and Blindheim, were beaten off with heavy loss. On the right Eugene's Prussian and Danish infantry were driven back across the stream in disorder, and his Imperial cavalry was no more successful. In these exchanges, the left Wing of the French and Bavarian army more than held their own in the slashing fights alongside the Nebel stream; Eugene's troops took heavy casualties and were undoubtedly badly shaken. Meanwhile, in the meadows beside the Danube, Cutts's column went into the attack on Blindheim again, regardless of loss. Under this pressure, the French commander in the village, the Marquis de Clérambault, began to pack into the narrow streets every infantry battalion he could lay hands on; before long, the French cavalry of the right Wing was left without sufficient support. This was crucial, for these squadrons, now exposed and isolated, were the real target for Marlborough's attack. The Duke was contriving a powerful mix of cavalry, infantry and artillery working together in close co-operation on what was, in Robert Parker's rather apt phrase: 'A fine plain, without hedge or ditch, for the cavalry on both sides to show their bravery.'

Marlborough could not push his troops forward very far beyond the Nebel stream, while the French infantry in Oberglau, under the confident and capable command of the Marquis de Blainville, remained active. Two Dutch brigades, commanded by the Prince of Holstein-Beck, were sent in to deal with the place, but were very roughly handled by the French and émigré Irish defenders, who put in a sharp counter-attack. Dr Hare goes on:

The Prince of Holstein-Beck was however wounded and taken prisoner in this attack; and the Duke of Marlborough seeing things in some confusion, galloped up, and ordered forward three battalions, commanded by Major-Gen. Averocks to sustain them, and caused a battery of cannon to be brought forward, affairs were re-established at this point.

Count Fugger was nearby, at Weilheim farm, with a brigade of Imperial Swabian cuirassiers. He had not responded to an urgent appeal from Holstein-Beck for help, feeling unable to move from the station allotted to him by Eugene. In a sense he was right, as the boundary between the two Wings of the Allied army was potentially a very weak spot at which the French might strike with good effect. Fugger's powerful presence at the farm was Eugene's guarantee against such a mishap to his left flank as he drove in against the Bavarians around Lutzingen. However, Holstein-Beck's Dutch brigades had been thrown into complete disarray, and had Marlborough not taken a firm grip, a disaster might well have occurred, with Marsin thrusting his powerful corps between the Duke and Eugene, splitting the Allied army clean in two. The Count now responded to Marlborough's summons, and brought his armoured horsemen cantering down towards the stream, and their menacing approach neatly deterred any attempt by Marsin to take advantage of the temporary Dutch confusion. The rent in the centre of the Allied line was repaired by Averock's Dutch and the Hanoverians under Hulsen. Francis Hare described the unfolding deployment of Marlborough's army:

> It was now past four o'clock, and the Duke of Marlborough had got the whole of the left wing of the allied army over the rivulet, and our horse were drawn up in two lines fronting that of the enemy; but they did not offer to charge until General Churchill had ranged all the foot also in two lines behind the cavalry.

Remorselessly, the infantry attacks directed against the three strongpoint villages were tying down the troops available to the Elector and the French Marshals. Marlborough retained the initiative with fresh horsemen ready to feed into the action, unlike Tallard, whose squadrons were exposed and increasingly worn out in the scrambling fights along the stream. The time had come for Marlborough's great effort to destroy the centre of gravity of the whole French and Bavarian effort on the Danube – Tallard's cavalry:

> About five o'clock the general forward movement was made, which determined the issue of this great battle, which until then had seemed to remain doubtful. The Duke of Marlborough, having ridden along the front, gave orders to sound the charge, when all at once our two lines of horse moved on, sword in hand, to the attack. Those of the enemy presented their fusils at some small distance and fired, but they had no sooner done so than they immediately turned about, broke one another, and betook themselves to flight.

It actually took several resolute charges by the Allied cavalry to break the French, but Hare rightly draws attention to their futile and antiquated practice of firing their pistols and carbines at the halt rather than, as the Allied cavalry did, moving to close with their enemy using shock action and cold steel. The adjutant of the Gendarmerie described the efforts of the French cavalry in his plaintive letter to Chamillart, writing that:

> All the army knows, that we had charged twice, before the cavalry had approached the enemy; that we faced them until six o'clock in the evening; and that it was in the centre, which was thin and weak, where the enemy pierced through ... Our body [the Gendarmerie], as they were posted, could do no more, than sacrifice themselves, as they did, without being able to succeed in their charges, being continually exposed to the fire of a close body of infantry sustained by several ranks ... We overthrew, indeed their first line, more than once, but it was still succoured, and animated again, by three others.

Supported by numerous infantry, the Allied cavalry squadrons came on again and again, wearing down the French horsemen. Suddenly, late in the afternoon, all was panic as Tallard's troopers turned about, disregarding the shouted commands of their officers, and galloped off the field. Merode-Westerloo remembered 'An unauthorised but definite movement to the rear by my troopers' and was caught up in the fleeing throng:

> So tight was the press that my horse was carried along some three hundred paces without putting hoof to ground, right to the edge of a deep ravine; down we plunged a good twenty feet into a swampy meadow; my horse stumbled and fell. A moment later some more men and horses fell on top of me. I spent several moments trapped beneath my horse.

As the French cavalry fled, Frances Hare described in vivid detail the dreadful destruction of the few battalions of French infantry they left behind on the open plain:

> The enemy had intermingled some regiments of foot with their cavalry immediately on the right of Oberglau. He [Marlborough] ordered some Hanoverian regiments of foot to halt and make head against the enemy's foot; and Colonel Blood was ordered at the same time to march a battery of cannon over the pontoons, and bring it to bear upon the enemy's battalions. This was done with good success, and made a great slaughter of the enemy. They stood firm, however, for a time, closing their ranks as fast as they were broken, until being much weakened, they were at last thrown into disorder, when our squadrons falling upon them, they were cut down in entire ranks, and were seen so lying after the battle.

Tallard tried to gather together some of his squadrons to make a stand, but all was in confusion. The Marquis de Maisonelle was sent galloping towards Blindheim to get some infantry out of the village, but he was never seen again.

Confronted soon afterwards by a group of Hessian dragoons near to Sonderheim, the Marshal was taken to the Prince of Hesse-Cassell, who sent him on to where Marlborough was directing the pursuit of the broken French army. The dignified exchange of courtesies between the two commanders, who were old acquaintances, is well known. Tallard bowed slightly and murmured 'I congratulate you, on defeating the best soldiers in the world.' The Duke, equally composed, drily replied 'Your Lordship, I assume, excepts those troops who have had the honour to beat them.' Tallard was then ushered into the privacy of Marlborough's own coach, where he could grieve for the disaster to his army, his loss of reputation, and for the young son he had seen shot down earlier that afternoon. Marlborough's chaplain wrote that the Marshal had:

> Surrendered himself to M. Beinebourg, aide-de-camp to the Prince of Hesse; and along with the marshal were taken some of his aides-de-camp and several other officers of note. They were brought immediately to the Duke of Marlborough, who desired that Marshal Tallard would make use of his coach; and his Grace immediately sent off Colonel Parke with a pencil note to the Duchess of Marlborough containing the announcement of the victory.

The 'pencil note' scrawled by the Duke on the back of an old tavern bill borrowed from an aide, was the famous 'Blenheim Despatch', and it read:

> I have not time to say more, but to beg you will give my duty to the Queen and let her know that her army has had this day a glorious victory. M.Tallard and two other generals are in my coach and I am pursuing the rest. The bearer, my aide de camp, Colonel Parke, will give her an account of what has passed and I shall do it in a day or so, by another, more at large.

Eight days later, a travel-weary Daniel Parke, having briefly visited the Duchess, handed the piece of paper to Queen Anne in Windsor Castle. Meanwhile, the Elector of Bavaria was also writing a note, but his message was of more sombre tone. He told his wife, who had once urged him to agree terms with Marlborough, of the catastrophe that had been endured: 'Wihr haben heute alles verhloren [We have today lost everything].'

The victorious army could not make an effective and vigorous pursuit though, partly due to the hard fighting that had taken place, and their resulting exhaustion. The inevitable fog of war so easily clouds operations, as Francis Hare described:

> The Duke having collected some squadrons from the pursuit, moved with them towards the flank of the Elector of Bavaria's wing of the enemy's army, which Prince Eugene had by a fourth attack succeeded in driving from its position ... But the right wing of our army, which was at no great distance behind that of the Elector, being mistaken for a part of his troops marching in good order and in such a direction as might have enabled them advantageously to flank our squadrons had they charged the other part of the Elector's force; and as it was now growing too dusk to

distinguish clearly the several corps, the retreat of the enemy was not further impeded in this direction. All this while the village of Blenheim had been incessantly attacked, but it still held out.

The village of Blindheim was, at this late stage, proving a persistent problem. Cutts had not the strength to force his way in, for he was quite outnumbered by the garrison, although his soldiers' musketry effectively prevented the French infantry from getting out from the narrow exits between the cottages. Marlborough's brother now directed the British infantry under George Hamilton, 1st Earl Orkney, which had supported the Allied cavalry on the plain, to swing to the left and take the village from the west:

> As soon as General Churchill saw the defeat of the enemy's horse, he sent to inform Lord Cutts that he was himself coming to attack the village of Blenheim in flank, and requested that his Lordship would make another attack at the same time in front ... An attack was at once made accordingly, and the Earl of Orkney and Lieutenant-General Ingoldsby entered the village at two different places at the head of their respective lines, but they were forced to retire.

Many of the cottages were on fire now, and those wounded who had taken shelter in them were in peril. John Deane wrote of the awful scenes in Blindheim as the flames took hold:

> We according to command fought our way into the village which was all of a fire, and our men fought in and through the fire and pursued others through it, until many on both sides were burnt to death ... The village was set on fire before we came to it by the enemy whereby they thought to have blinded our gunners, but great and grievous were the cries of the maimed, and those suffering in the flames after we entered the village and none is able to express it but those that heard it.

The French infantry and dragoons fought well, although the narrow alleys and yards meant that many were given no chance to use their weapons effectively. Around the walled churchyard a fierce hand-to-hand battle erupted as night drew on, but Orkney took advantage of a local truce, agreed to allow time to rescue wounded men from burning to death in the cottages, to attempt a parley with the defenders. The Duc de St Simon wrote that the Marquis de Blanzac, who assumed the command in the village as Clérambault was nowhere to be found, saw 'Denonville, one of our officers who had been taken prisoner, coming towards the village, accompanied by an officer who waved a handkerchief and demanded a parley.' James Abercrombie, an aide de camp who also witnessed the scene while serving with Orkney, wrote:

> As Lord Orkney having met with Marquis Denonville, who had commanded the French Regiment Royal [du Roi], but who was already a prisoner, he was suffered to go into the town upon his parole to return immediately. This he did, bringing with him to Lord Orkney several

French generals; but as they were discussing the terms of capitulation, General Churchill arrived, and telling them that he had no time to lose (it being now past seven in the evening), and that if they did not lay down their arms immediately, he must renew the attack. They submitted, and were with all the troops in Blenheim made prisoners.

De Blanzac was permitted by Orkney to go to the edge of the cottages, to see for himself that Tallard's army had disintegrated, while that of Marsin and the Elector was in full flight from the field. 'He returned to Blenheim, assembled all the senior officers, and told them what he had seen.' Effectively bluffed into surrender (for Marlborough feared the struggle for the village might have to be renewed in the morning), some 10,000 of France's best soldiers laid down their arms and gave up their colours, while their officers wept tears of frustration and shame at the humiliation of their plight. Their abilities and courage were never in doubt but, penned into the village all day long, they had little chance to demonstrate their devotion and valour, and for many the unhappy prospect of life as a prisoner of Imperial Austria now loomed ahead, unless an exchange could be arranged with Allied prisoners presently in French hands.

As darkness fell, the weary but victorious Allied soldiers could rest at last, and enjoy some of the fruits of their victory. Francis Hare remembered that the troops:

> Quickly possessed themselves of the enemy's tents, which were left standing, and which were found to contain great quantities of herbs and vegetables; and nearer to the Danube there lay about one hundred fat oxen ready skinned, which were to have been delivered out this day to the French troops, but which proved a welcome booty to the soldiers of the allied army after such long and hard service.

The Comte de Merode-Westerloo, having escaped from the debacle that engulfed the French cavalry, arrived in a very dishevelled state in Höchstädt village square, where he refreshed himself at the well. He was hailed by some French officers of his acquaintance who remarked that he had been slow in getting there, to which the Walloon nobleman waspishly replied that they, by contrast, had got there very quickly. Merode-Westerloo then busied himself with arranging a series of makeshift rearguards on the road to Diesenhofen, so that those troops that could still march had some chance of getting away. Meanwhile, Donald McBane lay wounded on the field of battle, on the outskirts of Blindheim village:

> About the middle of the night the Dutch of our army came a plundering, and stripped me of all except my shirt; a little after another came and took the shirt also. I besought him to leave me it, but he gave me a stroke with the butt of his gun.

It would be two days before his friends found the wounded man, and took him to a surgeon to have his injuries tended.

The Duke of Marlborough wrote to the Secretary of State, Robert Harley, from Höchstädt the day after the battle, Thursday 14 August, announcing the details of the victory in rather fuller terms than his famous despatch had done. Explaining the manoeuvres that combined the two Allied armies, the Duke went on:

> We resolved to attack them, and accordingly we marched between three and four yesterday morning from the camp at Munster, leaving all our tents standing. About six we came in view of the enemy, who we found, did not expect so early an onset. The cannon began to play about half and hour after eight. They formed themselves in two bodies, the Elector with M. Marsin and their troops on our right, and M. de Tallard with all his on our left; which last fell to my share; they had two rivulets, besides a morass before them which we were obliged to pass over in their view, and Prince Eugene was forced to take a great compass to come to the enemy, so that it was one of the clock before the battle began. It lasted with great vigour till sunset, when the enemy were obliged to retire, and by the blessing of God, we obtained a complete victory. We cut off great numbers of them, as well in the action as in the retreat, besides upwards of twenty squadrons of the French, which I pushed into the Danube, where we saw the greater part of them perish. M. Tallard, with several of his generals being taken prisoners at the same time, and in the village of Blenheim, which the enemy had entrenched and fortified, and where they made the greatest opposition, I obliged twenty-six entire battalions, and twelve squadrons of dragoons, to surrender themselves prisoners at discretion. We took likewise all their tents standing, with their cannon and ammunition, also a great number of standards, kettle-drums, and colours in the action, so that I reckon the greatest part of M. Tallard's army is taken or destroyed. The bravery of all our troops on this occasion cannot be expressed, the Generals, as well as the officers and soldiers, behaving themselves with the greatest courage and resolution. The horse and dragoons were obliged to charge four or five several times. The Elector and M. de Marsin were so advantageously posted, that Prince Eugene could make no impression on them, till the third attack, near seven at night, when he made a great slaughter of them. But being near a wood-side, a great body of Bavarians retired into it, and the rest of the army retreated towards Lavingen, it being too late, and the troops much too tired to pursue them far.

After asking that the Queen's wishes for the disposal of the captured prisoners, equipment, ordnance and trophies should be obtained, Marlborough went on to comment on the badly battered state of his own battalions, many of whom had fought a dreadfully hard battle, only a few weeks after the harrowing assault on the Schellenberg hill: 'You will easily believe that, in so long and vigorous an action, the English, who had so great a share in it, must have suffered as well in officers as men; but I have not yet the particulars.'

The reply sent by Queen Anne to the Duke of Marlborough, on receipt of the brief note brought by Colonel Parke, ran:

The good news Col. Parke brought me yesterday was very welcome, but not more I do assure you, than hearing you were well after so glorious a victory, which will not only humble our enemies abroad, but contribute very much to putting a stop to the ill designs of those at home.

On that same Thursday Marlborough went to see Marshal Tallard, to pay his compliments, and to enquire after his comfort. Dr Hare recorded the visit in his journal:

Reaching the Marshal's quarters, they [Marlborough and Eugene] found him very much dejected and wounded in one of his hands. His grace humanely enquired how far it was in his power to make him easy under his misfortune, offering him the convenience of his quarters, and the use of his coach. The marshal thankfully declined the offer, saying he did not desire to move, till he could have his own equipage. His grace accordingly despatched one of his own trumpets to the electoral army, with a passport for bringing it to the marshal. At this interview many of the French generals crowded about his grace, admiring his person, as well as his tender and generous behaviour.

During this interview, Tallard let it be known that several Allied prisoners, taken by de Silly's cavalry in the skirmishing on 12 August, had reported that their army was about to retire northwards to Nordlingen, rather than to advance to the attack on the plain of Höchstädt. Whether this was false information, deliberately planted by Marlborough to delude the French commander, is unsure, although it is sometimes hinted at as being fact.

Jean-Martin De La Colonie, who had missed the battle beside the Danube, as his regiment was now a part of the garrison in Ingolstadt, remembered the news of the defeat coming to the city:

A courier arrived bearing an order from the Electress [of Bavaria], to the effect that the Marquis de Massey was to return with his troops to Munich, by forced marches, so as to ensure the safety of the Electoral family. This courier told us, with tears in his eyes, that all was lost; the army of France had been totally destroyed of the plains of Hochstett, the Elector had fled to the French frontier, the Electress was in the saddest possible condition. It would be out of my power to find words strong enough to express the depression into which we were plunged at so unexpected a piece of news. All our manoeuvres, plans and conquests came to nothing in an instant; it was no longer possible to derive any advantage from our past efforts.

The Colonel commented with cynical, but worldly-wise, perception, that 'If Marechal de Tallard had been successful, no one would have found fault with him'. De La Colonie goes on to describe the operations necessary to conduct the Electress and her children to safety. The pursuit of the broken French and Bavarian forces towards the west, drawing the main Allied army away from the Danube, gave a kind of breathing space in which this could be accomplished.

The incredible tale of the defeat came to the French King in Versailles soon enough, in fact on the same day that Queen Anne received Parke at Windsor. St Simon remembered:

> The King received the cruel news of this battle on the 21st of August by a courier from the Marechal de Villeroi ... The entire army of Tallard was killed or taken prisoner, it was not known what had become of Tallard himself. Neither the King or anyone else could understand, from what reached them, how it was that a entire army had been placed inside a village, and had surrendered itself by a signed capitulation. It puzzled every brain ... We were not accustomed to misfortune.

The scale of the victory that Marlborough and Eugene gained that hot August day was staggering. Some 20,000 French and Bavarian troops were either killed or wounded, while another 15,000 surrendered as unwounded prisoners, most of them from the garrison penned into Blindheim village. Vast amounts of cannon, infantry colours, cavalry standards, wagons, horses and mules, ammunition and stores were captured as the French army fled from the field. The battle had been hard fought indeed, and the losses in the Allied army were about 13,000 killed and wounded, which gives a flavour of the severity of the fighting on the plain of Höchstädt.

The astounding news of such an unprecedented, and wholly unexpected, victory over the French, caused feverish celebration in London. John Evelyn noted in his diary:

> This week there was brought over the happy news of the French and Bavarian armies' defeat by the Confederates, and especially by the valour and conduct of the Prince Eugene and the Duke of Marlborough, who vanquished them and took Marshall Tallard, their general, prisoner. This news was immediately brought to the Queen, during the yet pursuit of the enemy, written by the Duke of Marlborough in such extreme haste that he could not particularly describe the rest of the circumstances and event, which we hourly expect. But this has so exceedingly overjoyed in that there is nothing but triumphs and demonstrations in the city, and everywhere.

A few weeks later Evelyn was able to write about the formal celebrations held in London to mark the victory:

> This day was celebrated the thanksgiving for the late great victory, with the utmost pomp and splendour by the Queen, Court, Great Officers, Lord Mayor, Sheriffs, [livery] Companies etc ... The Foot Guards; the Queen in a rich coach with eight horses, none with her but the Duchess of Marlborough in a very plain garment, the Queen full of jewels.

Back in the Danube valley, due to the exhaustion of the victorious Allied army, the pursuit of the broken French and Bavarian forces was less rigorous than might have been desired. This was unavoidable, as masses of prisoners had also to be catered for. Marsin and the Elector, by abandoning much of their ordnance and baggage train (although the Marshal reported getting 18 guns away from the field of battle), and by leaving important towns like Munich, Ingolstadt and Ulm to their fate, got back towards the Rhine, to combine their shattered army with that of Villeroi in Alsace, and to await there the approach of Marlborough and Eugene.

The Dutch States-General, so often unappreciative of the Duke's efforts, were loud in their praise of the triumph beside the Danube. They had:

> Never dared to carry our hopes so far, as to think of so glorious and complete a victory as you have gained over the enemy. The action that day has placed your merit in its true lustre. A day whose glory might have been envied by the greatest captains of past ages, and whose memory will endure throughout all ages to come.

Prince George, Queen Anne's husband and consort, wrote to Marlborough in warm and unmistakably sincere tones:

> I give you a thousand thanks for the great good news you send me, and assure you that nobody can rejoice more sincerely with you than I do, not only for the public good, but on your own particular being very sensible, after such disappointments as you have met with this year, success must be a double satisfaction to you. That you may never meet with any ill-fortune, but always make a glorious end of this campaign, is most heartily wished by your very affectionate friend.

Despite the weakened state of his own army, Marlborough moved quite promptly to breach the defences of the French frontier along the Rhine, while their field armies were in disarray. However, the Duke's health was far from good, perhaps a result of the strains of this daring campaign through the summer. On Sunday 17 August he wrote to Godolphin: 'Ever since the battle I have been so employed about our own wounded men and the prisoners, that I have not had one hour's quiet, which has so disordered me, that if I were in London I should be in my bed in a high fever.' A week later, although racked with a headache, the Duke looked forward to a continuation of the pursuit of his broken opponents:

> I am suffered to have so little time to myself that I have a continual fever on my spirits, which makes me very weak; but when I go from hence, I am resolved to go in my coach until I come to the Rhine, which I do not doubt will restore me to perfect health.

The pursuit of the battered French and Bavarian armies was, inevitably, not without occasional excitements, particularly as the Rhine was neared. John Deane remembered one incident on 28 August 1704, when the camp followers with the army were put into a state of great alarm:

> A partizan [foraging patrol or raid] of the enemy fell upon some of our sutlers and plundered them and so made them off, and our battalion of Guards marched by themselves that day and aforesaid sutlers coming thundering back and desiring our battalion to advance, swearing that all the French army was coming upon us, struck us into such a consternation

yet we were in a wood also knowing that we were all alone and a great distance from the army. In short it put us into great confusion; and at last it proved nothing but a strong partizan party and some parties of French Hussars who appeared. Our Grey Dragoons [Royal Scots Greys] followed them, came up with them and cut them down, and we marched by them and see them afterwards.

The Comte de Merode-Westerloo, who was still nursing his wounds from the recent battle, wrote of the retreat of the battered French and Bavarian army through the Black Forest, where Marshal Villeroi was coming forward to support them:

We were on our way, passing Villingen [where Tallard had lost four days in trying to take the place in June] below us to the right. We re-entered the gorges, finding Villeroi's men in full control of the passes. His army formed our rearguard. When we eventually emerged from the mountains, I was given leave on account of my wounds to ride ahead of the army, and I reached Strasbourg in one day ... The army reached Strasbourg three or four days later, and there it rested.

The Comte then told, with rather grim, possibly unintentional, humour, of how the fugitive Elector of Bavaria was received in the town: 'The Elector was housed in the Governor's residence, built overlooking the river, and there that very same night he was serenaded by the mayor from some boats. I do not think this was very well received on his part.'

At the beginning of September the Allied army began crossing the Rhine, using the pontoon bridges laid on Marlborough's orders during his march southwards to the Danube valley. The Margrave of Baden, convalescent still from his Schellenberg wound, and smarting with indignation at having been deliberately excluded (as he saw it) from the day of glory in August, moved with his Imperial troops to invest the town of Landau. Once again, as in July, the lack of a proper siege train hampered operations, as did the poor weather and sickness in the Allied camp. This was particularly so among the cavalry horses, and Captain Richard Pope wrote of Schomberg's Regiment of Horse that 'The left wing is entirely ruined, we have not above twenty horses or troops left, and probably not ten of those able to march.'

As the operations against Landau dragged on, the French were able to recover their poise, draw troops out of other garrisons and move them into the Moselle valley, guarding against any fresh Allied offensive there. Marlborough soon decided that to wait for the place to fall would be unwise. He wrote on 26 October 'I came this afternoon from Landau, where I have been ever since Tuesday. That siege goes on so very slowly, that I can give no news when it is likely to end.' Leaving Eugene to besiege Landau, the Duke's detachment was now threading its way through difficult country to invest Treves on the Moselle. On 20 October he wrote to Sidney Godolphin of his movements:

I have gone through the terriblest country that can be imagined for the march of an army with cannon. Had it rained, we would have left our baggage and cannon behind us .... If the siege of Landau had been ended, I should have marched with all the troops under my command; so that I might have been almost sure of success in this expedition. But as I have been obliged to leave one half of the Hessians, all the Hanoverians, and the English with Prince Eugene, I am now exposed to the enemy if they will venture, which I hope they will not [an uncharacteristic note for the Duke]. I should not have ventured to march with these troops, but I think the taking our winter quarters on the Moselle is as necessary for the good of the common cause as any thing that has been done this campaign [post Blenheim]. I shall have the satisfaction to know that I have acted for the best.

Marlborough was able to write to the Secretary of State, Robert Harley, on 31 October 1704 with news of more progress:

I marched before break of day this morning, with all the horse and four battalions, and as soon as our vanguard appeared the enemy quitted the fort [St Martin, overlooking Treves], and retired over the Moselle, after throwing much provision and ammunition into the river.

Adam Cardonnel, the Duke's private secretary, wrote of his daring advance with only a sketchy force under command:

It was very lucky that my lord duke hastened his march, for on the same day [29 October] Monsieur d'Allegre came with a detachment of horse within two leagues of Treves, having ordered a good body of troops to follow him, but on notice of our being here, he immediately retired.

On 3 November 1704, Marlborough's small army, which was still distinctly inferior in numbers to the forces the French could muster against him, had they been alert enough to combine and do so, was reinforced at last by the arrival at Bernkastel of twelve fresh Dutch battalions. The weakly-held town of Trarbach, further down the Moselle valley, could now be screened and the winter quarters for his own troops made secure. With cold weather coming on, the Duke felt he had accomplished enough; he wrote to Godolphin: 'I reckon this campaign is well over, since the winter quarters are settled on the Moselle, which I think will give France as much uneasiness as anything that has been done this summer.' The oblique reference to the victory at Blenheim, as being of only equal importance to lodging his army for the winter within arm's reach of this weak spot in France's frontier barrier, is striking, and illustrates Marlborough's acute grasp of strategic imperatives very well. Leaving his army in the Moselle valley in this way would leave a dagger pointing deep into the heart of France, ready for use early in the campaign to come in the following spring.

Coming so soon after the dramatic triumph on the banks of the Danube in August 1704, this daring and arduous advance to the Moselle, with the French generals, although numerically superior, wrong-footed at every turn, is often overlooked. This is a pity, as the Duke of Marlborough's abilities as a military commander of the first rank, able to discern strategic opportunities and seize them in good time and good order, are rarely seen to better advantage.

However, such successes were attended by frustrations and disappointment, as can be seen in a letter sent by the Duke from Landau, where he had hurried from the Moselle operations to bring the siege to a close before winter set in. On 7 November 1704, he wrote to the Prince of Hesse:

> I have arrived here last evening, but I do not find our arrangements are as advanced as those involved would wish. We are masters of the counter-scarp, and tomorrow all the batteries begin to fire on the breach, which should be widen enough by Wednesday [9 November]; then the enemy will be summoned to surrender; if not, the siege is likely to drag on another ten or twelve days.

Even this timetable was not achieved, for the garrison under the inspired command of the blind Marquis de Laubanie did not surrender until 29 November, on honourable terms, granted as they had held out for more than a very creditable seventy days.

On 15 November Marlborough left the army and travelled to Berlin, to confer with the Prussian king on ways to prosecute the war to best effect in the coming year. The Great Northern War, and the threat posed by the volatile King Charles XII of Sweden was a continuing worry; the Allies were concerned that Prussian troops would soon be leaving the Rhine and marching towards the Baltic. Frederick I was reassured by the Duke, and committed his troops to the service of the Grand Alliance for the next year at least; as evidence of this a strong Prussian contingent was soon moving to the support of Savoy.

Marlborough then travelled to Hanover to pay his respects to the Electress Sophia and her son, George. News came that Landau had at last fallen to Eugene, and the Duke could go on to the Hague, where he received the adulation of the States-General for his victory at Blenheim. Moving on to London, he landed at Greenwich on 14 December 1704, in company with the captive Marshal Tallard and several of his senior officers. The Duke was received in triumph for the unbelievable success gained four months earlier on the cornfields of the plain of Höchstädt.

The Comte de Merode-Westerloo though, was thoroughly disillusioned with life on campaign, after the rigours of the summer in the Danube valley. He wrote that: 'Since the battle [Blenheim] I had lost more than sixty horses, all my baggage had been burned; my personal expenditure during the campaign had been frightful. I just had no idea how I could honour my debts.' Meanwhile, Donald McBane had recovered from the wounds he received in the battle, and wrote of the close of the campaign that year:

> Our army marched to Holland. I had the good fortune to go to my old quarters, where I set up my old trade [fencing master and brothel keeper]; at this time her majesty Queen Anne, for our good service in that campaign, ordered every man two Guineas, which we called Smart Money.

In the light of the extraordinary successes in 1704, the new year would, by comparison, prove to be rather a frustrating disappointment for the Allied cause, although the Duke was to have, as shall be seen, a moment of undiluted glory.

Chapter Five

But Much is Yet to be Done –
The Lines of Brabant, 1705

Emperor Leopold died in the spring of 1705, and he was succeeded by his son, Joseph. The new incumbent was an admirer of the Duke of Marlborough, but the resulting distraction and delay to the Imperial war effort that this event caused was unhelpful. The Duke had found himself incapable of making the most of his victory at Blenheim the previous year; the exhaustion of his army, and the dogged determination of the French in the face of catastrophe had foiled him. Now, once again, the Dutch were overly concerned with the close defence of their frontiers and the security of the territory gained so far, rather than wanting to move out to attack their enemy.

The French had now recovered their strategic poise after the disaster to Tallard's army on the Danube. Their campaigns in northern Italy and in Spain were prospering, and their regiments were steadily being reinforced with fresh recruits, ardent efforts having been made to refill the depleted ranks. This was achieved with no little difficulty, and the Duc de St Simon wrote of the raising of fresh recruits that:

> The losses in Germany and Italy, greater in the hospitals than on the field of battle, made the authorities resolve to increase each company by five men and to raise a levy of twenty-five thousand militiamen. The King was fooled into believing that the people were willing and eager to enlist by being shown a few hand-picked samples, two, four and five men, who he passed on the way to Marley [his chateau]. He was told stories of the men's cheerfulness and valour. From my personal knowledge of my own estate and from what I heard the people say there, I knew the despair that this levy was causing, even to the point when men were mutilating themselves in order to gain exemption.

Despite such reservations the strength and morale of the French revived, although it suited them to play for time. As the rival armies gathered for the new campaign, and supply trains trundled along from depots to camps, John Deane recalled one skirmish in particular:

> The 28th [April] a French party of horse fell upon the lieutenant-general [Henry Lumley]'s baggage and cut off about twenty-three of the wagon

horses and carried them clear off, as they thought, and likewise took a shade [a small coach] very richly laden, but our army being upon the march, about a league behind, an express was sent immediately to the Lt. Genl. of what had happened. Whereupon the Lt. Genl. ordered the Scotch Dragoons [Greys] to pursue the French party. The which was done, and after hard riding for two or three hours our dragoons came up with the French party and fell upon them most furiously insomuch that they took and killed almost all of them.

The Duke of Marlborough's hopes were for a major campaign in the Moselle valley, bypassing the massive fortress belt along the border with the Spanish Netherlands, which had been deferred with the onset of cold weather the previous autumn. In exasperation at the all too familiar attitude of his cautious allies, he wrote to Sidney Godolphin on 2 April:

> [The Dutch] Generals' desire of keeping 50 battalions and 90 squadrons on the Meuse is very unreasonable; for if this should be complied with, I should have on the Moselle but 60 battalions and 79 squadrons to act offensively; and at the same time they do not do so much pretend to act otherwise than on the defence. I am sure I shall never consent to what they desire; but how I shall be able to get the troops out of their country is the difficulty.

The Margrave of Baden and his Imperial army were to join Marlborough, while Prince Eugene, in the meantime, campaigned in northern Italy to tie down French forces there. When the Duke got to the valley in May, marching by easy stages to spare the soldiers, he found that the army contractor in Coblenz had embezzled the stores and defected to the French. Colonel Cranstoune, commanding the Cameronians, wrote of the sorry incident:

> The States [General of Holland] had engaged to have a magazine both of meal for bread for the army and hay and oats at Treves sufficient to supply our whole army, when joined for four or five weeks, because it was foreseen that this being a mountainous bare country there could not be forage in the fields so early as to supply us. It is said the States really gave their orders for furnishing the magazines but the commissary employed there in chief to do it has either been in correspondence with France and treacherously neglected it, or else has spent the money and could not do it, so the magazines fall mightily short of what is necessary and the commissary for fear of punishment is deserted to the enemy.

It was not just officers charged with heavy responsibilities, such as the errant commissary, that were involved in mischief. The Duke wrote at this time to the Secretary of State, Robert Harley, in London:

> The weather is extremely cold, that I attribute to it, in some measure, the desertion we have among us. The English have their share; and as it is likely those who can get their passes will endeavour to make the best of

their way home, I wish some care might be taken, without making too much noise, to seize them in the sea-ports at their landing, and send them over in order to make examples of them, and prevent the like for the future.

On the Moselle, Marlborough had found that the depots were nearly empty, the rains heavy, and the promised contingents of Imperial German troops were slow in arriving at the rendezvous. The Margrave of Baden, suffering still from his wounded foot, sent his apologies (perhaps through necessity; he was very unwell). Despite this, the Duke could not delay while hunger gnawed at his troops, and he wrote to Godolphin on Tuesday, 27 May 'For want of forage and provisions, I shall be necessitated to march before all these troops can join me so that I have sent orders to the several commanders to hasten their march all that is possible.' Although short of supplies, the aggressive course Marlborough chose was to close with the French and try and force open battle; a risky strategy but one which promised high rewards.

So Marlborough advanced with his reduced army and confronted Marshal Villars, who had occupied a strong defensive position near to Sierck. The French commander could afford to wait, and presented a solid front to the approaching Allies; his cavalry having swept the region clear of provisions beforehand. Francis Hare was unimpressed by all that he saw on the march:

> You never saw so wretched a country. The soil barren, mountainous, fruitful in nothing but iron, and the air strangely cold, as if it had been the midst of winter. The towns have all the marks of poverty that French oppression and government can give; and to make the little accommodation an army could meet with in so wretched a country still less, there was not a soul to be seen in the villages, the peasants flying as we came, either into places of defence or to the woods.

Marlborough, probably wisely, did not attempt what would be a fruitless frontal attack on Villars' position. Despite his comment that 'Here is a fine place to meet an enemy' the French commander took no immediate action, thinking, with good cause, that for Marlborough's army to starve would do well enough, without the risk of open battle. John Deane remembered that in the Moselle valley 'Everything was very scarce, and the army gave it the name Hungry Hill.' Marlborough wrote on 2 June 1705 that 'We are much more afraid of starving than [of] the enemy, but we have yesterday sent expresses both to Coblenz and Mentz, to hasten with all speed corn and flour for one month.' By 5 June the Duke had begun to receive the long-expected reinforcements, but urgent news came a week later, that the French commander in the Spanish Netherlands, Marshal Villeroi, had stirred himself and stormed the Allied held town of Huy on 10 June, and moved on to occupy the town and threaten the citadel of Liège. Veldt-Marshal Overkirk was badly outnumbered, took alarm, and called to Marlborough for assistance.

The French assault on Huy had, in fact, been a hotly contested affair. Jean-Martin De La Colonie took part with his Grenadiers Rouge, and wrote that:

I had just time to join in the assault on an outwork belonging to the fortress of Huy, called the Red Fort, and commanded the grenadiers told off to carry it by storm. This assault was of a different character to which usually obtained in such cases, because it was necessary to employ escalading [scaling ladders], and I lost many men who were thrown from the tops of the ladders. A poor lad was shot while climbing the very ladder on which I was myself, and the ball entered the top of his breast and passed through the entrails. One could not believe his recovery possible, but the care taken of him, and the strength of his constitution pulled him through, so that his cure was regarded as a species of miracle. He was rewarded by promotion. The outwork carried, the town capitulated the next day, June 10th.

With such developments on the Meuse, the Duke had little alternative but to abandon his Moselle campaign and hurry northwards. Marlborough wrote to the Duchess on 16 June:

This moment is come Lieutenant-General Hompesch, from Marshal de Overkirk, to let me know that if I do not immediately help them they are undone, which only serves to show the great apprehension they are in; for it is impossible for me to send troops to them sooner than I have already resolved, but since they have so much fear at their army, I dread the consequences of it at the Hague.

The same day he wrote to Godolphin:

The deputies of the States in the army on the Meuse have sent an express to me to desire that 30 battalions of theirs may be immediately sent to them. This joined with the want of forage, and no hopes of having the horses and carts in less than six weeks for the drawing everything to the siege [Sierck], we have taken the resolution of leaving a sufficient number of troops at Treves, and marching with the rest to assist them on the Meuse.

In an uncharacteristically bitter tone, he added in his next letter to his friend the comment: 'Nothing has been performed that was promised'.

The operation to break contact with the French was fraught with difficulty; Marshal Villars, a most dangerous opponent, could be counted on to harass any withdrawal by the Allied troops. The move was conducted in very good order, though 'by marching all night' as Robert Parker remembered, and Donald McBane, who was there with Orkney's Regiment, wrote 'The French at this time took Houie [Huy], the Duke then ordered all the grenadiers in the Army, and so many men of a company that could march well, we marched night and day until we came to the Dutch.'

On 29 June, Marlborough wrote to his wife from Maastricht: 'I am extremely uneasy at the disappointments I have met with, for it is most certain the Moselle is the place where we might have done the French most hurt. I wish with all my heart that Prince Eugene were in Prince Louis's employment

[Baden's post].' Two days' later, he added 'I march tomorrow, and hope the cannon will go from hence the next day. When we have Huy, the Lord knows what we shall do next, for I am afraid the French will avoid all occasions of letting us be on the same side of the Lines with them.'

By 2 July 1705 Marlborough had rejoined Overkirk at Hanette, and Huy was recovered a week or so later. De La Colonie described the rapid moves taken by the Duke to recover the place:

> Milord Marlborough struck his camp on the night of July 8th, marched his army in several columns, so that no one was able to divine his intentions, and appeared at break of day in front of the force under the lieutenant general posted on our left flank. Our patrols by this time had returned to camp, which was wrapped in slumber; consequently when he arrived in sight of our lines he could see that we were making no movement or attempt to defend them. He then ordered his infantry to advance, who immediately rushed two of the gates and broke down a length of parapet to allow his cavalry to enter before the lieutenant-general's detachment had the chance of opposing them, or even warn the army to come to its help. So sudden was this action that the enemy were able to form up in our own lines before our people had left their camp, although immediately the news was brought to Monsieur de Villeroi he had the alarm beaten and marched to oppose them; but it was too late, the enemy had secured the position, and it would have been extremely rash to have attacked them as the flanking detachment, which was of considerable strength in itself, was in full retreat. We then occupied the camp at Lierre, a small town near Antwerp, and remained there while the enemy occupied Huy. Then, anxious for the town of Louvain, we marched to take up a position covering it.

Despite this skilful recovery of Huy on 11 July, with very little loss to his army, Marlborough's Moselle campaign that year, with his hopes of a strategic thrust into the heart of France, was lost beyond hope of recovery. Count D'Aubach had been left in command of a detachment to cover Treves, but he took alarm at a renewed French advance, and abandoned the stores gathered there, on 27 June. Any fresh Allied operation in the Moselle valley would require a great deal of new and time-consuming preparations. The opportunity would never come again.

Meanwhile, Villeroi was not dissatisfied. He had drawn the allies away from the Moselle, and could now shelter behind the extensive Lines of Brabant, constructed the previous year, stretching in a seventy-mile arc from Antwerp past Louvain to Namur. He could also draw reinforcements from Villars in the Moselle valley. Unless Marlborough could entice the French commander out from the defences, or breach the lines himself, he faced a dismal prospect during the rest of the year's campaign.

Marlborough now devised a subtle plan to snare his opponent. This project swung into progress when, on 17 July, Overkirk was marched with the Dutch corps, as if to threaten the French-held fortress of Namur. Allied pioneers laboured to bridge the Mehaigne river, and the French scouts could plainly see these operations, convincing Villeroi of the Allied threat in the south. The Marshal took the bait, and began to march his troops towards Merdorp and Namur. Meanwhile, Marlborough was hurrying his British, Danish and German troops through the night, heavy with mist and light rain, heading northwards across the old Landen battlefield to the Lines in the area of Elixheim. Here the water obstacles were less formidable than elsewhere, because of the local topography. By dawn on 18 July the grenadiers and pioneers of the Allied army were scrambling over the virtually deserted defences, while the French picquets in the area took themselves off to raise the alarm. Robert Parker remembered that: 'The pioneers fell to work in levelling the lines; so that in short time the Duke with the horse, and the detachment [of foot] were within them.' Marlborough's corps was soon under threat however. Donald McBane wrote: 'We marched in six lines making no noise, and attacked the Brabant Line, and took it about break of day, with little or no loss; when we were over on their side they attacked us.'

McBane's dry comments disguise the fact that it was a powerful French and Bavarian corps under Count Caraman and the Marquis d'Alègre, which threw itself at Marlborough's advanced guard with tremendous vigour as they crossed the obstacle belt. Kit Davies, still serving in Hay's dragoons, recalled that: 'Our horse and dragoons having openings to enter the lines, his grace led us on, and formed us to make head against the enemy; their corps nearest to the places of attack were in motion at the first alarm.' A brawling battle spread out along the narrow sunken lanes in the area. Marlborough's army actually outnumbered that of Caraman and d'Alègre, but Orkney wrote that the Allied troops had assembled in such haste that they were: 'A good deal mixed and not in their proper place.' The constricted lanes hampered a proper cavalry deployment; Marlborough was embroiled in the hacking close-quarter contest, and narrowly avoided being sabred by a Bavarian trooper. The man lost his balance and fell to the ground, and so the Duke's life was narrowly spared.

Not far away, the exiled Irishman, Peter Drake, had tired of service with his regiment in Lorraine (particularly as the rates of pay were less than he had expected) and absconded. He was, that very same July day, making his leisurely way with a forged pass in his pocket to try and enlist with an Irish regiment [de Courière's] in French service, who were quartered near to Louvain. The grenadier company of the unit was commanded by a namesake of his. Drake heard the sound of the battle at the Lines of Brabant, rolling across the fields in the early morning:

> I heard a report among the country people that the Brabant lines were surprised and entered by the Duke of Marlborough, which I thought incredible, and went on. In less than half an hour after I heard a smart firing, and soon perceived some troops, whether friends or foes I could not distinguish, but plainly saw they were in quick motion; and drawing nearer. I discovered a horse in a field of corn bridled and saddled, whose

rider I suppose had been killed. The creature did not stir, and I mounted him. By the furniture he must have been an officer's. Some of these troops rode towards me, and I turning to make the best of my way to Louvain, several shots were discharged without effect on me, but the horse was destroyed.

Walking onwards in some haste, the adventurous Irishman at last came to the French camp and, after brandishing his passport, asked for an old acquaintance. 'I took to inquire for de Courière's regiment, and Captain Sheehy; and having found him, he received me with open arms, and took me to Baron Drake's tent, introducing me to that gentleman.' After a number of discreet enquiries into Drake's background and military service so far in the war, the Baron enlisted him, once again, into the French army.

While Drake was arranging his affairs in this way, a few miles away Marlborough's troops had repulsed the attempt to drive them back over the Lines. The French and Bavarian cavalry was dispersed, and d'Alègre was captured. Count Caraman led the Bavarian infantry in a highly disciplined withdrawal to the shelter of the Mehaigne river. Robert Parker wrote admiringly of this skilful rearward manoeuvre:

> I must not omit taking notice of the gallant behaviour and good discipline of ten Bavarian battalions, who finding themselves abandoned by their horse, kept together, and observing that as we had marched all night, our foot was not able to come up with them, they formed themselves into a hollow square. In this form they marched, and notwithstanding that our right wing of horse and dragoons had surrounded them on all sides, yet they dared not venture within reach of their fire; for having divided their grenadiers into two bodies, which kept moving backward and forward to support the parts that were most in danger, the square kept marching on, driving the squadrons before them, out of their way, and so retreated safe to Louvain. This shows what the foot are capable of doing against the horse.

Marlborough did not pursue closely, a decision that attracted some criticism, but he had no way of knowing quite how close Marshal Villeroi was with his main army. The Duke wanted to combine his forces with those of Overkirk before moving forward. The Dutch corps was approaching, but was not yet on the field. Colonel Cranstoune wrote of the difficulty faced by Marlborough as the Bavarian infantry withdrew:

> There was rising ground before him [Caraman], to which he was retreating and the Duke really neither did nor indeed could at that time know how near the Elector and Marshal Villeroi were with their whole army and M. d'Overkirk's army were but marching up at distance and were not yet entered into the lines.

So, the Duke let the Bavarians go, and in the circumstances was right to do so. General Slangenberg, who galloped ahead of the toiling Dutch columns, was full of ardour however, and urged him to press on: 'This is nothing if we lie still here.' However, when Overkirk arrived, he was tired and ill-tempered after a long night-march, demanding that his troops be allowed to rest. The operation came to an end, although Marlborough's cavalry did press forward to seize the town of Tirlemont and take prisoner the French Régiment de Montluc before nightfall (Parker says two entire regiments, and McBane four). However, Overkirk paid full tribute to the Duke in his own despatch to the States-General regarding the action:

> I must do justice to the Duke of Marlborough, to give him all the honour of this enterprise, which he has carried on and supported, with a great deal of conduct and valour. We march again tomorrow. We made prisoners of war a regiment in Tirlemont.

Warm praise for a fair victory, and George Hamilton, 1st Earl Orkney, wrote afterwards of the Duke: 'See what a happy man he is, I believe this pleases him as much as Hogstet (Höchstädt/Blenheim).' Marlborough's comment, when congratulated on the success by one of his officers, was typical, 'All is well, but much is yet to be done.' The Duke wrote to Sidney Godolphin: 'I intend to march tomorrow towards Louvain, by which march I shall see what Monsieur de Villeroi will do.' The French commander was too quick, however, and fell back behind the shelter of the River Dyle before the Duke could intercept him. Villeroi was, however, forced to abandon in his withdrawal some rather curious pieces of artillery, which John Deane described as:

> Having three bores so that touching the match to one touch hole they fired out at each piece three balls at once. These murdering cannon were made the last year at the city of Brussels for the security of the line [Lines of Brabant], but by the providence of God we secured them so that they did our army but little mischief. At this time came many deserters from the enemy who declared that the enemy reckoned themselves twenty thousand men weaker than they were before we attacked them, for besides what was killed and taken, abundance run away from them to their own countries.

The Duke, with this neat operation, and with fairly modest loss, had burst through the vaunted Lines of Brabant, taken many prisoners, including their wounded commander, ten guns (some reports say eighteen), colours, standards and kettle-drums. He promptly put his soldiers to work at beginning to level the defences, so that never again could the French manoeuvre behind them and defy him with impunity. The chance was also taken by Marlborough to scout the surrounding countryside, making himself familiar with the very ground over which one of his greatest victories would be achieved before another twelve months had passed. Marshal Villeroi, his opponent on that occasion, had already done the same, both commanders appreciating the tactical importance and possibilities of the terrain. The Duke wrote to his wife after the battle:

I have this morning forced the enemy's lines and beaten a good part of their army, taken their cannon, two lieutenant-generals, and two major-generals, and a great many of their officers, besides standards and colours, all of which I shall have a perfect account tomorrow. It is impossible to say too much good of the troops that were with me, for never men fought better. Having marched all night, and taken a good deal of pains this day, my blood is so hot that I can hardly hold my pen. The kindness of the troops has transported me, for I had none in this last action, but such as were with me last year ... The troops with me make me very kind expressions even in the heat of the action, which I own to you give me great pleasure, and makes me resolve to endure everything for their sakes.

In London, the news of the victory was received with acclaim, and the Queen declared a Day of Thanksgiving, to be celebrated in August.

Despite such heartening success, Marlborough was unable to force a major battle on Villeroi during the remainder of 1705, the French commander clinging to the defence offered by the river lines. On those rare occasions when battle seemed imminent, the Dutch, as in previous years, intervened with cautious objections. The resulting delays allowed the French to escape from a tricky predicament on the Dyle river, where Marlborough had marched to outflank their position near Louvain. A strong detachment of English and Dutch infantry was put across the river on pontoon bridges at Neerysche, but a reluctance in the Dutch generals to engage enabled Villeroi to close up to the crossing place before the Allied advanced guard could be reinforced. Marlborough wrote to Godolphin on 29 July 1705:

It was unanimously resolved we should pass the Dyle, but that afternoon there fell so much rain as rendered it impracticable; but the fair weather this morning made me determine to attempt it. Upon this the deputies held a council with all the generals of Overkirk's army, who have unanimously retracted their opinions, and declared the passage of the river too dangerous, which resolution, in my opinion, will ruin the whole campaign. They have, at the same time, proposed to me to attack the French on their left; but I know they will let that fall also, as soon as they see the ground. It is very mortifying to meet more obstruction from friends than from enemies; but that is now the case with me; yet I dare not show my resentment for fear of alarming the Dutch.

Chaplain Samuel Noyes, who took part in the operation with Orkney's Regiment, wrote of the sorry incident a week or so later:

Our detachment came to the river, and under the cover of our cannon, which did great execution, laid six bridges. Colonel Godfrey with the grenadiers of the four English battalions passed over, as did also twelve of the Dutch battalions and beat all before them, cleared all the hedges and enclosed meadows and two villages, notwithstanding which Count Oxenstiern, who commanded all the detachments ordered the remainder of them to halt, and those who now passed to return, and the Duke commanded the copper boats [pontoon bridges] to be taken up again; the reason of which is variously reported. Some say the States refused to expose their army any further; others that the ground was so morassy [boggy] that our horse could never have got over; it is allowed they were morassy where the Dutch had made their four bridges, but very good hard ground where the English made their two. However, by this refusal of the Dutch General officers the whole thing fell to the ground.

Francis Hare's wry comment on the disappointment was 'Dyle, they say, in Scotch is Devil, as this paltry river has proved to be.' Henry St John had written from London a day or two later to Thomas Erle, saying that a letter he had recently received had:

> Found me rejoicing with my friends at the great and almost incredible success which my Lord Duke had in the affair of the lines, and I write this while I am cursing the stupidity, pique and cowardice of the Dutch officers and Deputies who labour all they can to make the advantage we have gained of no consequence. I hope Lord Marlborough will be able to cheat them into an engagement and when they are at the ball they must dance.

It was in vain. In mid-August, having loaded his wagons with bread, and cast loose from the formal supply lines for a week, Marlborough all but trapped the French on the Yssche river, just to the south of Brussels, as Deane put it 'On the road towards Brussels and near Waterloo.' Villeroi, who was still covering Louvain, was in great consternation, as the Duke's rapid march put his army in a position to attack Namur, Charleroi, Brussels, and even Mons if he stretched out that far. Uncertain for a time quite where Marlborough's blow would fall, the Marshal wrote to Versailles:

> It is necessary to make up one's mind to march to Brussels in order to save it, at the price of abandoning Louvain, it not being possible to defend them both. Supposing the enemy were to avail himself of the opportunity which we gave him by quitting our post in order to save Brussels, and made himself master of Louvain and after that the whole of Brabant, it still seemed to us that the loss of Brussels was yet more important.

Soon afterwards, Marlborough's rapid approach through Genappes towards the forest of Soignies was detected. Knowing that the position he held was bad, and fearing a catastrophe, the Marquis de Grimaldi, commanding the French forces on that flank, prepared to get his cannon and baggage away. Villeroi wrote to the Elector of Bavaria on 17 August: 'I believe that for centuries there has not been a more thorny hour.'

Instead of moving into the attack on 18 August, however, the Dutch insisted on holding a council of war. To makes matters worse still, General Slangenberg demanded precedence on the line of march for his personal coach and wagons, ahead of the slow-moving, but immeasurably more important, artillery train. Captain Parker wrote of this infamous conduct:

We were now drawing near the enemy, and his Grace had sent orders that the English train of artillery should make all possible haste up to him; but as they were just upon entering a narrow defile, Slangenberg came up to the head of them, and stopped them for some hours, until his baggage had passed on before them, a thing never known before.

Almost inevitably, the council of war decided after lengthy discussion that the enterprise was too risky. Even normally reliable Dutch officers such as Daniel Dopff were against an attack, apparently affronted that the Duke had not divulged his plans to them at an earlier point (not that they knew how to be discreet even when they were told these things). Marlborough appealed to the Dutch generals and deputies in impassioned tones:

> I have reconnoitred the ground and made dispositions for an attack. I am convinced that conscientiously, and as men of honour, we cannot now retire without an action. Should we neglect this opportunity, we must be responsible before God and man. You see the confusion which pervades the ranks of the enemy, and their embarrassment at our manoeuvres. I leave you to judge whether we should attack to-day, or wait till to-morrow. It is indeed late, but you must consider that, by throwing up entrenchments during the night, the enemy will render their position far more difficult to force.

So it proved: they talked through the afternoon and evening. In the morning, Villeroi had closed his main force up to Grimaldi, and when the Allied generals viewed the French position, it had plainly been well fortified in the night. An attack could no longer be made except at long odds against an easy success. Marlborough wrote to Duchess Sarah that same day: 'All the Dutch generals, except for M. Overkirk, were against it, so that the deputies would not consent to our engaging. We are now returning, for we cannot stay longer than the bread we have brought with us will give us leave.'

Justly indignant, Marlborough had to march his army off, reduced to overseeing the continued levelling of ten miles of the captured Lines of Brabant and looking to attack some minor fortresses. Louis XIV, almost fatally for his war effort, drew the wrong conclusions from all this, accepting Villeroi's report that Marlborough had been outwitted on the Yssche: 'The great noise that accompanied the Duke of Marlborough's march has all been ended in a shameful retreat.' So, the King learned to place less value in Marlborough's abilities – 'This mortified adventurer' as Chamillart smugly described him – and this was very dangerous.

For Marlborough, however, things could not go on in this way; writing to the States-General in the Hague, he said that he would no longer serve under such intolerable restrictions: 'I find my authority here to be much less than when I had the honour to command your troops, last year, in Germany.' The field deputies, concerned at the Duke's plain and furious impatience with them, also wrote to the Hague, attempting to excuse themselves:

We own that that my Lord Duke of Marlborough was of the opinion, as well as M. de Overkirk, that the attack was practicable, and might be attended with success. But we could not resolve to consent to a thing of so great importance contrary to the opinions of all the generals of that army, to which Your High Mightinesses have done us the honour to deputise us.

The States-General, in alarm that the Duke might resign his whole command, recalled Slangenberg and the more awkward of the field deputies, and promised full co-operation in future; Marlborough was to be allowed a much freer hand in the conduct of the operations. Henry St John commented on this in another letter sent to Thomas Erle at this time:

My Lord Duke has writ very plainly to the States [General] on this head by Monsieur Hompesch, and the letters from The Hague inform us the effect is that they have dispensed with his summoning councils of war and only expect he should advise with Monsieur d'Overkirk and the Deputies. He had ordered bread for twelve days and is now in action. God send us good news.

However, writing to Robert Harley on 10 September, Marlborough told him that 'We have for these three days past employed upwards of three thousand soldiers to assist in demolishing the Lines.' The Dutch had frustrated his attempts at anything greater for the time being. A few weeks later, as the work drew to a close, the Duke moved against the French held towns of Leau and Sandvliet, and he wrote again to Harley, on 20 October:

Tomorrow we intend to continue our march to Brecht and if the artillery and other preparations be ready to come up from Bergen Op Zoom, we shall make another motion the next day; in order to attack Sand Vliet, the taking of which place will be of good use to the States, for securing the navigation of the Scheldt up to Lillo, covering their frontiers, and will be a good curb to the garrison of Antwerp this winter.

The weather was worsening, Marlborough having written in late September 'The ill season being come in, our troops begin to suffer very much.' The condition of the horses, particularly those that laboured to drag along the artillery, concerned him: 'We are losing great numbers every day by sickness.' Despite this, both towns fell to the Allies without long resistance: 'Our men never leaving off cannonading and bombarding them' John Deane remembered, and the campaign began to draw to a close towards the end of October.

The Duke soon had to leave the army to go to Vienna for discussions with the new Emperor. But, before he went, there were many administrative matters claiming his attention. He wrote on 24 October to the Margrave of Baden with a recommendation for an Imperial cavalry officer, who had been on detached service with the army in the Low Countries:

Captain Panfi, who commanded a detachment of hussars in our army in the [recent] campaign, being sent to return with his men to rejoin their regiment, I do him the justice to assure your Excellency that we are very content with his conduct; he has comported himself with much bravery and zeal for the service, of a kind that causes me to recommend him as someone deserving of your favour.

Once in Vienna, Marlborough was presented with the Imperial dignity of the Prince of Mindleheim in recognition of his triumph the previous year on the banks of the Danube. Kit Davies, with evident relish, said that 'This news was brought to us before we left Tirlemont [for winter quarters], we were regaled with liquor, and made great rejoicings.' In the opposing army, Peter Drake was also now marching towards winter quarters also, where de Courière's Régiment settled in rather well. He remembered:

Ghent fell to our lot [to find quarters], and thither we marched ... there I had an elegant apartment, and a good table, and was shortly after furnished with a regimental suit like those worn by the officers. Being thus equipped and having the rank of cadet, I frequented the public places ... and thus passed the winter agreeably.

Kit Davies went on to recall that the cold months passed quietly enough, and time was available for the campaign-weary regiments to recuperate and replenish their ranks:

Our recruits, and horses to remount those who had lost them, arrived in Holland the 3rd of April 1706, and the Duke of Marlborough, with a number of volunteers, landed there on the 25th. The enemy, in the interim, lost no time; they had wrought hard all the winter upon their entrenchments behind the Dyle and on the fortifying Louvain, where they had brought together such prodigious quantities of flour, hay, oats and all sorts of ammunition.

How much use the French were able to make of these admirably complete preparations for a defensive campaign in Brabant during the coming year will be seen. Marshal Villeroi could continue to manoeuvre in comparative safety behind the Dyle river, and Marlborough would be hard pressed to get at him. However, strategic considerations were coming into play. Louis XIV was anxious to impress his opponents with the vitality of the French war effort, and his army commander in the Low Countries would soon march out to give battle in the open.

Chapter Six

The Miraculous Year – Ramillies and the Conquest of Belgium, 1706

In late spring of 1706, things were stirring on either side of the Dyle river in the Spanish Netherlands. The Duke of Marlborough was anxious to get the French army to stand and fight, while his opponent, François de Neufville, Marshal Villeroi, was receiving instructions from Versailles to go and seek battle. Peter Drake, still serving in an émigré Irish regiment in the French service, wrote of the opening of the season for war:

> We did not stir until the latter end of April, when we marched by the way of Brussels for Louvain, where the army was to assemble. We stayed some days to lay bridges over the Dyle, for the more convenient passing of the army and train, whilst the baggage marched through the town.

The Duke of Marlborough, with frustrating difficulty and delay, partially completed the concentration of his army near to Maastricht. A particular concern was that the dependable Danish cavalry were under instructions not to go on campaign until arrears of pay were settled, even though Queen Anne had written to her brother-in-law, King Frederick IV, on 13 April:

> The Duke of Marlborough is projecting an important undertaking against the enemy, and the friendship which I have for you making me rely on your own, I hope that you will consent to allow Your Majesty's troop[s] now under the said General's command to march wherever he thinks for the good of the service. The great concern which I always had for your subjects in my pay, should convince you that you can well confide them to my care.

Marlborough told his friend, the lord Treasurer, Sidney Godolphin, on 15 May 1706:

> When I left the Hague on Sunday [9 May] last I was assured that I should find the army in a condition to march. But as yet neither the artillery horses nor the bread wagons are come, so that we shall be obliged to stay for the English, which will join us on Wednesday [19 May], and then we shall advance towards Louvain. God knows I go with a heavy heart, for I

have no prospect of doing any thing considerable, when the French would do what I am very confident they will not, when the marshal de Marsin should return [from the Moselle], as is reported, with thirty battalions and forty squadrons; for that would give them such a superiority as might tempt them to march out of their lines, which if they do, I will most certainly attack them, not doubting, with the blessing of God, to beat them, though the foreign troops I have seen are not so good as they were last year, but I hope the English are better.

Other concerns crowded in upon the Duke, in large degree a consequence of the imperfections of alliance warfare, and he wrote to Secretary of State, Robert Harley, in London on 17 May: 'I find the King of Prussia is as obstinate as ever against his troops serving in Germany; or even letting them advance into these parts.' However, the troops in English and Dutch pay were steadily gathering, even if Marlborough eventually had to pledge his own credit to secure the services of the Danish squadrons.

The Duke thought it unlikely that Villeroi would risk battle, but the Marshal now had orders from Versailles to do just that. Louis XIV wanted peace, and the best way to put pressure on his opponents to negotiate with him was to intimidate them, or so it seemed. All the French field commanders were expected to take the offensive this spring, and demonstrate to the whole world the vitality of France and the French war effort. The King had written 'I can think of nothing which can better induce them [the Allies] to come to an agreement which has become necessary now than to let them see that I have sufficient forces to attack them everywhere.' The rather pointed letters sent to Villeroi by both the King and Michel de Chamillart, the French War Minister, aggravated the Marshal, who seemed to feel that his own courage was being impugned. The Duc de St Simon wrote that:

> Villeroi was wounded by these reiterated admonitions. He had the feeling that the King doubted his courage since he judged it necessary to spur him so hard. He resolved to put all at stake to satisfy him, and to prove that he did not deserve such hard suspicions.

It was also felt, both at Versailles and in the French army, that the inability of Marlborough to achieve very much in 1705, other than the Elixheim success, indicated that the victory at Blenheim in 1704 had been due to luck, rather than to the Duke's skill. This, perhaps, led Villeroi to risks that otherwise he would not have thought of taking.

As Marlborough indicated in his letter of 15 May to Godolphin, he had information that Marshal Marsin would march from the Moselle valley to reinforce the French in Brabant. Should this take place, and some of Marsin's cavalry certainly did join Villeroi in mid-May, his opponents might well feel powerful enough to take the field. The Duke was not very optimistic that this would be so, however, not yet aware of the urging coming from Versailles to the French commanders. Louis XIV, in fact, did caution Villeroi not to move until the reinforcements from the Moselle had joined him. In the French camp, Colonel Jean-Martin De La Colonie commented on the attitude of easy confidence that filled the French at this time:

> The last campaign had been so favourable to France that she became convinced the wheel of fortune was turning in her favour, and that she should therefore take the opportunity to strike terror in the hearts of her enemies. To bring this about a battle in Flanders would be necessary; she had in reserve, should a reverse occur, a number of fortified towns which would be a means of defence for the frontier by checking the enemy's advance and giving us time to replace our losses, and in case of success Holland and the German frontier lay open to us.

Rather against early expectations then, it was learned in the Allied camp on Wednesday 19 May that the 60,000-strong French army had left its camp near Louvain the previous day, and crossed the Dyle river, apparently heading for the Allied-held town of Leau, lost by Villeroi the previous year. The French then swung southwards, past Tirlemont, heading for the convenient watershed at Ramillies, where easy passage across dry ground could be found between the marshy Mehaigne and Gheete rivers. By this route he might turn the left flank of the Allied position on the borders of Brabant, and catch his opponent off-balance. Marlborough wrote to the Duke of Württemberg, commander of the absent twenty-one squadrons of Danish cavalry, on that same day: 'Having just been advised that the enemy have passed the Dyle, I send this express to request your Highness to bring your cavalry forward by a double march.'

The Allied army, which would number 62,000 men when the Danish cavalry caught up, was put on the road, and moved to take possession of the very same watershed at Ramillies that Villeroi was heading for. The reason is plain; for this dry ground gave the only convenient route from east to west, or vice versa, in the region. Whichever army held the ground would be at an advantage when moving swiftly to the attack. On Thursday Marlborough wrote to Godolphin as the fateful campaign began to unfold:

> The French knowing that it is not in our power, in less than three weeks, to have the Hanoverians or Hessians from the Rhine, they have taken the resolution of drawing as many of their troops out of the garrisons as is possible, and marched yesterday out of their lines, and are now camped at Tirlemont. The English join the army this day, and the Danes two days hence. We shall be 122 squadrons and 74 battalions ... I hope for success, being resolved to venture; for as yet they have but twenty squadrons of the marshal de Marsin's detachment [from the Moselle].

Marlborough delayed his army's advance for a day at Corswaren, to enable the Danes to close up. Württemberg had responded to the Duke's call like a loyal lieutenant, and his cavalry would join the Allied army in time to participate in the attack the following day. Meanwhile, Marlborough wrote from Borchloen to Robert Harley in London, telling of the urgent concentration of his army in face of the French moves:

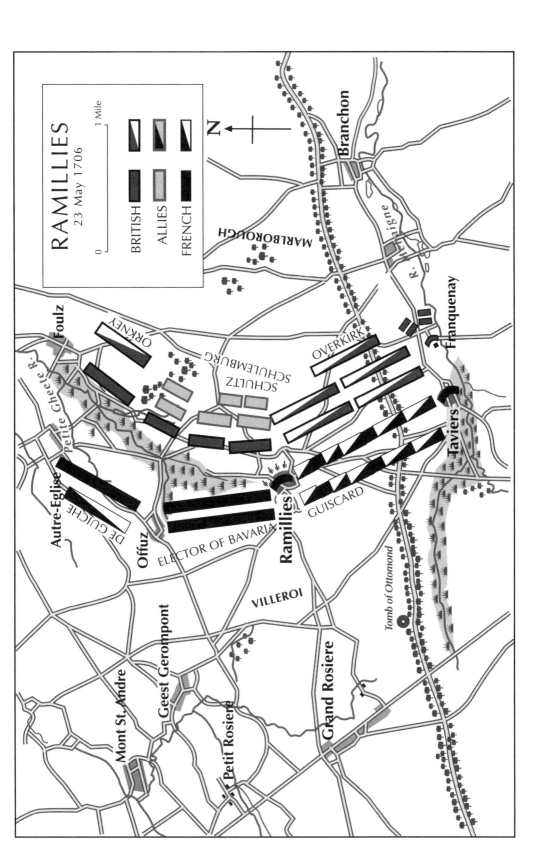

RAMILLIES
23 May 1706

BRITISH
ALLIES
FRENCH

0   1 Mile

N

Foulz
ORKNEY
Autre-Eglise
DE GUICHE
Offuz
ELECTOR OF BAVARIA
SCHULTZ SCHULEMBURG
OVERKIRK
Franquenay
Taviers
Ramillies
GUISCARD
VILLEROI
MARLBOROUGH
R. Mehaigne
Branchon
Mont St. Andre
Geest Gerompont
Petit Rosiere
Grand Rosiere
Tomb of Ottomond
Petite Gheete R.

> The English troops came to Bitsen within a league and a half of Tongres, from whence the Dutch marched to-day, and we joined at this place. The enemy having drained all their garrisons, and depending on their superiority [in numbers], passed the Dyle yesterday and came and posted themselves at Tirlemont, with the Gheet before them, whereupon I have sent orders to the Danish troops, who are coming from their garrisons, to hasten their march. I hope they may be with us on Saturday, and then I design to advance towards the enemy, to oblige them to retire, or, with the blessing of God, to bring them to a battle.

The Duke saw, with sparkling clarity, what was the vital ground, and what was the likelihood of a sudden clash, as the two armies surged towards each other. On 21 May 1706, he had prophetically written to a friend: 'We design to advance in order to gain the head of the Gheete [the Ramillies watershed], to come to the enemy if they keep their ground. I can think nothing could be more happy for the Allies than a battle.' The absence of the Prussian troops, so steadfast and brave in action, still perturbed the Duke, and he wrote with some asperity to Lord Raby, the English Ambassador in Berlin, the following day:

> You will see from our journal the situation we are in. If it should please God to give us victory over the enemy, the allies will be little obliged to the King [of Prussia]; and if, on the other hand, we should have any disadvantage, I know not how he will be able to excuse himself.

However, the gravity of the situation, and the many things with which he had to concern himself as his armies moved forward to confront the French, did not prevent the Duke from exerting himself to help the families of the soldiers he commanded. The same day he wrote again to Raby:

> M. de Ruchat, who commanded the Prince of Nassau-Dillenburg's regiment in the King of Prussia's service, where he behaved himself with a great deal of reputation and had been wounded in several actions, being dead some time since, and his widow, who is thereby reduced to very low circumstances, being now at Berlin, in order to solicit a small pension from the King of Prussia. I pray your Excellency will please to intercede in her behalf, either with the King or the Count de Wartenberg, not doubting but that your Excellency's great credit with both will procure her the relief her condition seems to deserve, which shall be esteemed as a great obligation [by me].

The coming clash of arms at the Ramillies watershed was by no means unexpected. That the French felt that they might have to fight that Sunday is plain, as it was known that Marlborough and his army were on the move eastwards, though no-one knew quite how far they had got. Peter Drake wrote of the preparations in Villeroi's camp that Saturday night:

> On Whitsun Eve (22 May 1706) we were furnished with sixteen charges of ball and powder a man; orders were given out at night for the General

[reveille] to beat at dawn of day; the chaplains to say Mass at the heads of their respective regiments; the tents to be struck, the baggage loaded, all sure tokens there was work cut out for the following day. At four [o'clock am] the whole army was in motion, marching in columns; viz., the two lines, first and second, in order of battle, the train of artillery between the lines, a proportion being assigned to each brigade, and our baggage on our right, between us and our garrisons [i.e to the west]. Thus we did proceed without the least interruption until twelve o'clock.

Despite this apparent state of alert, Maximilien Wittelsbach, the Elector of Bavaria, was not present, as he was attending Pentecostal celebrations in Brussels, and he would not join Villeroi until the deployment on the Ramillies position was well underway. In the opposing army meantime, John Deane recalled that 'The Danish troops came up with our rear this evening [22 May] and encamped at a small distance from us.' Tom Kitcher, a Hampshire farm labourer turned soldier with Meredith's Regiment, told of his march to battle that Sunday morning: 'When the call of arms sounded, he and his comrades made many complex movements the purpose of which he understood nought and which he and his companions, grumbling, derided but carried them out without fault.' The exasperation of the common soldier, faced with the seemingly incomprehensible and unreasonable demands of their officers, is plain; little has changed over the centuries, as soldiers today will testify.

That misty Sunday morning the French army was on the march onto the Ramillies ridge, and its quartermasters were scouting the area ready to set out a good campsite for the night. They were first on the ground, an important tactical consideration, and Colonel De La Colonie, whose Grenadiers Rouge were brigaded with the Cologne Regiment, wrote of the magnificence of the scene, marching as part of:

> One of the finest armies ever seen, which took up a position overlooking the Plain of Ramillies, its left resting on the wood of Waterloo [probably in the area around Fouz le Caves] with the right in the plain itself. The enemy appeared in the plain, the left of their army resting on a marsh [the Mehaigne river] near the village of Tavier, whilst in front of their right they had a series of deep ravines [the line of the Petite Gheete, running northwards from Ramillies to Offuz and beyond]. The ground bordering on these ravines, although dry to all appearance, was none the less impractical, and in this position they awaited our attack.

The Colonel was rather mistaken; at about 7am that morning, the Allied Quartermaster-General, William Cadogan, had ridden forward with an escort of 700 dragoons, 'the correct number appointed for such a task', to scout the Ramillies watershed for signs of the advance guard of the French army, and, like them, to find and mark out a camp ground for the night. Marlborough plainly expected Villeroi to be further north than he was, and, given Drake's evidence of the preparations for battle, it may be said that, on this occasion at least, French intelligence of the respective manoeuvres was a little better than the Duke's. Villeroi was deploying into battle formation, while Marlborough was still on the march, looking for a campsite. What counted most now, was the reaction of the two army commanders to the impending collision; which would make the best decisions and put them into practice first.

As Cadogan's party cantered across the Plateau of Jandrenouille from the overnight encampment near to Merdorp, they ran into a group of French foragers who, after a brief exchange of shots, quickly made off to the west. They took word of the encounter back to Villeroi, on the Plateau of Mont St André. He acted swiftly to occupy what was a naturally very sound defensive position. Peering through the mist towards them, the big Irishman could dimly make out the massed ranks of Villeroi's army on the march, heading for Ramillies. At once, messengers went spurring back to Merdorp to bring Marlborough forward to where he could see the French movement. The Duke and his aides joined Cadogan at about 10am, by which time the mist had lifted. The French were deploying into line of battle, stretching in a shallow arc from Taviers in the south to Autre-Eglise in the north, a distance of about four miles in all. Paradoxically, the Dutch had warned Marlborough against making any attempt to force the French from this very position three years earlier, when they described with some accuracy the natural strength of the terrain Marshal Villeroi was now deploying to occupy. They were worried that 'where their right being extended to the Mehaigne, near Taviers, and their left towards Ramilles and Autre Eglise, they will have a narrow aperture of but 1200 paces to defend.' The deputies were right, but Marlborough had no intention of avoiding a clash of arms.

Flying in the face of these cautionary words, Marlborough without hesitation ordered his cavalry forward into position, ready to mount an attack. By doing this so promptly, he firmly fixed Villeroi to fight on the ridge-line from which he first saw the Allied approach. The French commander was given no chance to draw off and avoid battle, as he had so carefully done in the past. Marlborough's army, slightly larger than that of the French, covered a smaller frontage, and so their punch, when it came, would be more compact and carry more weight than their opponent could muster. Also, the French and Bavarians would have to march around the outside of the arc when shifting troops from one flank to another, while the Allies could cut across the middle. St Simon, who was plainly well briefed, wrote that 'There was a marsh [the Petite Gheete] which covered our left, but which hindered our two wings from joining.' Although Villeroi was first on the ground, he was wrong-footed from the start.

Despite this tactical disadvantage, not particularly serious on its own, the dispositions made by Villeroi were sound enough, as he moved quickly to arrange his army in line of battle. His excellent cavalry and dragoons were massed on the open level plain in the south, between Ramillies and Taviers, while the bulk of his infantry took up position on the low ridge-line between Ramillies and Offuz, where the ground to the front was broken up by the marshy rivulets of the Petite Gheete. Bavarian cavalry stood in reserve to support the infantry in the north, while the two villages on either flank, Autre-Eglise and Taviers, were packed with veteran infantry and prepared for defence, as were both Offuz and Ramillies in the centre. Colonel De La Colonie remembered the French deployment well:

> So vast was the plain at Ramillies that we were able to march our army on as broad a front as we desired, and the result was a magnificent spectacle. The army began its march at six o'clock in the morning, formed into two large columns, the front of each consisting of a battalion; the artillery formed a third [column], which marched between the infantry columns. The cavalry squadrons in battle formation occupied an equal extent of ground, and there being nothing to impede the view, the whole force was seen in such a fine array that it would be impossible to view a grander sight. The army had just entered on the campaign, weather and fatigue had hardly yet had time to dim its brilliancy, and it was inspired with a courage born of confidence. The late Marquis de Goudrin, with whom I had the honour to ride during the march, remarked to me that France had surpassed herself in the quality of these troops; he believed that the enemy had no chance whatever of breaking them in the coming conflict; if defeated now, we could never again hope to withstand them.

Walloon officers accompanying Marlborough's party assured the Duke that the valley of the Petite Gheete was quite impassable. This echoed the advice he had received three years earlier, but the Duke still directed the British infantry under the 1st Earl of Orkney, and the cavalry and dragoons under Lieutenant-General Henry Lumley, to close up to the stream, ready to attack the small villages of Offuz and Autre-Eglise. German infantry, Hessians and Saxons under Count Schulemburg, and Dutch led by Schultz and Spaar, were sent to form up in front of Ramillies itself, as were brigades of Protestant Swiss and Scottish troops in the Dutch service. Veldt-Marshal Overkirk's Dutch cavalry and Württemberg's Danish squadrons confronted the massed French cavalry on the open plain to the south of Ramillies, supported by the Dutch infantry. Private John Deane, who marched into battle with the 1st English Foot Guards, wrote:

> His Grace the Duke of Marlborough, judging by the situation of the ground that the stress of the action would be on the left, ordered that beside the number of those Horse belonging to that wing [the Dutch], the Danish squadrons, they being twenty [actually twenty-one, although Parker says fourteen] in number, should also be posted there. It was about two in the afternoon before our army could be formed in order of battle, and then began to attack on our left.

Jean-Martin De La Colonie, although he was standing close to Ramillies with his battalion, described the potentially fragile situation on the French right flank:

There was yet another point to which no attention had been paid, but which had an important bearing on the result, and that was the village of Taviers, which lay beyond the marsh [on the French right], nearly equidistant from the enemy and ourselves ... The cavalry were formed on the extreme flanks of both armies on the edge of the marsh, which was but a pistol-shot in breadth and only practicable for infantry; hence, whichever infantry occupied the village, they could line its edge, open a destructive fire, and destroy the cavalry without any risk whatever. The enemy, who were the first to appreciate this fact, sent fourteen battalions [actually four battalions initially, together with some squadrons of dismounted dragoons] across the marsh to seize it, and then our generals realised the result this would have on the course of the battle, and resolved to drive them out before the action began.

The Colonel was as yet unaware that Swiss troops in French service had already been sent forward to hold Taviers. He makes no mention of the small hamlet of Franquenay, which, being several hundred metres forward of Taviers, was even more exposed to any Allied assault. Shortly after midday, a detachment of Swiss was moved forward to occupy Franquenay; they were too far in advance of Taviers to be properly supported, and so were wasted. A brigade of Dutch Foot Guards, under Colonel Wertmüller, went into the attack on Franquenay at about 2pm, as John Deane mentions; supported by a pair of field guns, the Dutch promptly drove the Swiss out of the hamlet and back over the marshy meadows to seek refuge with their comrades in Taviers.

Wertmüller's Guards were in close pursuit, and the vicious struggle was renewed at bayonet point around the cottages and barns of the village. Losses were severe on both sides, and Colonel De La Colonie remarked that the fighting there was almost as murderous as the rest of the battle put together. The Dutch soon had a firm hold on Taviers, and the right flank of the whole French army was now dangerously exposed. General Guiscard, commanding the French cavalry on this part of the field, promptly two sent more Swiss infantry battalions and fourteen squadrons of dismounted French dragoons to retake Taviers; the effort went in piecemeal, with no attempt at mutual support, and it was broken up by the Dutch without great difficulty. De La Colonie's brigade of French and German infantry was ordered by Comte de la Motte to move southwards from Ramillies to support the counter-attack: 'We set out, and passed along the right of our line to reach the marsh.' As they neared the fighting, the Colonel wrote that the ranks of his men were disrupted by the fleeing soldiers who had been routed by the Dutch Guards. He now suffered the mortification of seeing his own veterans break:

It appeared they had attacked the village without waiting for us, and had been repulsed with much loss ... The runaways threw themselves among my men, and carried them off with them, and I was never more surprised in my life to find myself standing alone with a few officers and the colours. I was immediately filled with rage and grief; I cried out in German and French like one possessed; I shouted every epithet I could think of to my grenadiers; I seized the colonel's colour, planted it by me, and by the loudness of my cries I at last attracted the attention of some few of them. The officers who had stood by me rushed after the fugitives, also shouting and pointing out the colonel's colour which I still kept in my hands, and at last they checked the stampede. I gradually rallied my grenadiers and several companies of the Cologne regiment, making in all four small battalions, very much shaken.

De La Colonie's battered troops (his own brigade commander had been taken prisoner by the Dutch, after imprudently galloping on ahead and getting his horse stuck in the mud of the nearby Visoule stream) had to take up a fresh position across the marshes to the west of Taviers, unable to participate to any great extent in the battle any further 'Although it was out of my power to attack the enemy in Taviers, yet I detained them in that village, from which they did not dare to emerge, and thus protected the right flank of the Maison de Roi.' The Colonel exaggerates the effect he had, elbowed aside at one end of the field of battle, but he adds the pithy comment on the example to be set by officers on a battlefield: 'It is absolutely certain that a commanding officer cannot exhibit too much firmness in such perilous circumstances, for upon him all eyes are fixed, and it is usually by his example that the cowardice or courage of his men is decided.' The Colonel apparently did not realise that a number of the Dutch Guard battalions did move, with some squadrons of dismounted dragoons, to cover the Danish advance around the exposed flank of the French cavalry as the afternoon wore on.

This whole shambles of an operation not only failed to re-establish the security of the French right flank, but fourteen squadrons of French dragoons, four Swiss battalions of infantry, and much of the Bavarian brigade of infantry, at the very least, had been lost to any participation in the cavalry battle looming on the plain. The Grenadiers Rouge were, though, able to rescue some of the French dragoons and Swiss who were floundering about in the marsh of the Visoule stream:

> The enemy's squadrons appeared on the further edge with the intention of shooting down the fugitives. I ordered a volley to be fired by the whole of my line, which threw them into disorder. A singular feature connected with this volley was the astonishment of the enemy, who were under the impression that my troops, dressed as they were in blue and red, belonged to their side and that we had fired on them by mistake ... I saw that the remains of their squadrons had taken up a position still sufficiently within range of the marsh to enable them to knock over our bogged people with stray shots; I therefore sent a captain and a hundred grenadiers to line their side of the marsh and keep down the enemy's fire.

At the far end of the battlefield the opposing batteries were hammering remorselessly at each other. Ramillies was under heavy attack by the Dutch and

Saxon brigades: 'Attacked by detachments of 12 battalions of Foot commanded by Lieutenant-General Schultz, who entered at once with great bravery and resolution' according to John Deane. A Scottish brigade commanded by the 2nd Earl of Argyll moved forward in support, as did a small Swiss brigade (in Dutch service) commanded by General Murray. The fighting in the narrow streets was ferocious, and the French and émigré Irish defenders were difficult to move. In the village, Peter Drake remembered:

> Lord Clare's [Irish] which engaged with a Scotch regiment in the Dutch service [Borthwick's] between whom there was great slaughter; that nobleman having lost two hundred and eighty nine private centinels, twenty two commissioned officers and fourteen sergeants; yet they not only saved their colours, but gained a pair from the enemy.

The contest was bloody indeed, and two British regiments, the Buffs and Churchill's, were sent to bolster the attack. The colour-ensign of Borthwick's Scots-Dutch regiment, James Gardiner, was shot in the mouth and left for dead. He was saved by two French soldiers who, intending to plunder his pockets, believed him to be a fellow-Catholic as he spoke to them (probably with some difficulty, as he had a mouthful of broken teeth) in Latin.

To the north, between Offuz and Ramillies, Captain Robert Parker of the Royal Irish remembered the gradual unfolding of Marlborough's plan:

> The Duke had a fair view of the enemy and saw, evidently, that the stress of the battle must be on the plain where they were drawn up in a formidable manner. He also saw that things must go hard with him, unless he could oblige them to break the disposition they had made on the plain … Although he knew the ground along the Gheete was not passable yet he ordered our right to march down in great order, with pontoons [fascines] to lay bridges, as if he designed to attack them in their weak part.

Orkney's British infantry descended the easy slope to the valley of the Petite Gheete. Struggling through the marshy ground, the soldiers began to climb the slope to the ridgeline, under a heavy musketry fire. The Hampshire-born soldier, Tom Kitcher, spoke of engaging in brutal fighting that afternoon, and he afterwards told the curate of his home village that:

> They were commanded to cross the marsh by means of fascines and many were shot and maimed or killed, by the French outposts, which they carried and laid down their foundations. He told me that limbs and bodies which it was impossible always to ascertain whether or no they were dead were used to pack the quagmire at some points and that one redcoat that he knew of raised himself from the supposed dead at the indignity of this treatment and turned upon the pioneers who had thought him one of their bundles of faggots and flayed them with his tongue. He went on, the Frenchies seemed surprised and showed no mind to fight much. Some of

them I saw turned tail and I spiked one of their officers through the gullet and another through the arse, where he spun like bacon upon a spit.

Kitcher plainly did not know that the soldiers the British drove up the slope towards Offuz village were a brigade of Walloon infantry commanded by Major-General de la Guiche. These tough troops gave ground rather more slowly than the young soldier remembered, making Orkney's battalions pay a suitable price for their passage of the Gheete stream.

Steadily Orkney's troops pressed upwards towards Offuz, fighting hand to hand against superior numbers of French and Walloon infantry, drawing Villeroi's attention firmly to the threat posed by this British attack which, if successful, might overwhelm his left flank. Fatally, the Marshal was driven by his concern for the security of his left flank to neglect his right. Kitcher remembered the fighting in grisly detail:

> Our cavalry did not come up to help us, but even without them we quit ourselves I reckon in a seemly way. One fellow's guts got round my ankles and I had to despatch them like a snake. He showed how poorly he thought of this by cursing me mightily. I suppose a man has an affection for his guts, even when he's quitting them for an angel's halo.

Having thrown a heavy punch against Villeroi's left, Marlborough was now putting the full weight of his attack onto the French right. Unable to be strong everywhere, he had to call back the British infantry who were making slow progress against de la Guiche's infantry around Offuz. Orkney could not believe the order to retire at first, although a string of aides (the last being William Cadogan) were sent to him by the Duke, to ensure that there was no misunderstanding. The Earl was indignant, as Tom Kitcher tells us:

> We were making forward without a single horse to our aid, when we had the order to give ground and make way back to the river. 'Pray, what's this?' said my Lord Orkney, so his servant told me after. He had no mind to give ground when we were giving no quarter, nor we hadn't neither, being up to our necks in deadliness and noise. But, so it was ordered and we went back across the stream and there we stayed awhile.

The withdrawal of the British infantry down the slope was well handled, and the French and Walloons were unable to disrupt the movement, although they came forward into the valley once again. There they met solid volleys of musketry from the 1st English Foot Guards and Orkney's Regiment, who covered the withdrawal. Orkney wrote to a friend of his infantry's attack on the villages:

> Where I was with most of the English foot, there was a morass and ruisseau [stream] before us, which they said was impossible to pass over. But however we tried and, after some difficulty, got over with ten or twelve battalions; and Mr Lumley brought over some squadrons of horse with very great difficulty; and I endeavoured to possess myself of a

village, which the French brought down a good part of their line to take possession of, and they were on one side of the village, and I on the other; but they always retired as we advanced. As I was going to take possession, I had ten aides-de-camp to [tell] me to come off, for the horse could not sustain me. We did it very well and in good order, and, whenever the French pressed upon us, with the battalion of Guards and my own [regiment], I was always able to stand and make them retire. Cadogan came and told me it was impossible I could be sustained by the horse if we went on then, and since my Lord could not attack everywhere, he would make the grand attack in the centre and try to pierce there.

The British battalions reformed on the ridge-line from where they had started their advance, and now Marlborough's intentions became clear. The second line of infantry began to move southwards towards Ramillies, taking advantage of a shallow fold in the ground which hid them from the eyes of the French, Walloons and Bavarians on the opposite ridge. This was part of Marlborough's massive reinforcement of his centre and left in the crucial battle in the south, where the French cavalry were increasingly exposed. Villeroi was simultaneously moving his own reserves of infantry to the north, marching them to support the battle for Ramillies and to hold the ridge-line to Offuz and Autre-Eglise.

Marlborough's attention was directed at the huge swirling cavalry battle that had erupted to the south of Ramillies. Here, De La Colonie had already noticed that the gaps between the French cavalry squadrons were greater than was customary, as they had to cover so much ground on the mile-wide plain. He wrote of the fighting:

I now saw the enemy's cavalry squadrons advance upon our people, at first at a rather slow pace, and then, when they thought they had gained the proper distance, they broke into a trot to gain impetus for their charge. At the same moment the Maison du Roi decided to meet them, for at such a moment those who await the shock find themselves at a disadvantage.

Despite their lack of numbers compared with their Dutch and Danish opponents, the French troopers fought vigorously under the inspired command of General Guiscard, but, De La Colonie ruefully commented, 'What a contrast was shown in the melee … The enemy, profiting by their superiority in numbers, surged through the gaps between our squadrons and fell upon their rear whilst their four ranks attacked in front.' However, with a tremendous effort, the French household cavalry, despite the lack of real infantry support, threw back Overkirk's Dutch squadrons, a number of whom scattered. Marlborough was close to Ramillies, having given the orders to bring his reserves of cavalry from the north to bolster the Dutch attack. While awaiting their arrival, he rode forward to encourage the disordered troopers and, conspicuous in his red coat, became exposed with a small group of aides on the edge of the fighting. The Duke's horse stumbled at a ditch and he was thrown heavily to the ground, where the French cavalry nearly rode over him.

Colonel Cranstoune, who saw the exploit, wrote that the Duke 'Exposed his person like the meanest soldier' and:

> Put himself at the head of the Dutch horse; and the gardes du corps, mousquetieres, and gens d'armes, happening to encounter them, ten of the Dutch squadrons were repulsed, renversed and put in great disorder. The Duke, seeing this, and seeing that things went pretty well elsewhere, stuck by the weak[er] part to make it up by his presence, and led still up new squadrons there to the charge, till at last the victory was obtained. It was here where those squadrons were renversed and in absolute déroute and the French mixed with them in the pursuit, the Duke, flying with the crowd, in leaping a ditch fell off his horse and some rode over him. Major-General Murray, who had his eye there and was so near he could distinguish the Duke in the flight, seeing him fall, marched up in all haste with two Swiss battalions to save him, and stop the enemy who were hewing all down in their way. The Duke when he got to his feet again saw Major-General Murray coming up and ran directly to get in to his battalions. In the meantime Mr [Captain] Molesworth quitted his horse and got the Duke mounted again, and the French were so hot in their pursuit that some of them before they could stop their horses ran in upon the Swiss bayonets.

A little later, as Marlborough mounted a fresh horse, a round-shot fired from a French battery in Ramillies skimmed the saddle, narrowly missing the Duke's cocked leg, and decapitated the officer who held the stirrup for him. John Deane said of the incident:

> My Lord Duke had still a greater escape, for my Lord Duke just as he was remounting of his horse again and Major Brinfeilde [Bringfield] attending of him, he being my Lords gentleman of the horse, the ball came so near that it took off Major Brinfeilde's head just by my Lord Duke's side.

As the pressure increased on the French cavalry to the south of Ramillies, a gap steadily opened in the cornfields on the far right of their flank, where the Dutch had seized Franquenay and Taviers earlier in the afternoon. Into this space had been thrust the battalions of Dutch Guards, and Opdham's regiment of dragoons. Württemberg's Danish cavalry now found the way open, and slipped through, virtually without any molestation. The Duc de St Simon wrote 'All this time our left had been utterly useless with its nose in the marsh [the Petite Gheete].' By 6pm, the Danish cavalry were formed up in the open fields at the rear of the French right Wing. Marlborough and Overkirk rode over to join them, and in a solid disciplined body the squadrons surged forward against the exposed flank of the Maison du Roi. De La Colonie recalled that:

> Naturally our right was soon crushed. I noticed numbers of rider-less horses make their escape, and in a short time [this] became general. The

enemy took our lines in flank, rode them down, and completely routed them; each trooper thought only of retreat. Brigade after brigade broke.

Villeroi's army was desperately off balance, and his right Wing was in utter disarray. He hurriedly tried to redeploy part of his left Wing from the Plateau of Mont St André to meet this sudden threat; the baggage of his army, neglectfully left behind at Offuz and Ramillies at the onset of the battle, hampered the Marshal's belated efforts, and chaos ensued. Peter Drake was with one of the regiments which had been held back behind Offuz, and now tried to move to a fresh position so that a stand could be made against the onrushing Danish horsemen:

> We were commanded to face to the right about, and retire. We had not got forty yards in our retreat, when the word sauve qui peut [fly that can – run away], went through the great part, if not the whole army, and put all in confusion. Then might be seen whole brigades running in disorder, the enemy pursuing almost close at our heels.

Across the wide battlefield the two armies were in close and deadly conflict, but the French and Bavarian army was in peril and being overwhelmed, their commander dazzled by the many blows aimed against him. Villeroi was unable to react in time as his more skillful opponent put forth his full strength, with subtle arrangements that were now taking awful and devastating effect. James Campbell, who fought with Borthwick's Scots-Dutch regiment in the capture of Ramillies, commented that 'The action was very hot for two hours, afterwards the enemy was repulsed with the greatest imaginable loss, they lost all the cannon and the baggage what in killed and taken prisoners is not yet known, but in short it is a most glorious victory.'

In Ramillies village the German, Swiss and Scots infantry had forced their way into the alleys between the cottages, and the garrison now began to melt away with the rest of Villeroi's broken army. One brigade though, comprised of veteran Bavarian and Cologne Guards, fought on valiantly from the shelter of a sunken lane leading onto the Plateau of Mont St André. Their commander, the Marquis de Maffei, who had distinguished himself by his gallant conduct as D'Arco's second-in-command at the Schellenberg fight two years earlier, was in no mind to flee and tried instead to make a stand against the Allied cavalry. However, he mistook the identity of some horsemen nearby, and rode over to give them orders. Years later he wrote, not without a certain wry humour:

> I then saw coming towards us a line of hostile cavalry, who having broken our right were advancing to surround the village. I thought at first they must be our people, and I had not even the slightest suspicion to the contrary when I saw that they stopped two or three hundred paces from us without doing anything, although they could have attacked us from the rear. I did not notice the green cockade which they wore in their hats, which was indeed so small that it could hardly have been discerned at the distance ... I went towards the nearest of these squadrons to instruct their

officers, but instead of being listened to I was instantly surrounded and called upon to ask for quarter.

The horsemen were Dutch, and Maffei was made a prisoner and led away. His leaderless brigade soon joined the throng of fugitives fleeing to the north and west. Robert Parker remembered the plight of the French and German infantry in the village, as Marlborough's attack engulfed them. 'The troops in Ramillies defended themselves to the last, until they saw their troops drove out of the field; upon which they drew off, and made towards their left wing; but were most of them cut to pieces before they could reach it.'

Parker is plainly referring to the period after Orkney's infantry withdrew from their savage assault on the Offuz ridgeline, which Tom Kitcher described in such vivid and salty detail (although he served in a different regiment, Meredith's). The British infantry were pushing forward once again to take possession of Offuz. As they did so Ross's and Hay's dragoons rode forward at full tilt to break the Régiment du Roi as it tried to extricate itself from the village of Autre-Eglise. Peter Drake, who plainly had no very high opinion of this supposedly elite Régiment du Roi, wrote rather scathingly 'I saw one of their best, called the King's Regiment, composed of four battalions, lay down their arms like poltroons, and surrendered themselves prisoners of war.' This unit was on the very left of the French and Bavarian army, and John Deane wrote:

> Our folks charged them so quick and with so much bravery that the enemy's Horse clearly abandoned their foot, and our dragoons pushing into the village of Autreglise made a terrible slaughter of the enemy. The French King's own regiment of Foot called the Regiment du Roy begged for a quarter and delivered up there arms and delivered up there colours to my Lord John Hay's Dragoons.

The commander of the Spanish [Walloon] Guards, the Marquis de Guertière, was taken prisoner by the British cavalry, together with many of his officers. Marshal Villeroi and the Elector of Bavaria were nearby, attempting in vain to rally their shattered troops. They almost fell into the hands of their enemies, as Lieutenant-General Wood remembered; he saw the two commanders only a few yards away, but did not realise the prize almost within his grasp, turning aside instead to take other officers prisoner:

> One of the [French] Lieutenant-Colonels, who was much wounded, remembering me since the last war, called out to me to save his life, as I did; the other Lieutenant-Colonel came to me, and yielded himself prisoner also. Both these assured me, the day after the battle, that the Elector himself, and the Marshal de Villeroi were in the crowd, not ten yards from me, when they two called out to me for quarter, and that they narrowly escaped. Which, had I been so fortunate to have known, I had strained Corialanus on whom I rode all the day of the battle to have made them prisoners.

Kit Davies's comment on all this was 'The enemy was everywhere entirely routed, and never victory was more complete.' She was unable to participate in the pursuit for very long, however, as her active career as a soldier was about to come to a close. Davies goes on with her tale:

> I escaped unhurt, though in the hottest of the battle, until the French were entirely defeated; when an unlucky shell from a [church] steeple struck the back part of my head and fractured my skull. I was carried to Meldert, a small town in the quarter of Louvain, five leagues north-west from Ramillies, upon a small brook which washes Tirlemont.

Although she was restored to health, her sex had been discovered while under treatment, and she was obliged to leave the regiment and give up the apparently congenial life of a roving soldier.

Earl Orkney wrote of the immediate aftermath of the victory, when the suddenness of the French collapse and the speed of their headlong flight posed a problem in carrying out a proper pursuit through the darkening evening:

> I don't know myself what prisoners we have; I am told several major-generals and others of less note. Lord John Hay's dragoons and others got in upon the Regiment de Roy, which they beat entirely. There is at least 7 or 800 of 'em prisoners, and everywhere you see colours and standards, and I hear there is at least forty pieces of cannon and a great deal of their baggage. We pursued them until dark night, but their horse was impossible to get at. It vexed me to see a great body of 'em going off, and not many horse with them; but, for my heart, I could not get our foot up in time; and they dispersed.

The cost to Villeroi's army of this shattering defeat was truly considerable. Some 13,000 of the French and their allies were casualties or taken as prisoners, and the numbers of those reported to have deserted the ranks over the following few days came to another 15,000. In reality half the French army ceased to exist that afternoon, and the rest were severely shaken as a fighting force; dozens of guns – virtually all the French artillery train – were abandoned on the field, together with a huge amount of stores and baggage. By comparison, the losses in the Allied army were light, amounting to 3,642 killed and wounded, of whom only eighty-two were officers. One of these, however, was the Hereditary Prince of Hesse-Cassell, cut down in the milling cavalry battle on the plain. John Deane wrote of the Allied army's pursuit:

> The next morning May the 13th [24th N.S] our army at break of day, having laying upon our arms for some four hours, just to repose a little, we got up again, and pursued the enemy … This day we took abundance of the enemy on our march.

Marlborough's army had engaged in a breathless, hectic pursuit of the broken French and Bavarian forces through the night. So fast was the pace of the victory and the follow-on operations that proper orders could not be issued; Allied commanders just pressed onwards through the darkness, heading for the vital crossings over the Dyle river. The following day, the Duke wrote to Queen Anne with his report of the victory:

> I humbly crave leave to congratulate your Majesty with all humility and respect on the glorious success wherewith it pleased God yesterday to bless Y.M's arms and those of your allies over the enemy, who were equally desirous to come to a battle with us, having got together all their strength in these parts. I have been on horseback the whole day and last night, in order to press the enemy in their retreat, and am just come to my quarters to send Colonel Richards to Y.M. with an account of this action, wherein all the troops, both officers and soldiers, have behaved themselves with the greatest bravery and courage, but I must humbly beg Y.M. will permit me to refer to the Colonel for the particulars. I hope the troops will be able to march again to-night, in order to see if the entrenchments behind the Dyle may be attacked.

Peter Drake was among the fugitives making his way to the shelter of the Dyle river, and he remembered very well the pitiful state of the French army on the morning of 24 May:

> We never halted until break of day, near Louvain, when we crossed the river dispirited and weary having been on our feet twenty-four hours without the least rest. It was indeed a sight truly shocking to see the miserable remains of this mighty army.

After a hasty council of war with the Elector of Bavaria, held under torchlight in the market-place of Louvain that Sunday night, Villeroi burned his stores or had them dumped in the Dyle, then abandoned the town and the line of the river, and fell back towards the shelter of the Senne and the Dender. The Elector of Bavaria, in tears of shock at the defeat inflicted on the French and Bavarian army, wrote 'We had the finest army in the world, but the defeat is so great, and the terror of the troops so horrible, that I know not what the morrow may bring.' Peter Drake described the bedraggled retreat of the remnants of the army:

> We marched with the shattered remnants of our troops to Brussels, in the neighbourhood of which we remained ten days; during which we were detached to every place where there was the least probability of the confederate [Allied] army's approaching us, to fell trees, and by other means obstruct the roads. From Brussels we marched to Ghent and Oudenarde.

Marlborough was unavoidably busy with sending news of his astonishing victory on the Ramillies-Offuz ridge-line. To Sidney Godolphin, he wrote on the day after the battle:

On Sunday last we came in presence with the enemy, who came with the same intentions I had, of fighting. We began to make our lines of battle about eleven o'clock, but we had not all our troops until two in the afternoon, at which time I gave orders for attacking them. The first half hour was very doubtful, but I thank God after that we had success in our attacks, which were on a village in the centre, and on the left we pursued them three leagues, and the night obliged us to give it over ... I am going to get a little rest, for if our bread arrives by six this evening, I will march to Louvain this night.

Shortly afterwards, writing to the King of Denmark with news of the victory, Marlborough gave fulsome praise to the valiant efforts of the Danish cavalry in the battle: 'Who distinguished themselves so eminently, and acquired so much glory in the battle, that I cannot excuse myself from writing ... I hope your Majesty will excuse the liberty I take in commending them to your favour.' Queen Anne's own reply to the Duke's message of victory, received a few days later, and in her scribbled handwriting, ran:

The Great Glorious Success which God almighty has been pleased to bless you with, and his preservation of your person, one can never thank him enough for, and next to him all things are owing to you; it is impossible for me ever to say as much as I ought in return of your great and glorious services to me.

In the meantime, the Duke's troops were pressing onwards against makeshift French rear-guards and delaying tactics. Louvain fell, despite, as Jean-Martin De La Colonie described, the hasty construction of fresh defensive works: 'A new palisaded covered-way had certainly been constructed, together with some earthen outer-work, but the whole was of very little consequence.' Disregarding such efforts Marlborough was able to move rapidly forward and summon the magistrates of Brussels to submit to his army just three days after the battle, while resting at the chateau of Beaulieu. Meanwhile, the Duke could not avoid the many mundane tasks required within an army on operations, especially when working with such a small staff. On 27 May 1706 he wrote to one of his commanders, Sir Richard Temple, about the handling of French prisoners:

I doubt not but you have received my orders of the 25th inst. For marching from Bitsen to Louvain, but understanding there are a great many French prisoners at Tirlemont, I desire you will remain there with your regiment, and take them under your care until further orders. If you find any number in a condition to march, I would have you send them with an escort to Leau ... From whence the governor will have orders to send them forwards to Maastricht. As soon as you come to Tirlemont, pray let me have a list of the names and qualities [ranks] of all the officers you find there, with the numbers and conditions of the private men.

The same day a letter was sent to Sidney Godolphin, with quite understandable renewed optimism, as the whole long season of good campaign weather stretched ahead:

> The consequences of this battle are likely to be greater than that of Blenheim; for we have now the whole summer before us, and, with the blessing of God, I will make the best use of it. For, as I have no council of war before this battle, so I hope to have none during the whole campaign; and I think we may make such work of it, as may give the Queen the glory of making a safe peace.

The Duke plainly had no intention of allowing Dutch caution, whether stemming from nervous general officers or interfering field deputies, to get in the way of his onward dash into the heart of the Spanish Netherlands. He took the submission of the magistrates of Brussels and of the States of Brabant on 28 May, when the keys to the city were handed to him on a golden platter. The Duke wrote to the Queen that evening:

> Not only Brussels, the capital city of Brabant, with Louvain, Mechlin, Alost and several other places, have submitted to your Majesty's victorious arms, but the Three States of this duchy of Brabant, the Sovereign Council, and the city of Brussels have actually declared for King Charles.

Villeroi, in the meantime. had fallen back from the Senne river to the Dender, but Marlborough's fast marching columns cut across his opponents' lines of communication with France. Unless he was alert, the Marshal faced being trapped along with his crippled army in northern Flanders. Captain Blackader (soon to be made a major), taking part in the hectic pursuit, noted in his journal on 30 May:

> A fatiguing march this Sabbath. All the day I met with what I fear and hate in this trade viz; cursing, swearing, filthy language etc. Yet though it was a hell all around me, I bless the Lord, there was a heaven within. We are still pursuing our victory, and they are still fleeing before us … Towns that we thought would have endured a long siege are giving up and yielding without a stroke.

Crossing the Dender at Alost (Aalst), the Allies had reached Gavre on the Scheldt by that same day, forcing Villeroi to fall back past Ghent to the protection of the Lys river. The Duke wrote to Sidney Godolphin the following day:

> We did this day design the passing of the Scheldt at Gavre [a few miles downstream from Oudenarde], by which we should have cut the French army from their old lines; but they rather chose to abandon Ghent, which they did this morning at break of day … I shall send tomorrow a detachment to Bruges, they having also abandoned that town. As soon as

we have the cannon, and what is necessary, we shall attack Antwerp; after which I should be glad the next place might be Ostend; for unless they draw the greatest part of their army from Germany, they will not be able to hinder us from doing what we please.

The breathless pace, almost unprecedented in European warfare, of the Duke's pursuit after the victory at Ramillies shines through all this. Despite Villeroi's best efforts to recover his army's composure after the disaster of that Whit Sunday, he was given no time, no breathing space, in which to do so. The best that could be done was to save what was left of the French army and that meant, in effect, that the whole, immensely valuable, territory of the Spanish Netherlands had to be abandoned to Marlborough and to the Austrian claimant. The shock to the interests of the French-born King Philip V, the loss of prestige, and of rich tax-gathering territories, could not be overstated; it equalled in effect, and may well have exceeded, that of Blenheim two years previously. Furthermore, as the Duke remarked, the victorious Allied army had the whole summer before it, and was now moving rapidly towards the French border.

The awful tale of defeat had carried to Louis XIV in Versailles of course, the King being given the news on 26 May when Villeroi wrote to a friend at Court to assure him that his son, although wounded, was safe. St Simon wrote of the tense waiting for the full details to arrive: 'Never had one seen such anxiety and consternation,' he wrote, 'in everyone's fears for kith and kin, the days seemed to be years.' Michel de Chamillart, the French War Minister, was sent to confer with Villeroi, and the Duc de St Simon wrote that the King:

> ... determined to despatch Chamillart to Flanders to ascertain the true state of affairs. Chamillart accordingly left Versailles on Sunday 30th May, to the astonishment of all the Court, at seeing a man charged with the war and the finance department, sent on such an errand. He astonished no less the army, when he arrived.

The two men met on 31 May 1706 at Courtrai on the Lys river. The King, who wrote with magnificent understatement to his grandson in Madrid, 'We have not been fortunate in Flanders', was now taking steps to stabilise things and Marshal Marsin soon arrived on the scene with reinforcements from the Moselle valley. Other theatres of war were being stripped to the bone to rebuild the French army in the north.

On the day that Chamillart and Villeroi met to confer, Marlborough was able to write to the Duchess: 'We are now masters of Ghent, and tomorrow I shall send some troops to Bruges. So many towns have submitted since the battle that it really looks more like a dream than the truth.' A dream now made awful reality for the French commander, a competent and honest soldier, whose reputation was shattered for ever. Chamillart approved the decision, in the dreadful circumstances, to fall back, abandoning territory, so as to save the army for future operations. Villeroi was soon removed from command; after such a catastrophic defeat no-one retained confidence in his abilities. He was a close friend of Louis XIV, who wanted him to be removed, the official line being that Villeroi had asked to be replaced. Colonel De La Colonie wrote that:

> Notwithstanding Monsieur de Villeroi's misfortune, it would have been more in accordance with the King's wishes if this general had remained in command of the army in Flanders, but he begged His Majesty to dispense with his services, and obtained permission to retire to the Court.

The King was gracious with his unfortunate general, and greeted Villeroi on his return to Versailles with the kind words 'At our age, Marshal, we must no longer expect good fortune.' Villeroi would never be offered another command.

In the Low Countries the speed and power of the Allied advance could not for long be sustained. The bringing forward of supplies and heavy guns depended to a very considerable degree on the use of the waterways, the canals and rivers of the region, and French garrisons had first to be cleared out of the towns which dominated these vital arteries of war. Antwerp's magistrates presented the keys of the town to Marlborough on 11 June 1706, but operations against Dendermonde proceeded rather slowly. The Marquis de Tarazena, until very recently the Governor of Antwerp, but now declared for King Charles III, prepared to emplace his siege guns before the defences. He protested that he had insufficient troops to properly invest the town. Brigadier-General Meredith, who accompanied Tarazena, was unable to exert very much influence, and the overly-proud Marquis was reluctant to ask Marlborough for assistance. In the enemy camp though, the Elector of Bavaria, soon aware of the Allies' lack of numbers before Dendermonde, took the chance to send in 400 dragoons and infantry as reinforcements for the garrison. Marlborough, in exasperation, sent a letter from the camp at Rousselaer to the Secretary of State, Robert Harley, on 21 June: 'I have advice that a detachment of the enemy are marched to relieve Dendermonde, but I hope they will find Brigadier Meredyth, who commands the blockade of that place, so well upon his guard as to prevent their design.'

As it turned out, the Elector brushed aside the rather feeble attempt by Meredith to intercept the reinforcing column and so, on 23 June, Marlborough felt obliged to detail William Cadogan, with a strong force of cavalry and infantry, to take charge of the operations. Marlborough wrote to Harley the following day, about the sorry episode:

> The Elector of Bavaria has taken advantage of the siege of Ostend and the army's being here to cover it, to put a reinforcement of about four hundred foot and one hundred dragoons into Dendermonde. Brigadier Meredyth was upon his guard, but had not strength enough to prevent it; he had five or six men killed, and as many, with a captain, taken prisoners. The detachment who conducted these men consisted of at least three thousand horse and two thousand foot. They returned immediately to rejoin the Elector, but lost at least six or seven hundred men by desertion in the expedition. Brigadier Cadogan came too late to seize the bridge at Alost, the enemy having possessed themselves of it two hours before he

could get thither, so that he returned the next morning to Oudenarde, whither I have now sent him orders to march with a detachment of horse and foot to concert and take measures with M. de Tarazena and Brigadier Meredyth for the strengthening the blockade.

The bombardment of Dendermonde began as the Duke wrote this letter, but Tarazena was now concerned at a lack of ammunition for sustained battery firing and, although scores of peasants had been conscripted to labour on the trenches, the blockade of the town was still far from complete. Negotiations with the Governor, the Marquis de Delvalle, proved fruitless, and Tarazena was apparently not much help, for Marlborough wrote to Cadogan on 30 June: 'The sooner Tarazena goes [back] to Antwerp the better, for his staying can be of no use but a trouble.'

Meanwhile, Charles Churchill, Marlborough's brother, was installed as Governor in Brussels and, with the Allied armies pursuing their headlong campaign of conquest, the rear areas were laid bare and were potentially vulnerable; he felt obliged to take stern measures for the security of the city, and to maintain order. On 14 June he issued a proclamation:

> For the service of His Catholic Majesty, Charles III, and to prevent many inconveniences, to command all Frenchmen, military and others, not burghers or house-keepers in the city, not to stir out of their dwellings, on the said 14 June 1706, in the afternoon, on pain of imprisonment; having directed passes, for their retiring safely, to be given to such as should desire the same; Declaring, that if twenty-four hours after that time, any Frenchmen, not burghers or house-keepers, should be found in that city, they should be treated as spies, and hanged ... All Spaniards, who were come thither from the garrison of Antwerp, and would not acknowledge Charles III for their lawful Sovereign, nor could produce passes from Brigadier Cadogan, should be treated as the aforesaid Frenchman; and the wives of all French officers, or soldiers, except such as by reason of sickness, were confined to their beds, were to retire from thence in three days on pain of imprisonment, and forfeiture of all their goods and effects.

Ostend capitulated on 4 July, to Overkirk, whose operations had been assisted by two Royal Navy bomb-ketches offshore. Menin, a strong Vauban-designed fortress, could now receive Marlborough's attention; the investment of the town was complete on 22 July. The heavy guns came up from Ghent a week later, and the Allied attack began on 4 August. The garrison put up a stout resistance, and the Duke of Marlborough supervised some of the activities in the trenches in person. Captain Robert Parker's regiment, the Royal Irish, took an active part in the siege operations:

> It was a regular and well-fortified place, with a garrison of 5,000 men, and well equipped with all manner of necessaries. The Governor disputed every inch of ground with us, until we carried our approaches to the foot

*Marlborough and his staff oversee the crossing of the Scheldt, 11 July 1708.
(Oudenarde tapestry, Blenheim Palace, by kind permission of His Grace The Duke
of Marlborough.)*

Queen Anne of Great Britain. Loyal and stubborn, her close friendship with Marlborough was a great asset, but she dismissed him in the end.

Louis XIV, King of France. His ambitions brought war back to Europe, when he permitted his grandson to accept the throne of Spain in 1700.

Detail from the Blenheim Tapestry. Marlborough and his staff await the submission of Marshal Tallard on the field of battle, 13 August 1704. (Blenheim Tapestry, Blenheim Palace, by kind permission of His Grace the Duke of Marlborough.)

John Churchill, 1st Duke of Marlborough. Mezzotint by J. Smith after Godfrey Kneller. Queen Anne's Captain-General 1702–1711.

Prince Eugene of Savoy. Marlborough's close friend and comrade. Victor of the battle of Turin, 1706. Present at Blenheim, Oudenarde, Lille and Malplaquet.

James FitzJames, Duke of Berwick, Marlborough's nephew. Marshal of France. One of Louis XIV's best field commanders, he defeated Allied efforts in Spain.

The Comte de Merode-Westerloo, Field-Marshal of the Holy Roman Empire. Author of entertaining and informative memoirs. Viewed Allied deployment at Blenheim from his camp bed.

Claude Louis-Hector Villars. Marshal of France. Held the line for France 1709–1713. Gravely wounded at Malplaquet. Victor of Denain 1713.

Louis-Joseph de Bourbon, Duc De Vendôme. Cautious and cunning, he foiled Marlborough in 1707, but mishandled the battle at Oudenarde in 1708.

Louis-François Boufflers, Marshal of France. Failed to hold Marlborough 1702–1703, but conducted epic defence of Lille, August - December 1708.

George Hamilton, 1st Earl of Orkney. Highly competent British infantry commander, fought at Schellenberg, Blenheim, Elixheim, Ramillies and Malplaquet.

Christian (Kit) Davis, Welsh etc. Adventurous female Dragoon who followed her man to war. Ended life as a Chelsea Pensioner.

William, 1st Earl of Cadogan. Marlborough's Quartermaster-General and Chief of Staff. Pierced line of the Scheldt at Oudenarde 1708. Succeeded Marlborough as Master-General of the Ordnance.

The British Cavalry rout the Spanish Guards and the Bavarian Electoral Guards, near Autre-Eglise, late afternoon, 23 May 1706.

The Battle of Malplaquet. Marlborough's massed cavalry move towards the French centre, early afternoon, 11 September 1709.   *(Artist: H. Dupray)*

Detail from the Wynendael Tapestry. Webb's infantry hold the French back as a vital supply convoy hurries on to the Allied camp before Lille, 28 September 1708. (Wynendael Tapestry, Blenheim Palace, by kind permission of His Grace the Duke of Marlborough.)

of the glacis; and then we made an attack on the covert way. Our regiment was engaged in this attack, and here we paid for our looking on at Ramillies; having had two captains, and five subalterns killed, and eight officers wounded, among whom I was one ... The day after we had lodged ourselves on the covert way, the Governor beat the chamade and honourable terms were granted ... I was on this occasion made Captain of our Grenadiers.

The defences having been steadily battered down, on 23 August 1706 Marlborough was able to write to Sidney Godolphin:

Yesterday morning the army at Menin planted a white flag on their breach, and as I was there I immediately ordered an exchange of hostages. We have this morning possession of their gate, and on Wednesday they are to march out with the usual marks of honour. We must have eight or ten days for the levelling our lines [siege works] and putting the place in a posture of defence. In the meantime, I am taking measures for the siege of Dendermonde. If the weather continues dry, we shall take it; but if it should rain, we cannot continue before it.

The Duke was referring to the problem of the extensive water defences at Dendermonde, which had dried up in the heat of summer. The place was blockaded by Charles Churchill, and siege operations there were concluded, without the hindrance of bad weather, on 5 September 1706. The town was given up a few days later, and the day after the capitulation, it began to rain heavily. The Allied army next moved to the siege of Ath where the garrison was apparently caught unawares. The Duc de Vendôme, who, St Simon wrote, 'had orders to leave Italy, and succeed to the command in Flanders,' was an astute and bruising campaigner, and he soon sought permission from Versailles to take the field with what troops could be gathered together, and challenge the Allied advance towards the French border. Louis XIV, made cautious by adversity, refused his consent and replied, 'The Duke [of Marlborough] is only seeking an opportunity for a battle, he attacks places in the hope of enticing you thither.'

Marlborough wrote to Robert Harley on 23 September, with an account of a successful opening to these siege operations:

The trenches were opened before Ath on Monday night [18 September] with all imaginable success, the enemy having not discovered where our men were working before the next morning; the batteries will be perfected this night, and we shall begin to fire from them to-morrow.

Donald McBane took an active part in the operations against Ath, with the grenadier company of Orkney's Regiment: 'I was in several storms; I was throwing grenades eight hours together, when I got a ball in the head, which will remind me of it while I live.' Kit Davies, meanwhile, had recovered from her wounds and put off her red coat to became a cook in the allied army, but this homely role was plainly a little too dull for her enterprising spirit, and she recalled:

I undertook to cook for our regiment, returning to my husband's quarters every night. I did not long carry on this business, as the close attendance it required prevented my marauding, which was vastly more beneficial. After I had given over my cooking, I turned sutler, and by the indulgence of the officers was permitted to pitch my tent in the front, while others were driven to the rear of the army.

The Irishwoman's gift with words and her ability to exercise a certain feminine charm over the officers is plain. She gives an entertaining account of how adventurous the routine could be in the trenches before the town:

General Ingoldsby broke ground, at night, with the loss of one man only; for the enemy imagining we should open our trenches on the side where the Lord Overkirk was, had drawn their strength to that quarter, to prevent, or impede, his works. When my husband marched with General Ingoldsby to the side where they were to break ground, he left me boiling the pot.

While taking the broth to her husband in the front line, Davies dallied in the trenches, exchanging banter with the officers and soldiers she met on the way. She plainly could not resist getting into the action whenever the chance offered, and tells us:

Looking through the sand-bags, [I] saw a soldier, who, ignorant of our being on the side we were, came out of the town to gather turnips. I took a piece [musket] out of one of our people's hand, and called to the officer to see me shoot him, for we had pushed our trenches within thirty-three paces of the palisades. I suppose we were just then perceived; for the instant I killed the man, a musket-shot, from the town, came through the sand-bags, split my under-lip, beat one of my teeth into my mouth, and knocked me down. My husband, and some of his comrades, ran to take me up, and seeing me bloody, imagined I was shot through the head; but I convinced them to the contrary, by spitting the ball and tooth into my hand.

Meanwhile, word had come in to Marlborough's camp of Prince Eugene's stunning victory at Turin on 7 September 1706, when that city and the whole of northern Italy was saved for the Grand Alliance, and Marshal Marsin was mortally wounded, just after receiving a premonition of his own impending death; he had died soon after capture. The Duke wrote on 18 September to Harley:

A trumpeter, who returned last night from the French camp, brings an account that they had received news yesterday of a battle in Italy, wherein the French army is said to have been defeated with the loss of their cannon and baggage; that the Maréchal de Marsin was killed, and the Duke d'Orleans wounded. Some part of it is confirmed by people come last night out of Tournai, so that I make no doubt but the siege of Turin is raised, which is so considerable, that though we must wait some days for the particulars, I thought it my duty in the meantime to give the Queen the earliest account I could of it, and to congratulate her Majesty upon the good news.

This deliverance for Savoy, one of the newer partners in the Grand Alliance, and which had seemed certain to fall to a French offensive, added to the sense of wonder with which the world viewed the victorious Allied campaigns in 1706. Meanwhile the soldiers in Marlborough's army continued to be busy, and John Deane, serving still with the 1st English Foot Guards during the operations against Ath, wrote in his journal:

> Our men broke ground expeditiously; and entrenched themselves almost up to the palisades of the enemies works, being so near that they could easily call to each other and throw their grenades into each others works. Our guns and bomb batteries were finished by 15th of September [O.S.], and then gave the besieged an account of it by the noise of their thunderbolts. For they continued firing day and night until the town surrendered up all prisoners of war, and on the 23rd [O.S] they marched out, and were sent prisoners to our garrisons. There was in the town six regiments of French and Spaniards who made a brave defence and killed abundance of our men.

It was a spirited defence, as Deane testifies, which had included two fierce French sorties on 27 September, but the place could not hold out, and, in accordance with the King's cautionary words, there was no attempt by Vendôme to lift the siege. The garrison submitted to the Allies on 2 October 1706, and Marlborough wrote to the States-General in the Hague with the welcome news:

> The Good Lord continuing to acknowledge the justice of the cause of the Grand Alliance I again have a new occasion to give congratulations to your High Mightinesses: it is the prize of Ath, where the garrison are obliged this afternoon to submit as prisoners of war. Veldt Marshal Overkirk will have the honour of giving your High Mightinesses more details.

Overkirk's letter to Baron Fagel, the Secretary to the States-General, told of the negotiations leading to the surrender:

> After we had made ourselves masters of the covered way of the Counter-scarp, and while I was in the approaches about six o'clock, last night, the enemy beat a parley, and sent out two officers to demand an honourable capitulation. I let them know, that they were to hope for no other terms, than to be received prisoners of war; That out of consideration, however, for the officers, I would allow them their swords and baggage, and the soldiers their knapsacks, and gave them half an hour's time to resolve what to do ... the governor would not agree to it; upon which the

hostilities were renewed. But today, towards noon, the besieged having beat a second parley, and sent back the two officers that came out to treat with me last night, one of whom was a colonel, the other an adjutant to the Duke de Vendôme , it was agreed, after some debate, that the garrison should surrender themselves prisoners of war. We shall take possession of a gate tomorrow, and the garrison is to march out on Monday … p.s. The garrison consisted of 2,100 men, of which 500 were killed and wounded, in the siege. On our side 8 or 900 men were killed or wounded.

Three days after, the Veldt-Marshal wrote to Fagel again, with details of the capitulation, and the arrangements for the distribution of the prisoners taken:

Yesterday, the Garrison of Ath marched out, as prisoners of war, consisting of 150 officers [a rather high figure, Overkirk perhaps included the NCOs], and about 600 soldiers, besides almost 300 sick and wounded, left in the hospitals. I have sent them to Ghent, to be embarked there for Bergen op Zoom, where one half of them is to continue, and the other half is ordered for Breda, until their High Mightinesses think fit to dispose of them in other places. Yesterday, the baggage, which I granted to the officers, was sent to Mons and Conde.

Marlborough had intended to move on to attack Mons, but logistical problems and a certain reluctance among his allies to do more that year, with so much achieved already, prevented this project. Even as late as this, in October, the Dutch were proving difficult allies, for all their undoubted bravery. The Duke was to write to Sidney Godolphin on 14 October:

If the Dutch can furnish ammunition for the siege of Mons, we shall undertake it; for if the weather continues fair, we shall have it so much cheaper this year than the next, when they have had time to recruit their army. The taking of that town would be a very great advantage to us for the opening of the next campaign, which we must make if we would bring France to such a peace as will give us quiet hereafter.

The necessary stores were not forthcoming and so no operation against Mons could take place in 1706, or indeed, would take place until 1709, when the Dutch infantry would pay a price in full and bloody measure to secure that town, in the terrible dark woods at Malplaquet. The place might have been had cheaply three years earlier, without the trouble of a major battle.

With winter coming on, the season for active soldiering in 1706 gradually drew to a close. Marlborough wrote to Robert Harley later that month that 'The continual rains we have had for several days have made it impracticable to undertake another siege.' So, after a grand review of the army, the Allied troops went off to their quarters early in November. There, Kit Davies stoically recalled that 'Our regiment was quartered in Ghent where I was delivered of a child before my time, which lived about half a year.'

The Comte de Merode-Westerloo, pleading poverty after the expenses of the Blenheim campaign, had retired from the service of Philip V in the previous year. Now, like many others, he declared his allegiance to the Austrian claimant. Such shifts in loyalty, while not uncommon and quite legal if done in proper form, inevitably caused some friction with those who maintained their original allegiance. The Comte wrote of an incident at this time, when a trap was laid for him and his entourage:

> Aix was riddled with French sympathisers, and Maguinet, a friend of theirs in the Namur garrison [which had resisted Marlborough's onslaught after Ramillies] took it into his head to take me prisoner … I was on the point of setting out following the arrival of 250 infantry and fifty cavalry sent by the Governor of Maastricht, when a courier from that same officer brought news warning me that the enemy were reported to be considerable stronger than my escort, and that he would send a further 300 men the next day to meet us … I set out at about 7 o'clock and on reaching the forest of Aix we discovered the enemy in position. I descended from my coach and mounted a horse, divided my infantry into five platoons supported by the cavalry, and then marched the first two platoons forwards towards the enemy.

To the Comte's surprise the French then turned and rode off without waiting to engage him. He then saw more troops on the move in the distance:

> We then discovered that this was the second escort coming from Maastricht to join us – the enemy having spotted them first. We left our advanced guards with them, and made our way peacefully to Genappe, where I refreshed my household and escort. I ate some fine trout there, I remember.

Before Marlborough could retire from the campaign, he had, as usual, to attend to a mass of routine administration, including petitions for advancement and promotion, with the Duke's recommendations of the fine qualities of the individual petitioners being eagerly sought. Not all these requests came from highly placed officers, as can be seen from this letter, written to the Commissioners of the Royal Hospital in Chelsea:

> Being informed that one of the cooks of the Royal Hospital is lately dead, I pray leave to recommend to you William Daniel to succeed him. He served the late king in his family abroad all the late war, and has been with me every campaign since, and likewise attended me in my journey to Germany. I therefore willingly contribute towards his settlement. Your favour on this occasion will very much oblige.

A few days later the Duke was concerning himself with the advancement of the career of one of his stalwart aides, writing from London to Lord Raby in Berlin:

> M. de Pouguet, who will have the honour to deliver this to Your Excellency, having behaved himself perfectly well at the battle of

Blenheim, where he commanded a squadron of Bothmar's dragoons as eldest [senior] captain, having met with some hardships, as he pretends, in the Elector of Hanover's service since the decease of the Duke of Zell, and being desirous to serve in the Prussian troops, I could not refuse to give him my recommendation to Y.E., and to pray you will forward his pretensions and give him all the countenance you can at your [Prussian] court, making use of my name at the same time, if you think it will do him any good.

The year had seen an extraordinary turn of events, oversetting the entire French strategic balance in the north. The victory at Ramillies, by breaking the back of the only French field army in the Low Countries – an army that had been substantially reinforced from the Moselle valley just before its defeat – laid bare almost the whole of the Spanish Netherlands, a wide and rich region over which long and expensive campaigns might quite legitimately have been fought for possession, to conquest by Marlborough's thrusting columns. Major towns and fortresses that had, in the past, defied their enemies for months and sometimes years – Louvain, Brussels, Antwerp, Ostend, Dendermonde, Oudenarde, Menin, Ath – had fallen to the Duke's commanders in mere days and weeks. Robert Parker commented that 'Never was an enemy so fairly pushed out of a country.' Nothing like it had been seen before, and it remained to be seen whether the French could again recover their poise.

Of the campaign, Jean-Martin De La Colonie wrote ruefully: 'Such were the melancholy results which followed on the Battle of Ramillies.' An equally sombre Duc de St Simon commented on 'Our military history of the year 1706, a history of losses and dishonour. It may be imagined in what condition was the exchequer with many heavy demands upon its treasures.'

Chapter Seven

So Great a Blessing – Flanders, and the Battle of Oudenarde, 1707–1708

In the wake of Marlborough's conquest of the Spanish Netherlands in 1706, Emperor Joseph, on behalf of his younger brother, offered the Duke of Marlborough the Governor-Generalship of the province. This was tempting, not just in terms of prestige, for the annual stipend alone was 60,000 Crowns. The Duke refused the offer, primarily because the Dutch were jealous and suspicious of Austrian influence on their borders, both in terms of tax-gathering potential (to help cover their ruinous costs in the war) and the security of the Barrier towns in which they placed such faith. Despite the Duke's refusal of the lucrative post, the Dutch were resentful of what appeared to be unwarranted Austrian interference on their very border. This was a region conquered for the Grand Alliance largely by the efforts of their own troops during the post-Ramillies campaign, when Imperial troops had been engaged rather unproductively elsewhere.

The Duc de Vendôme had replaced Marshal Villeroi in command of the French field army on the northern border of France. Described by the Duc de St Simon as 'Of ordinary height, rather stout, but strong, hearty and active', Vendôme was under orders to keep Marlborough occupied, but to avoid open battle. In this he was to prove quite successful, although Marlborough strove for an aggressive campaign; the old problem of Dutch caution recurred and their field deputies were as unco-operative as ever. Bad news would, before long, come from the Rhine, where the French were on the move, while there was ill-feeling and mistrust between the Imperial Court in Vienna and their field commanders. This can be seen from a rather sad letter, dripping with irony, written to Marlborough by the ailing Margrave of Baden, in the autumn of the previous year:

> His Imperial Majesty, my master, seems unconvinced of the truth of the lists [troop numbers] which I have sent to him about the army under my command. I have been made to feel in terms which are plain enough that his Majesty has received contrary accounts from his Quartermaster-General, who has assured him that this army comprises 40,000 combatants equipped with everything. As for the figures I have given, I

am sure that I have not made a mistake. I have been forced by his Majesty's orders to hand over to Field-Marshal Thungen charge of affairs, not doubting that the 40,000 men which the Imperial Court knows with scientific certainty are massed upon the Upper Rhine will succeed in all that is desired of them.

Baden died at his home in Rastadt on 4 January 1707, shunned and villified by the Imperial Court that he had served for so long in a valiant military career. The gunshot wound to his foot, sustained during the valiant flank attack at the Schellenberg fight nearly three years earlier (and mockingly known to the world as 'the Margrave's toe'), had festered, and at last killed the doughty old general in the most pitiless and agonising way.

Marlborough joined the army at Anderlecht on 21 May 1707, and six days later advanced to Soignies to challenge the French. Once in the field though, he found the task of catching Vendôme no easy matter. 'Their camp is very strong, and I believe they will not stay in any place where they may with reason be attacked.' The Duke wrote on 30 May to Robert Harley in London:

My last to you was on Thursday night [26 May] from Soignies. I went out at four o'clock the next morning, with a strong detachment of horse and dragoons, to endeavour to observe the enemy's camp and to get certain knowledge of their marches, and found they were marched to the plain of Fleurus, having drained all their garrisons and quitted their lines with a design, in case we should sit down before Mons or any other place, to ravage all Brabant, which they might do in less time than our great artillery and ammunition would be bringing up for a siege. It was therefore thought most advisable to return this way [to Beaulieu near Louvain], and accordingly on Saturday [28 May] the army marched to Lembecq, and yesterday we passed the canal of Brussels, and having now secured the great towns, we shall advance tomorrow to the Dyle, and by our next march approach nearer the enemy, who are generally allowed to be stronger than we, but on the other side I hope the goodness of our troops will balance their numbers. Our hussars have had two lucky recontres more with the enemy's parties, and have brought in several prisoners with a good booty of horses. The desertion is very great among their troops.

He added, with his usual patience, but not without a hint of weary resignation, the news that the Lines of Stollhofen had been stormed and French forces were flooding into central Germany on a grand raid:

We had an account this morning of the misfortune of the German troops on the Rhine, who had let the French pass that river by surprise and were all dispersed. This must give new courage to the enemy, and certainly put the Empire under great consternation.

Plainly, it suited the French to play for time in Flanders, tying the Duke down with fruitless marching to and fro, while they attacked his less able colleagues and caused havoc elsewhere. Marlborough was obliged to be patient, and watch for whatever moves Vendôme might make. In the meantime, John Deane of the 1st English Foot Guards tells us, he kept the army in fighting trim by reviewing the troops, and having them put through their exercises:

> On the 29th of May [O.S] his Grace viewed the English foot, and the Earl of Orkney, posting himself at the head of our battalion of Guards, saluted the Duke. And afterwards all the English foot exercised by signal of colours and beat of drum, and every brigade fired in platoons before his Grace; in which exercise the English got great applause of the foreigners.

The weather soon proved unkind, with heavy rain and high winds, and this unavoidably exerted a drag on the movements of the armies. Deane recalled that some few weeks later:

> About seven o'clock in the evening there happened a very terrible storm of wind, rain and hail to that degree that it did great damage in our camp, especially in the lines, blowing down and tearing to pieces the officers and sutlers tents, driving their beds and bedding, clothes and their effects about the streets. And some of it swimming away with the streams for the fall of water in a small space of time run so fierce off the hilly ground down to the valleys that it was sufficient to have drove a watermill – to the admiration of the army.

In early August it was learned that French troops were being sent from Flanders to the south of France, to deal with Prince Eugene's offensive against Toulon, and the Duke at last got Dutch agreement to take the field. The Allied army lay at Louvain, with a detachment covering Brussels. Vendôme's army was now at Genappe. The weather remained unseasonably bad for high summer, and Marlborough wrote to Godolphin on 4 August from camp at Meldert: 'We have had so much rain, that I can hardly stir out of my quarter, the dirt being up to the horses' bellies, which is very extraordinary in this month.' Four days later he could report that:

> The duke of Vendome had detached 12 battalions and 9 squadrons [towards the operations at Toulon] but continues still in camp. I hope this detachment will encourage the [Dutch] deputies, so that I may make the march which I have been proposing for these last six weeks.

On 11 August 1707 Marlborough began his advance, attempting to get around the left flank of the French position. Vendôme promptly withdrew from Genappe, and the Dutch cavalry commander, Count Tilly, was sent ahead by Marlborough with a strong force of cavalry and grenadiers to maul his rearguard. Tilly got the message to move too late in the day to act and the French escaped from a potentially very tight spot with relatively slight loss. Jean-Martin De La Colonie remembered the episode:

> General Tilly would undoubtedly have attacked our rearguard had he had a chance, but we escaped this owing to the darkness. As it was the whole

of our army had not passed by daybreak, a nasty little stream with difficult banks constituted our defile, which M. de Vendome had lined with dismounted dragoons to cover the retirement of our rear-guard in the case of attack by General Tilly. The few that still remained to cross were supported by our dragoons who checkmated the attempts of the enemy to interfere with them.

Vendôme got to a good position near Mons, from which to turn and face the approaching Allied army. Frustrated in this opening move, Marlborough halted his army at Soignies the same day that the French got in place near Mons; the operations were hampered still by the bad weather, which took a toll of the foot soldiers in particular, and the Duke was obliged to bide his time, looking for a weak spot in the French dispositions.

In rather downcast mood, made worse by the persistent rain, the Duke wrote to Sidney Godolphin on 15 August, with details of the campaign so far:

> I was in hopes this might have given you an account of some action; for this Friday we marched to Nivelle, and camped about half a league from Seneff, where the French army was encamped. We came too late for attacking them that evening. As soon as it was dark they began to make their retreat, without making the least noise, not touching either drum or trumpet; so that the Count de Tilly, whom I had detached with 40 squadrons and 5000 grenadiers, to attack their rearguard, in case they should march, knew nothing of their marching until daylight, so that there was very little done. Our loss was three officers and some few soldiers. I believe theirs was also very inconsiderable; but by these four days march they have lost very considerably by desertion; for we gave them no rest.

In fact, Tilly's aides had been unable to find a light with which to read the Duke's message, when it was received in the middle of a dark and rainy night in a strange orchard. Colonel Cranstoune, whose unit was part of Tilly's detachment, wrote that 'It rained heavily, was pitch dark, and no house near.' The Dutch cavalry commander might be forgiven some hesitation in the circumstances. A measure of confusion and delay was the inevitable result and the French slipped away. Colonel De La Colonie remembered the barely avoided encounter that night rather vividly, as the following morning his own troops almost put an end to his military career for good:

> The few that still remained to cross were supported by our dragoons, who checkmated the attempts of the enemy to interfere with them. Our army marched about a league further on after passing this defile, in order to reach the plain of Roeulx, where a halt was made to reassemble the various regiments which had become dispersed, and to bring order into our line of march. The Allies, who were moving on our right, were separated from us by several woods, and seeing us forming up on the plain, and not knowing our motive, took up a battle position in case of accidents. The Duke de Vendôme noticing this thought they intended to

attack us, so ranged the men likewise, who meantime discharged their pieces preparatory to re-charging them, in case they got damp. I was at this moment walking with [Captain] Quemin in front of the line when we were startled by the fire brought to bear upon us, for they were all firing in our direction; I believe that I never had a better chance of being killed than on this occasion; a battle even would have been no more dangerous.

The Colonel goes on to recount some of the hardships of this campaign, at a time when, as Marlborough had noted, the weather was unseasonably very bad. De La Colonie gives a flavour of the urgency attending the French movements in order to avoid battle with the Allies:

> No camp was marked out or tents pitched. Each regiment spent the night under a constant downpour of rain, on the spot where it found itself in the order of march, so as to be the sooner ready to resume the march next day and attain our lines. Success attended our efforts, and the manoeuvres carried out by M. de Vendôme gave the enemy no opportunity of attacking us or even making an attempt to seize any town, for he was ever on the alert, and fore-stalled them everywhere. It is true the army had had to forego the luxury of a baggage column for some time and lacked every comfort, but our country's safety was assured thereby.

The poor weather cleared at last, and Marlborough was once again on the march, moving from Soignies to cross the Dender river at Ath by 1 September. John Deane wrote rather dismissively that:

> As soon as they heard of our marching towards them they began their old trade of setting their camp on fire and running away by the light of it. And to hinder our following them, there being a bridge of stone over the river Dender, at the end of which they had digged a deep trench cross the road and made breastworks on each side, and felled a great many trees across the same as if they had designed a great contest. But of no effect, they being surprised to a great degree, otherwise they would not have left such moveables behind them, as, namely, casks of wine, tubs of beef, and hogsheads of Brazil tobacco and many other things very welcome.

Vendôme fell back once more before the Allied approach, moving towards the shelter of the Scheldt river. His moves at this time, drawing his opponent on, but refusing to give Marlborough the chance to strike at his army, were well thought-out and very effective. They refute some of the criticism routinely levelled at him for indolence and neglect of his military duties. Meanwhile, the Duke wrote again to Godolphin, from Ath:

> The enemy decamped in great haste [from Mons], and I believe our march tomorrow will oblige them to pass the Scheldt. The deputies are convinced that if we had made the march to Genappe two months ago, when I pressed for it, the duke of Vendôme would have been obliged to retire as he now does.

The bad news from the south of France, of the abject failure of the Allied attempt on Toulon, reached the Low Countries at this time. On the same day that Marlborough crossed the Dender in pursuit of the French, he wrote to the Comte de Rechteren in rather sombre mood:

> I have received the honour of your two letters of 10 and 17 of the last month, the latter of which did not arrive till this morning. I do not doubt you have heard the same news that we have from Paris, that the Duke of Savoy has had to leave the siege of Toulon on 22 August. We have no details yet of his march.

As it turned out, the operations against Toulon, while falling well short of expectations, did have some positive results for the Allies. French troops were drawn away from Spain to counter the operations against the port, so preventing their use in following up their recent success at Almanza properly, and the French fleet was burned or beached in the harbour, to prevent the ships falling into Allied hands.

On 5 September, Marlborough's army resumed its advance, and the Scheldt was soon safely crossed, under the protection of the guns of the Allied-held fortress of Oudenarde:

> We have made three marches in order to pass the Scheldt, which we have done this morning. We shall stay in this camp [Petteghem] to-morrow, and the next day march to Helchin, by which we shall oblige the enemy to eat up [forage in] his own country, which I am afraid is all the hurt we are likely to do them; for I am very confident they will be careful not to give occasion for action.

Marlborough took up a strong advanced position between the Scheldt and Lys, with a flank of his army resting on each river; Vendôme had lost the line of the river beyond hope of early recovery. He was unable to attack the Allies in such a stout position, so on 7 September 1707 the French army had begun to fall back once again, to the protection of the Marque river, near to the great fortified city of Lille well inside the border of France itself. Trading ground for time, the French commander was eating up the season for campaigning very well.

At this time, Donald McBane got a pass to get together a party of volunteers and go out and raid the French outposts, and perhaps gather a little booty at the same time:

> That night we went very quietly to try what we could make. Before day we came near the French camp, and hid ourselves in a wood all the next day. At night we went to the rear of the French camp, and hid ourselves as well as we could in a little wood by the highway side. Presently appears a colonel of French dragoons with sixteen horsemen and his own baggage. I desired them to surrender, but they were unwilling which obliged us to fire, wherewith we wounded four, and took the other twelve and the colonel prisoner, and made the best of our way for our own camp.

Three days later, McBane and his band had permission to go marauding again:

> I ordered my guide to go to the French camp to see what they were doing or when they went to forage; about twelve at night he returned and told me that the Household [cavalry] of France was to forage near where I and my men lay, they had the best horse in the camp; about five in the morning we removed a little nearer the highway where they were to pass. I thought fit to attack them in the centre, which we did, and took sixty of the horses, one of them fired and wounded one of my lads slightly in the face; we went off with all speed for that shot alarmed the camp.

The enterprising grenadier was able to sell the horses to his officers for a good price, but, as he ruefully admits, he very soon drank, whored and gambled the money away.

Elsewhere in the war, far away from Flanders where Marlborough was having such a lack of success, Allied campaigns were also faring badly. In Spain, the French were securing victories, and the sympathy and support of much of the population was strongly for King Philip V. The grand project to seize the French naval base at Toulon had miscarried, and along the Rhine, French armies had taken fire and sword into central and southern Germany, and were now ravaging those same minor principalities that provided such excellent troops for the Allied armies. Once again, French cavalry watered their horses in the Danube, and some of their officers strolled over the Schellenberg hill, as sightseers of the scene of the dreadful battle there three years earlier.

Most significantly for the Allied war effort in 1707, Marlborough had been unable to fix Vendôme long enough to force a battle. Through the skill of his field commanders, Louis XIV, while actively seeking an advantageous peace for France, was playing his cards rather well. John Deane wrote of the French conduct of the campaign that 'As we advanced they retracted [retreated] from one place to another, still threatening what they would do, but all proved but wind.' The season was growing late and the weather worsened yet again. The Duke wrote of his concern to see 'The poor soldiers march in dirt up to the knees, for we have had a very great deal of rain.' Robert Parker complained at one point in the campaign that 'We lay for three weeks weather-bound, before our artillery could be raised off the ground.' All that could really now be done was to go into winter quarters, and make plans for the next campaign season when, with good fortune, Vendôme might be brought to battle and defeated.

The recently concluded Treaty of Union between England and Scotland saw an expansion in the Scottish army establishment, and Marlborough had responded to an appeal from the eldest son of the Duke of Atholl, to be recommended for the command of a regiment newly raised from among his father's retainers. The Duke wrote to the Marquis of Tullibardine: 'I shall readily use my endeavours that justice be done you in relation to the command of your regiment.' While writing to Major-General Murray on the subject 'I shall not be wanting in my endeavours that my Lord Tullibardine be easy in the command of the regiment.' This favour would pay a bleak dividend, one misty autumn day, two years later in the woods at Malplaquet.

The Duke of Marlborough's plans for his 1708 campaign hinged on combining his army in the Spanish Netherlands with that of Prince Eugene, whose Imperial troops had been operating in the Moselle valley. The Elector of Hanover would remain to hold the front on the Rhine, while Eugene brought his army to combine with the Duke, and confront the French commander in Flanders before he, in turn, could also be reinforced. Not surprisingly, a series of delays, political and practical (mostly, but not entirely, unavoidable) detained the Prince in Vienna and Marlborough was obliged to allow the initiative to pass to the French, for the time being. Vendôme, however, was also confronted with difficulties, as he had to share the command of his army with a royal prince, the Duc de Bourgogne (Burgundy – Louis XIV's eldest grandson). Colonel De La Colonie wrote of the preparations for the campaign:

> It had been discovered that the Allies had a great scheme in hand for an invasion of Flanders with superior forces. The Duke of Burgundy together with the Duke of Berry [his younger brother], now arrived to place themselves at the head of the army of Flanders during the campaign, in joint command with the Duke of Vendome. They arrived about May 20th, but neither our German reinforcements [troops from the Moselle valley], nor those of the Allies [Eugene's army] were on the ground until the end of June.

Unless the Colonel was speaking with the valuable clarity afforded by hindsight, the plans for Eugene's march northwards to join Marlborough were plainly an ill-kept secret.

Vendôme (who was never made a Marshal of France) was a formidable campaigner with an army nearly 100,000 men strong. He was also a man of the most sordid personal habits, tolerated at the fastidious court of Louis XIV only because of his ancestry – he was the grandson of an illegitimate offspring of King Henry IV of France – and because of his undeniable skills as a military commander. Vendôme's infamously idle and gross conduct was described by St Simon:

> More than once he was nearly captured by the enemy because he refused to leave headquarters that were comfortable, but isolated, and he often hazarded the success of an entire campaign because he would not move from a camp when once he had settled there. In the field he saw little for himself, relying for information on his staff, whom he more often than not disbelieved.

St Simon's detestation of Vendôme, and his prejudice against him, is evident, and he was plainly an easy man to dislike. Still, it has to be admitted that the general was often, if rather erratic in his behaviour, a very successful campaigner and no mean opponent. St Simon goes on:

He was excessively filthy in his habits and boasted of them, his custom was to rise late and at once take his seat upon his chaise-pierce [camp lavatory], and in this curious custom he wrote his despatches and issued his orders for the day. Anyone who had business with him, even general officers and distinguished visitors, found this the best time to talk to him.

Louis XIV was concerned to forestall the junction of the two allied armies. He pressed Vendôme to take the offensive in the Low Countries while there was still time to do so with a superiority in numbers, and the general's first inclination was to swing to the west, and threaten Marlborough's lines of communications and supply with Ostend and Antwerp. However, Burgundy expressed a preference for a straightforward advance on Brussels. This would almost certainly entail a stand-up fight with Marlborough, who could field 90,000 troops, on ground more or less of the Duke's own choosing. Vendôme, resenting the presence of the royal prince with the army, tried to ignore his opinions, and so the French, too, lost time. Meanwhile, in the Allied camp:

> The Duke had to be patient while he awaited the arrival of Eugene's army. With his comparative lack of numbers, and particularly with regard to the French superiority in cavalry, he was unable to venture forward and engage Vendôme with any real chance of success, unless forced to do so.

Marlborough had been too optimistic about the speed with which Eugene could gather his troops, and had to employ patience while waiting for the French to move. John Deane, who commented on the recent arrival in the Low Countries of the 2nd English Foot Guards (the Coldstream) to form a brigade with the 1st Guards for security duties at headquarters, wrote that 'We lay at Terbanck from 23rd May [O.S.] until the 24th June still waiting the enemy's motion, who had possessed themselves of very strong ground, so that we could no-ways come at them.' On 28 June the Duke wrote in some exasperation to Sidney Godolphin:

> By letters I received last night from Prince Eugene, he gives me hopes of being in a condition of beginning his march either tomorrow or the day following ... Prince Eugene thinks the Elector [of Hanover, later George I] will not approve of his march, which is the reason of his not acquainting him sooner ... That which gives me the greatest uneasiness is, that I find Prince Eugene thinks that their horse cannot join me in less than ten days, and that their foot must have fourteen or fifteen days. If they cannot make greater expedition, I fear the horse of the duke of Berwick will get before them, which I have writ to the Prince, by express, this morning.

He was quite right, and once Eugene got his troops on the road northwards, Marlborough's nephew was hard on their heels with a powerful French force, striving to either overtake the marching columns, or to cut across the route and interrupt their progress. A damaging running battle along the roads leading from the Moselle would disrupt the Allied campaign well enough. Berwick did not have to win such a desperate contest to frustrate the Allied plans; he just had to delay Eugene. So Marlborough prepared to operate without the increment of Eugene's full strength if need be, even though the odds against success lengthened by doing so; the Duke wrote to his son-in-law, Lord Sunderland, on 2 July:

> I expect the Prince himself on Thursday or Friday [5 or 6 July], to concert matters with me, and reckon his horse will not be above two or three days behind him. As soon as they are at hand, we shall begin to move towards the enemy, in hopes to bring them to a battle, which I fear they will avoid.

The Duke was aware that, as his plans could not be disclosed to a wide audience, the seeming inactivity of his army would attract adverse comment in London. So, that same day, he found time to send a note to the Paymaster-General of the Army, James Brydges. After congratulating him on his recent return to parliament as Member of Parliament for Hereford, Marlborough went on:

> I believe our long continuance in the camp has been a great disappointment to our friends at home. I assure you it has been no less to me, after the measures I had concerted with the Elector of Hanover and Prince Eugene in April last, but I hope we shall be able in a little time to send you some good news, for I have an account that Prince Eugene's army has been on the march towards us these four days. The Prince himself designs to be at Maastricht the 4th, in order to come directly to the camp, and the horse three or four days after, and if they can join us before the enemy have their troops from the Saire, I think we need desire nothing more.

At this time, the Duke also set out his plans for the coming campaign in a letter to the States-General in the Hague:

> I have imparted to Prince Eugene and to Count Rechteren, that it will be more advantageous to the interests of the common cause, for the army on the Moselle to join us in Brabant, without delay, and entreated them, should they be of my opinion, to communicate the same to the Elector of Hanover, and to begin their march as soon as possible. These measures being taken in conformity with the approbation of the [Dutch] field deputies, I doubt not but they will give notice to your High Mightinesses … His army commenced their march last Friday, the cavalry advancing by long forced marches, which the infantry rapidly followed. We shall move directly upon the enemy, and bring on a battle.

In the opposing camp, Vendôme and Burgundy still could not agree on the best course of action, so the matter was referred to Versailles for consideration. In the meantime, the French commander could manoeuvre to put Marlborough off-balance, while nurturing a plan put to him by the French War Minister, Michel de Chamillart. It was generally known that the civilian population of the Spanish Netherlands were resentful of Dutch occupation, and particularly of the heavy taxation imposed on them by the States-General. The important towns of Ghent and Bruges, in particular, were susceptible to French persuasion. The waterways of northern Flanders, so useful to the Allies when transporting supplies and heavy ordnance, were controlled by these two places, and Vendôme planned to seize them right out from under Marlborough.

The Comte de Merode-Westerloo claimed to have warned Marlborough of what the French commander was intending to do:

> I received news from a reliable source advising me to take good care of Ghent and Bruges, which were soon to be betrayed to the enemy. This information came to me from Lille, and from such a quarter that its validity could not be doubted. [Marlborough] treated my news as something of no account, telling me that it was impossible, and I could say nothing to make him change his mind.

Marlborough did not entirely trust the Comte, a man who had quite recently left the service of his opponents, and it was understandable that he should treat his advice with some caution. Soon afterwards, though, on 4 July 1708, the French army sprang into action, with flying columns under Comte de la Motte and the Marquis de Grimaldi riding ahead to try and surprise the small and unprepared Allied garrisons in the two towns. At Ghent, the next day, the French advanced party under Brigadier-General la Faille bluffed their way in and disarmed the town guard. Summoning the magistrates before him, La Faille flourished under their noses a pardon from the Governor-General, the Elector of Bavaria, absolving them of blame for defecting so promptly two years earlier to the Austrian claimant to the throne in Madrid. The cowed citizens, understandably fearing for their necks, yielded to the bold coup, and a party of la Faille's soldiers took possession of the citadel. Too late, a column of Allied troops were seen approaching to secure the place, but they drew off when they found the French already securely in occupation.

Meanwhile, de la Motte was cantering headlong with a column of cavalry and dragoons towards Bruges, which he took by surprise later that same day. The town of Damme, nearby, shut out his troops and resisted the summons, but de la Motte quickly went on to seize Plas Endael, a small but important fort on the road leading southwards from Ostend. De La Colonie wrote of the audacious stroke:

> We took by surprise the towns of Ghent and Bruges. M. de Fouille, a leader of the Walloon troops, who had been Grand Bailly of the first-named place when the enemy took it [in 1706], entered the town, in company with ten officers in his confidence, disguised as peasants. With the connivance of the burghers they managed to introduce a detachment of our troops by a gate which they at once seized and thereby secured the town ... The Count de la Motte with a body of troops approached Bruges on the same day, and this town, which found itself at the time unprepared, capitulated on the same conditions as the Fort of Ghent.

Marlborough, undeniably wrong-footed on this occasion, had written to Major-General Bothmar on 6 July urging that Bruges be reinforced:

> I have received your letter written at seven o'clock last evening, and it is well that the commandant of Dendermonde has listened to your advice to send another detachment to the garrison in the citadel of Ghent. I am writing now to be assured that the place is sufficiently provisioned.

The Duke was too late, as the place was in French hands already. On 7 July a letter arrived from Major-General Murray, whose brigade it was that had been unable to prevent the French seizure of Ghent:

> I had the account of the enemy's being entered Ghent at seven o'clock that morning [5 July], and at eight o'clock I was before the Bruges port [gate] with four hundred dragoons, and had ordered all the foot to be ready to follow; and when I called myself to the burghers at the barriers to open the ports, otherwise the Grand Bailiff and all of them should answer for it with their heads; but they answered, in the presence of the Baron d'Audignuies and several other officers, that they would open the ports for no man; and as I am informed since, there were only six dragoons of the enemy within at that port who kept guard with the ordinary guard of the burghers, so it is clear that the burghers were resolved to assist the enemy.

Colonel De La Colonie wrote of the Allied response to this French success: 'It was not long after we had taken these two towns that we learned of the junction effected by the Allies at the camp at Anderlecht.' The Colonel was mistaken, as only Prince Eugene would join Marlborough at this time. Meanwhile, the Duc de St Simon remembered how the glad news reached Fontainebleau:

> We took Ghent and Bruges by surprise and the news of these successes was received with unbridled joy. It appeared easy to profit by these two conquests, obtained without difficulty, by passing the Escaut [Scheldt], burning Oudenarde, closing the country to the enemies, and cutting them off from all supplies. Ours were very abundant, and came by water.

Vendôme's main army was now marching towards the Dender river to combine with the flying columns, and to cover these conquests. Marlborough, temporarily on the tactical back foot, was pushing his troops to overtake him and regain the initiative. He also sent Prendergast's Regiment and Waleff's Dragoons to reinforce Oudenarde on 7 July, under the stern command of Brigadier-General Chanclos, the Governor of Ath. The Brigadier promptly explained to the citizenry where their loyalty and interests lay, and these fresh troops successfully entered the town before the French could intervene. Adam Cardonnel, Marlborough's secretary, had replied on 8 July to Murray's letter of explanation of the failure to prevent the seizure of Ghent, as the Duke was unwell:

> His Grace sees that the burghers of Ghent have chiefly contributed to our misfortune in the loss of that place. I hope before the campaign is over we

> may be able to make them repent it ... We have just now an express from Brigadier Chanclos, that he has got into Oudenarde, and also some reinforcements from Ath. p.s. We march at two in the morning towards Ath.

However, Marlborough could not catch and overwhelm the French rearguard on the march, other than to engage in a skirmish at the Dender river crossings, and Vendôme was able to retire in good order towards the Scheldt. Once over that river, he would have leisure to select a strong position from which to defy the Allies, while covering Ghent and Bruges, and simultaneously awaiting the arrival of Berwick's army from the Moselle.

On 7 July 1708 Eugene arrived at last in the Allied camp at Alost, but he was accompanied only by a small cavalry escort of dragoons and Imperial hussars. His arrival cheered Marlborough, who was quite unwell with headaches and a high temperature; he was also understandably downcast at the loss of the two important towns. The Allied operations had dragged rather up to this point. The Duke's chaplain, Dr Francis Hare, wrote: 'His Grace has been confined to his bed all day by his fever-fit, but something he took this afternoon carried it off, with a gentle sweat, and he was much mended.' Eugene's arrival was timely and fortunate, for once in conference with his close friend the Duke's spirits revived rapidly, and decisive steps were agreed to engage the French army before it could be reinforced, even if this meant bringing on a battle before the Prince's own troops arrived from the Moselle.

The French success in northern Flanders, and their necessary march to cover their conquests, put their army in a position where their extended lines of supply and communication with France were exposed to Allied attack. Until the French decided on their next move, Marlborough's army was now closer to their frontier than Vendôme. The French commander had plans to besiege Oudenarde, but Burgundy now preferred to move against Allied-held Menin, comfortingly closer to their depots and magazines in northern France. The decision had to be referred to Versailles as the two could not agree; in the meantime, they could manoeuvre to cover the line of the Dender river, and prevent any attempt at a crossing by Marlborough.

While the French decided what to do next, Marlborough's army was on the march against them, and the move was too fast for Vendôme to counter. The Duke left the Earl of Albemarle with a strong force of cavalry to guard the rear of the army along the road from Brussels, and put his advance guard, under William Cadogan, across the Dender at Lessines on 10 July 1708, only a couple of hours before the French cavalry got there. The Duke wrote to Godolphin the same day:

> The head of the army is got hither. I have received advice this morning from the governor of Oudenarde, that he was invested on both sides of his town yesterday morning. I should think myself happy, since I am got into this camp, if they continue their resolution of carrying on that siege [as that would fix the French army in position there while the Allies closed up to strike at them].

Having lost the line of the Dender, Vendôme now had no option but to fall back behind the Scheldt; a siege of Oudenarde was no longer practical as Marlborough drew nearer, but Menin could still be a target, while stout French garrisons were left to hold on to Ghent and Bruges in the north.

Marlborough was driving forward now; he sent Cadogan and his detachment on ahead at a fast pace, and by mid-morning on 11 July, his pioneers were bridging the Scheldt a mile or so downstream from Oudenarde; the French army was also crossing the river, at a leisurely pace, about six miles away at Gavre. Vendôme was, at first, unaware of the Allied approach. John Deane wrote:

> The front of our army passed that river and as fast as they came over was drawn up in brigades, in order of battle ... The enemy having passed the Scheldt at Gavre marched at the same time towards Oudenarde to dispute our passing that river, little dreaming of our having so strong a detachment over.

As Vendôme and Burgundy were hardly on speaking terms, it is not surprising that the direction of the French forces in this sudden confrontation alongside the Scheldt was a poorly co-ordinated affair. The Marquis de Biron had been sent to cover the left flank of the army as it moved away from the crossing place at Gavre towards the higher ground at Huyshe. He had two brigades of Swiss infantry under command, together with a detachment of French cavalry. The leading brigade, led by Major-General Pfeiffer, headed towards the small villages of Heurne and Eyne, just downstream from Cadogan's own crossing place at Eename, an area described by Robert Parker as being 'A marshy piece of ground, full of trees and brushwood.'

By midday Cadogan had got his pontoon bridges across the river and his Dutch and British infantry were swarming across to the far bank. Marlborough and Prince Eugene joined the advanced guard at the pontoon bridges at about this time. The Duke approved Cadogan's arrangements and went to scout the higher ground near Oudenarde. A French dragoon officer, whose letter home was found in abandoned baggage later on in the campaign, wrote that:

> The action was ill-managed on our side. At 11 in the morning we let them come over the river quietly, which they would not have ventured to do, had we, in any tolerable manner, offered to dispute their passage; but seeing us standing still, they were encouraged to prosecute their design, and begin to pass over two bridges, which they had laid. As fast as their horse and foot came over, they ranged themselves in order of battle against us.

Four Prussian battalions under Brigadier-General Evans were left at the pontoon bridges as guard, while pioneers were sent into Oudenarde town to help Chanclos lay additional bridges so that Allied troops could use that route also, and lessen the pressure on the pontoons at Eename. Jorgen Rantzau's Hanoverian cavalry also crossed the river and pressed forward to the Ghent road and the line of the marshy Diepenbeek stream, which ran to its confluence with the Scheldt near to Eyne.

At about 1pm that afternoon, 11 July 1708, Cadogan's infantry were ordered forward to clear the village, and so expand the Allied bridgehead to allow the troops pouring down the road from Lessines to deploy properly. Joseph Sabine's British and Plattenberg's Dutch brigade moved smartly forward. Almost immediately they clashed with the forward companies of Pfeiffer's Swiss, and a savage firefight broke out along the boggy Diepenbeek stream. John Deane wrote that: 'They throwed one brigade into a village near the Scheldt to keep our detachments in action ... Thinking to have beat us before we were drawn up in any order.' In fact, there was no such neat French plan, as Pfeiffer's brigade, not fearing that the Allied troops were nearby in any strength, just drifted into an action with Cadogan's force. The Swiss did, however, try and erect a barricade of a kind to strengthen their rather inadequate position, Robert Parker recalling that 'They cut down a number of trees, and laid them in such a manner to prevent our coming at them.' As the noise of musketry grew louder, the Marquis de Biron came forward towards Eyne to see for himself what was happening and, thoroughly alarmed at what he found, hurried back to Heurne to summon his reserve brigade into action.

The Duc de Vendôme and his entourage were at this point enjoying a brief luncheon at the roadside – Burgundy and his elegant party were nearby – as the army marched past towards the high ground. Once there, if it was necessary, they could turn and take up a firm defensive position and defy Marlborough to come at them. There appeared to be no urgency, for the Allied army was thought to be many miles distant, at Lessines. Now, messengers came to Vendôme, that his flank guard was being driven in by Dutch and British infantry; the mutter of musketry from the direction of the town a few miles away was swelling to a roar, and, if it had been giving concern to the French commander at all up to that time, it plainly no longer indicated some insignificant affair of outposts. Taking to his saddle, Vendôme rode towards Heurne, and was able to see for himself the dust rising above the hills beyond the Scheldt; a large force was on the march towards the river, and tactically his own army, caught unawares, was suddenly quite off-balance. Yet Jean-Martin De La Colonie felt that the battle need not have taken place: 'As the time of day was somewhat advanced, it was possible, had it been wished, to have avoided giving battle.'

Despite the shock of the audacious Allied approach – 'If they are there, the Devil must have carried them' – had been Vendôme's scornful exclamation, his actual response was swift and correct. Rapid action to crush the impudent Allied bridgehead over the river should set all things right. Instructions were sent to Biron to use his Swiss brigades to drive back the Allied infantry from Eyne and the shelter of the Diepenbeek stream, while the cavalry of the left Wing of the army moved forward to support their attack. Vendôme had no notion that Pfeiffer's brigade was already in broken retreat from that stream, with the Hanoverian cavalry harrying them ruthlessly as they fell back.

The Marquis de Biron was now moving forward with the reserve Swiss brigade to help Pfeiffer, when Marshal Puységur, Vendôme's chief of staff, rode up and commanded him to halt his troops, not far from Heurne. The

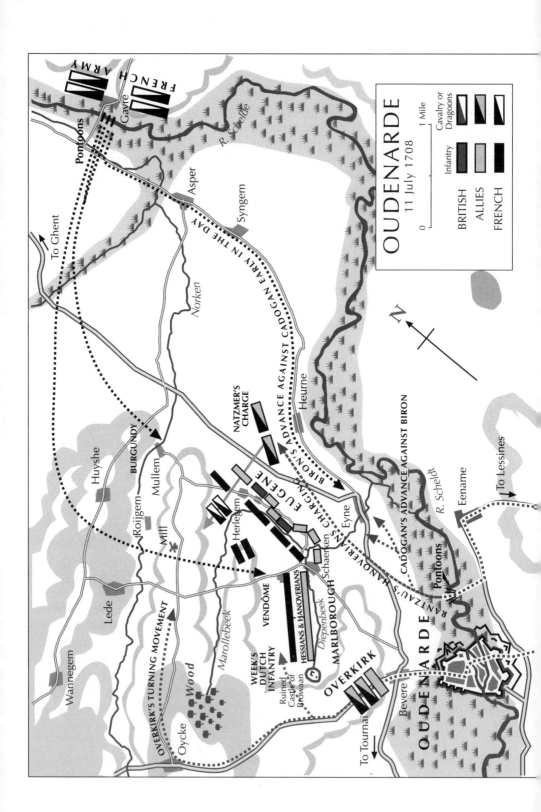

OUDENARDE
11 July 1708

0   1 Mile

BRITISH   Infantry   Cavalry or
ALLIES   Dragoons
FRENCH

N

FRENCH ARMY

Gavre

Pontoons

To Ghent

R. Scheldt

Asper

Syngem

Norken

NATZMER'S CHARGE

BIRON'S ADVANCE AGAINST CADOGAN EARLY IN THE DAY

Heurne

Huyshe

BURGUNDY

Mullem

Roijgem

Mill

Herlegem

EUGENE

BIRON'S CHARGING

Eyne

CADOGAN'S ADVANCE AGAINST BIRON

R. Scheldt

Eename

To Lessines

Lede

Wannegem

OVERKIRK'S TURNING MOVEMENT

Oycke Wood

Marollebeek

VENDÔME

WEEK'S DUTCH INFANTRY

HESSIANS & HANOVERIANS

Diepenbeek

Schaerken

MARLBOROUGH

RANTZAU'S HANOVERIANS

Pontoons

Ruined Castle of Bevoaan

OVERKIRK

OUDENARDE

Bevere

To Tournai

ground ahead, he declared, was too marshy and impassable for cavalry, so that any further advance would be unsupported and bound to fail. They were then joined by Marshal Matignon, who was looking for a camping ground for the night, and he agreed with Puységur, ordering Biron to go no further. Vendôme then came up, with the leading squadrons of cavalry summoned to the support of the Swiss attack, and he angrily demanded to know why the infantry were not pressing forward. Deferring to Puységur's apparently superior knowledge of the state of the ground ahead, he reluctantly countermanded the order for Biron to advance, and went off to find Burgundy, to try and co-ordinate a proper attack against the Allied bridgehead.

Pfeiffer's isolated brigade meanwhile was in ruins: 'It was about three in the afternoon that our detachment engaged the brigade in that village which, after a very mean defence were all taken prisoner' was John Deane's dismissive comment on their performance. Driven out of Eyne, the Swiss troops fell back in disarray across the meadows towards Heurne, but Rantzau's dragoons cut in at their flank and the infantry dispersed in panic, many being taken captive or cut down; Pfeiffer was among the prisoners. Finding no real opposition the Hanoverian horsemen surged ahead, along the general line of the road to Ghent, and went at full tilt into the ranks of the Royal La Bretache Régiment. They burst through the French troopers, scattering them in disorder and seizing both their standard and the mortally wounded commanding officer, before going on to engage the French cavalry brought forward a little earlier by Vendôme to support Biron's abortive advance.

Rantzau's dragoons were badly over-extended and outnumbered by the massed French squadrons, and they had to break contact and hurriedly withdraw towards the shelter of Cadogan's infantry around Eyne. Their headlong retreat was covered by the Earl of Stair with a party of quartermasters, who were looking for a camping ground for the night, and was unable to resist the temptation to take part in the action. The Electoral Prince of Hanover (who, one day, would be George II of Great Britain) was thrown from his wounded horse in the scramble, and would have been sabred by a French trooper had not the prince's squadron commander, Colonel Losecke, come to his rescue at the cost of his own life; John Deane, who remembered that it had been a 'wet morning', wrote of the Hanoverian exploit:

> A noble action it was, and the behaviour of all from the highest to the lowest the same. The royal Prince of Hanover in this action behaved himself with undaunted courage, exposing himself in the thickest of the fire until his horse was shot from under him.

As the afternoon went by, the main body of the Allied army came streaming down the road towards the pontoon bridges. Returning from his reconnaissance to the high ground on the left, Marlborough directed that some of them should take the route through Oudenarde itself, to ease the congestion as troops waited to cross the river. Cadogan's detachment was still rather exposed, but he was now able to bring forward from the bridges the four battalions of Prussian infantry that had stood guard there since that morning. As they approached the hamlet of Groenewald, the Prussians saw a column of French infantry approaching. These had been sent forward by Burgundy who, affronted at the impudent sally by Rantzau's squadrons, intended them to turn Cadogan's vulnerable left flank along the Diepenbeek stream. St Simon, commenting with the eye of the veteran soldier that he was, and appreciating the worth of line versus column when fighting in such close country, wrote that the French battalions:

> As soon as they arrived, they threw themselves among the hedges, nearly all in column. The columns that arrived from time to time to the relief of these were as out of breath as the others, and were at once strongly charged by the enemy, who, being extended in lines and in good order, knew well how to profit by our disorder. The confusion was very great, the new-comers had no time to rally; there was a long interval between the platoons engaged and those sent to sustain them.

Evans's Prussian troops got into line just in time to receive the advancing French, and to drive them back with heavy loss from their devastating and disciplined volleys of musketry; the leading files of French seemed to melt away in the blast. Here, perhaps, was the key to the puzzle surrounding the lamentable lack of success by these fine French troops at this crucial time, when Cadogan was still heavily outnumbered, and the main Allied army not yet in position to help him. The French, coming in on these clumsy columns, simply could not operate effectively in the close country beside the Diepenbeek. The anonymous French dragoon officer wrote that 'Our infantry advanced, and the ground was disputed two or three hours with a terrible fire, and great obstinacy.' John Deane, marching with the composite Foot Guards brigade, remembered that 'the fight was very desperate on both sides.'

As the six French battalions recoiled from contact with the Prussians, Vendôme came upon their disordered ranks. Already fuming with frustration at the delay in eliminating Cadogan's bridgehead, he ordered the infantry back into the attack on Groenewald, and sent a further six battalions from the right Wing of the army to bolster the effort. Cadogan, alert to the threat to his left, began feeding British and Dutch infantry from the area around Eyne towards the teeming battle, and Groenewald was held, for the time being, as the French were thrown back once again. Vendôme, on the other side of the Marollebeek stream, was now beside himself with frustration and fury, and personally led a further twelve battalions into the fray, having lost both his self-control and his grip on the wider direction of the battle at this early stage.

While all this was going on, John Campbell, the 2nd Duke of Argyll, was leading 20 battalions of British and German infantry into place along the Diepenbeek stream, parallel with the Scheldt at this point, spreading them out westwards past the French right flank towards Oycke and the low, domed hill known as the Boser Couter. At about 5pm, they pressed forward and the French infantry suddenly found their flank turned; they recovered with great gallantry, fresh troops were fed into the brawling battle and Argyll's troops were in turn driven back across the Diepenbeek. They were soon joined by 20 more German battalions, hot and sweating from their urgent march, led into action by Count Lottum. At one point Burgundy asked the Marquis de Grimaldi to advance with some squadrons of the French right Wing to support Vendôme's infantry in their battle between Groenewald and the hamlet of Schaerken, but they found the ground marshy and halted prematurely; Vendôme was left without support. Yet Louis XIV's grandson knew he was wrong, being heard to mutter, half to himself 'What will M. de Vendôme say when he hears that, instead of charging, I entrenched myself?'

John Deane said of the fighting for Schaerken that 'Our forces pressing vehemently on them at once gave them such a vigorous attack and furiously rushing into the village, drove them cleanly out.' It was not quite so simple, as the place changed hands several times and all the buildings were burnt to the ground in the process, together with the luckless wounded who had taken shelter there: 'The enemy vigorously maintained that village on the left still pressing fresh forces therein that we might not have any suspicion of their stealing off, which supplies did us considerable damage for a great while.' All this while, the British cavalry, commanded by Henry Lumley, took post to guard the left flank of the Allied army as it fed, battalion by battalion, into the rapidly escalating conflict.

By late afternoon, the entire right Wing of the French army had been drawn into a confused and brawling battle in the meadows, gardens and orchards beside the Scheldt, while the left Wing stood idle, lacking any instructions, on the track leading from Gavre. Vendôme was busy in the firing line shouting orders and thrusting soldiers into position, while Burgundy had neither the experience or the character to grip the situation and fight it properly. As De La Colonie remembered: 'One hardly knows how the battle began, but it did so about four hours after midday and lasted until night, being resumed more than once. We lost some excellent troops, far more than the enemy.' At about 6pm, another 18 German battalions deployed to support the hard-pressed battle-line along the Diepenbeek, and Marlborough was able to move Lottum's troops to reinforce his fragile right flank, where only a few squadrons of Prussian and Hanoverian cavalry had faced the entire French left Wing.

As Marlborough, with Eugene's skilled assistance, held the right Wing of the French army firmly in place, engaged in such an expensive and entirely unproductive infantry battle, Veldt-Marshal Overkirk moved around Vendôme's right flank with a powerful corps of Dutch and Danish horse and foot, out onto the empty slopes of the Boser Couter, the approaches to which had been secured by Lumley's cavalry. On the way, Overkirk paused, at Marlborough's urgent request, to detach Week's brigade of Dutch infantry to support the hard-pressed German troops near Brouwaan chateau. Meanwhile, the attention of the French was caught by a second daring cavalry raid on the other flank, when Dublislaw Natzmer's Prussians scattered two French battalions and captured a battery near the Ghent road, before being driven off with heavy loss.

Some time after 7pm, and in teeming rain, Overkirk's cavalry and infantry smashed down, in an entirely unexpected attack, behind the French line of battle. At the same time the British and Dutch infantry around Schaerken pressed forward in renewed attack. The French dragoon officer wrote in his letter:

> We were obliged to endure the continual fire of the enemy's foot and cannon, without daring to stir, because we were on the right of the King's Household [near to the windmill at Royegem], who suffered as much as we. Towards the evening we were fallen upon by a great number of the enemy's horse, to hinder us from succouring the rest, who were put to rout, and of the seven regiments of dragoons we have lost above half.

Neither Vendôme or Burgundy had sufficient troops in place to meet the massive assault, from either direction, and the right Wing of their army was virtually encircled; they were only saved from total annihilation by the onset of night. Kit Davies's laconic comment on the affair was 'Being taken in rear by 18 battalions and some horse, they began to lose courage.'

Now the left Wing of the French army, which had scarcely had a chance to fire a shot all day long, trickled off in the darkness, along the road towards the safety of the Ghent–Bruges canal. As they did so, Vendôme met the young royal Duke and his party at the roadside. The two men had not spoken together all that long, dangerous afternoon, and now the old general urged that their army should stand firm on the high ground around Huyshe, and gather itself to renew the battle in the morning. No-one spoke in support of him and, seeing that it was no use, Vendôme said, at last, 'Very well gentlemen, I see clearly that you all wish it. So, we must retreat, and you, Monseigneur [to Burgundy] have long desired it.' There was a long, horrified, pause at the insulting remark, but Burgundy made no reply. At last Puységur broke the silence, asking how the retreat was to be conducted, and the officers began calling for their horses and making off. With the cover of night the broken French army scrambled away northwards, leaving large numbers of dead, wounded and captives on the field. Vendôme's private secretary, Du Capistron, wrote of the bewilderment and collapse in morale that was evident in the French army, after the turbulent and disastrous day that had been endured:

> As to the retreat, the Duc de Vendôme was not for it; but, as he was backed in his opinion by the Comte d'Evreux only, he was obliged to submit. No sooner, therefore, had he given the word, for the army to retreat, but all got on horseback, and with astonishing precipitation, fled to Ghent.

John Blackader remembered that 'Night put a screen of darkness between us and them' while the Duc de St Simon, many of whose friends were present at the defeat, wrote of the disorder in the French army that reigned that evening:

> Every man was separated from his troop, cavalry infantry and dragoons were mixed higgledy piggledy; not a battalion, not a squadron managed to keep together, all became entangled and embroiled with one another. When night fell, an immense amount of terrain had been lost, and half

the army had not yet reached the battle-front. So great was the confusion that the Chevalier de Rozel, Lieutenant-General at the head of one hundred squadrons, received no orders. In the morning he found himself utterly forgotten; he at once commenced his march, but to retreat in full daylight was very difficult. Elsewhere fighting went on at various points.

Meanwhile, on the high ground over which led the road to Ghent, the French dragoon officer remembered that:

> We had no other expedient left, than to force our way through the enemy … Some of the enemy's adjutants summoning us to yield ourselves prisoners of war, we submitted to it, seeing no other way to save our lives. At least forty of our regiments are reduced to a wretched condition, the greatest part of them being killed or taken.

The day after the battle, 12 July, Marlborough, who had spent the night on the field in the rain, was received by Brigadier-General Chanclos in the town square of Oudenarde, which seethed with hundreds of French prisoners. Before conferring with his senior officers on the next moves of the army, the Duke sent the Earl of Stair with a note to Sidney Godolphin in London:

> I must acknowledge the goodness of God in the success he was pleased to give us; for I believe Lord Stair will tell you they were in as strong a post as is possible to be found; but you know when I left England I was positively resolved to endeavour by all means a battle, thinking nothing else would make the queen's business go well. This reason only made me venture a battle yesterday, otherwise I did give them too much advantage; but the good of the queen and my country shall always be preferred by me before any personal concern; for I am very sensible if I had miscarried, I should have been blamed. I hope I have given such a blow to their foot, that they will not be able to fight any more this year. My head aches so terribly that I must say no more.

Marlborough's words, prophetic in a way, illustrate plainly his own understanding that his whole position, at home and abroad, rested on his continued ability to produce victories, while pointing at the same time to his failing health. Veldt-Marshal Overkirk's report of the battle, written to Baron Fagel from Oudenarde town itself on the day after the battle, ran:

> On Monday last [9 July] we broke up [camp] with the army from Herfelingen, near Enghien. We marched the whole night and the next day, passed the Dender at and above Lessines. Yesterday morning [11 July] we marched again, from Lessines towards Oudenarde where we arrived about noon. We had received intelligence that the enemy broke up on Tuesday, from the neighbourhood of Alost, and were encamped at Gavre, and that they, also, passed the Scheldt, yesterday, at that place. Which, indeed, we found to be true, perceiving, upon our arrival at Oudenarde, the enemy upon a full march, towards Tournai. We laid the bridges over

the Scheldt in their sight, and our troops passed the river with an unspeakable speed and courage. About two o'clock, the greatest part of the army had passed, with which the Duke of Marlborough and Prince Eugene formed the right Wing near Brouwaan castle, about half a league from the town, and began to engage the enemy in battle. In the meantime I marched, likewise, with the troops of the States, which composed the left Wing, in order to attack the enemy, which I did, about five o'clock, having been obliged to make a great round to come at them, and God has been pleased so to bless the arms of the High Allies, that we have entirely beaten the enemy, and forced them to retire, in great confusion; some towards Courtrai, and others towards Ghent. We sent out a body of horse and foot this morning, to pursue the runaway enemy, and scatter them yet more, but they were got too far away by the favour of the night.

Overkirk's statement that he got his troops into position and attacked at five o'clock is not supported by other accounts of the action, most notably that Marlborough was waiting for him to go in well after seven o'clock that evening; the delay in getting the Dutch and Danish corps through the cramped streets of Oudenarde may have cost Marlborough a decisive victory. The same day, the Duke wrote to his wife in London:

I have neither spirits nor time to answer your last three letters; this being to bring the good news of a battle we had yesterday, in which it pleased God to give us at last the advantage. I do, and you must, give thanks to God for His goodness in protecting and making me the instrument of so much happiness to the Queen and nation, if she will please to make use of it.

The Duke was tired after the extraordinary exertions of the previous day, and many operational matters clamoured for his attention. Still, the closing phrase was very unfortunate. Duchess Sarah, engaged in a futile squabble with the Queen over her role and perquisites, promptly showed her the Duke's letter with its implied criticism of his friend and patron. Anne, who had written to Marlborough 'I want words to express the joy I have that you are well after your glorious success', now indignantly asked her Captain-General for an explanation of these words:

You say, after being thankful for being the instrument of so much good to the nation and me, *if I would please to make use of it* [Author's italics]. I am sure I will never make an ill-use of so great a blessing, but, according to the best of my understanding, make the best use of it I can, and should be glad to know what is the use you would have me make of it, and then I will tell you my thoughts very freely and sincerely.

Marlborough's urbane and courteous reply smoothed things over – 'I was in great haste when I writ it, and my fullness of heart for your service made me use that expression' – but such unnecessary troubles were very unhelpful, and an irritating distraction at a time when he had begun conducting operations within the very borders of France itself.

Marshal Berwick had hurried ahead of his marching army and reached the Sambre river the day after the battle, with an advanced guard of cavalry, which he promptly sent on to help hold Mons. The rest of his force, as it toiled along the hot roads from the Moselle, was directed to concentrate at Valenciennes. Berwick wrote in some despair at the situation he found, so suddenly changed from the euphoria which had accompanied the seizure of Ghent and Bruges only a week or so earlier:

> I went post to Tournai, to have a nearer view of the situation of things. There I found a great number of straggling parties of the army, which were subsisted by M. de Bernières [the commander of the garrison]. Upon a review of them, the whole number at Tournai, Lille and Ypres, amounted to upwards of nine thousand men; the enemy had made as many prisoners. As it would be some days before my infantry could come up, and the frontier was entirely destitute of troops, I divided these parties among the three places. M. de Vendôme, in order to outnumber the enemy, had carried all into the field, scarcely leaving men enough behind to guard the gates. I cannot absolutely blame him for this yet, from the year 1706, it had always been found that the loss of one battle was followed by the loss of all Flanders, for want of garrisons.

Marlborough, of course, saw Berwick's arrival rather differently, as posing a real threat to the flank and rear of his army as it pressed onwards. The Duke was therefore relieved when Eugene's troops arrived at Brussels on 15 July 1708; with the rear-areas now more secure, he could move forward into France. Marlborough's satisfaction at having Eugene's army covering his back is shown in a letter sent to Count Zinzendorf at this time. 'The Prince of Savoy has been with us nearly a fortnight. All his troops are on this side of Brussels, where they render us essential service, by keeping the enemy in check, while we are so far in advance.'

The Duke had already sent Count Lottum ahead, late in the evening of 13 July, with 40 cavalry squadrons and 30 infantry battalions, to seize and destroy the unoccupied French lines of defence between Ypres and Warneton. Marlborough's own headquarters was moved to Helchin the following day, going on to Werwicq two days later. Disregarding an impractical plan put forward by some of the Dutch field deputies to try and blockade Vendôme's army in northern Flanders and then starve them out, Marlborough moved towards the French border. By 15 July work had begun on levelling the French defensive lines, and several hundred prisoners had been captured in the process. Matthew Bishop, who took part in the operations, wrote afterwards that:

> We slung our firelocks and every man had a shovel in his hand, and when we came to the place appointed, we ran up upon their works. It was like running up the side of a house. When we got to the top we began to throw it down as fast as possible in order to make way for the army.

The Duke hoped that such a move, so threatening to the security of the border districts, and before the arrival of Berwick's main force from the Moselle, might entice Vendôme out to give battle once again. He wrote to Godolphin:

> They leave all France open to us, which is what I flatter myself the King of France and his council will never suffer, so that I hope by Thursday [19 July] M. de Vendôme will receive orders from court not to continue in the camp where he is, from whence we are not able to force him.

On 16 July 1708, the Duke sent to his wife a letter, apparently begun some days earlier, with a full report of the battle beside the Scheldt river:

> I hope before this you would have had the news by Lord Stair of the good success we had on last Wednesday. I have been obliged ever since to be in perpetual motion, so that I am a good deal out of order. I was in good hopes that the diligence I have made in getting into the French country (for I am now behind their lines), would have obliged them to have abandoned Ghent; but as yet it has not had that effect, but, on the contrary, M. de Vendome declares he will sacrifice a strong garrison rather than abandon that town, which, if he keeps his word, he will give me a great deal of trouble; for till we are masters of Ghent, we can have no cannon [the heavy ordnance could only be brought forward to the Allied army by water, unless enormous effort was used to bring it by road]. The governor of Oudenarde, to whom we sent our prisoners, assures me that the number is above seven thousand, besides seven hundred officers; and we have a great many killed and wounded on both sides. They were forced to leave the greatest part of theirs on the place where they fought. We did take care to send all ours into Oudenarde, after which I ordered that such of the French as were yet alive should be carried into the town. I have no account of what that number might be, but it being a wet night, I believe a great many of them suffered very much. If we had been so happy as to have had two more hours of daylight, I believe we should have made an end to this war. However, I believe the French will be careful not to venture any more this year; but the greatest mischief they can do is, the venturing all for the preserving of Ghent.

The attention of Vendôme and Burgundy, at this crucial time, seemed to centre on presenting their own, quite different, accounts to Versailles of the mishandled battle at Oudenarde. Vendôme's report, not surprisingly, skimmed over his own indisciplined failure to take a grip on the situation as it unfolded, and concentrated instead on the lack of support from the left Wing of the army: 'I cannot comprehend how 50 battalions and 130 squadrons could be satisfied with observing us engaged for six hours and merely look on as though watching an opera.' It is difficult not to feel sympathy with him over this point.

Marlborough's operations were now, as he had predicted, hampered by the inability to use the waterways of the Scheldt and Lys rivers. The Duke wrote to Godolphin on 23 July 1708 of the difficulties encountered in the preparations for aggressively pushing the campaign forward:

We continue still under the great difficulty of getting cannon, for whilst the French continue at Ghent, we can make no use of the Scheldt and Lys, which are the only two rivers that can be of use to us in this country. We have ordered twenty battering pieces to be brought from Maastricht, and we have taken measures for sixty more to be brought from Holland. The calculation of the number of draught horses, to draw this artillery, amounts to sixteen thousand horses, by which you will see the difficulties we meet with; but we hope to overcome them. In the meantime, we send daily parties into France, which occasions great terror. The duke of Vendome's army is so frightened, I am very confident if we could draw them out of their entrenchments, even from behind the canal of Ghent and Bruges, we should beat them with half their numbers, especially their foot. This is one of the reasons for their staying where they are.

Then, a very intimate touch, showing again the strain under which Marlborough operated while achieving such significant results on campaign: 'It looks affected to complain in prosperity, but I have so many vexations, that I am quite tired, and long extremely for a little ease and quiet.' There was no rest, no pause in the pace of operations. Vendôme's battered army lay behind the Ghent-Bruges canal, cowed but still dangerous, while Berwick was in the field with the troops brought from the Moselle, and those he had drawn out from the garrisons along the French border to replace the losses at Oudenarde. With all this to contend with, Marlborough drew steadily nearer to Lille, while Eugene watched his back. Unlike the leadership of the French army, the Allied commanders operated in close harmony. The Marquis de Biron, whose attempt to throw back Cadogan's advanced guard had miscarried so badly, now a prisoner of Marlborough, was struck by the closeness between the Allied commanders: 'A perfect agreement between the two captains for the conduct of affairs.'

Despite such accord, a dispute had now arisen between the two men, on how best to progress the campaign. Marlborough had already sent his cavalry deeply into northern France, gathering supplies and seizing cattle and horses. Such towns as La Bassée, Lens, St Quentin and Peronne were occupied, briefly, and the suburbs of Arras were raided. Now, despite the obvious low state of the French armies, a plan the Duke put forward to thrust deep into France, even as far as Paris, met with no approval from the usually intrepid Prince Eugene. On 26 July, the disappointment plain in his words, Marlborough was writing once again to Sidney Godolphin in London: 'I have acquainted Prince Eugene with the earnest desire we have for our marching into France. He thinks it impracticable, until we have Lille for a place d'armes and magazine.' The Prince's concerns were far from being trivial. To advance into France while a powerful fortress belt lay undisturbed behind them, and field armies (however cowed) in virtually equal strength threatened flanks and lines of supply and communication, seemed adventurous to the point of rashness. The Allies turned their attention, instead, to Lille, the second city of France, which now lay in the path of their army.

Chapter Eight

That Pearl Among Fortresses – The Siege of Lille, July–December 1708

As Marlborough was unable to convince Prince Eugene, or the Dutch generals, of the worth of his plan to advance deep into France, he reluctantly turned aside to assault the great city and citadel of Lille. At first glance this seemed a less promising project, likely to tie down the Allied armies for some months. However, Lille was a prize of considerable worth, and if it seemed likely to fall the French army might have to come out to fight in the open again. The capture of Lille in the 1670s had been one of the high points of Louis XIV's long military career, a triumph the King cherished, and he had lavishly improved its fortifications, employing all the considerable skills of Marshal Vauban. Captain Robert Parker wrote that:

> The [French] King had expended vast sums of money in pulling down the old buildings, and laying out the streets in a most regular and spacious manner. His famous engineer Vauban had exerted his utmost skill, as well in the beautiful and exact model of the new buildings, as in its noble and extraordinary fortifications.

Marlborough, however, was unable to invest Lille properly before Louis XIV became aware of the growing danger to the town, and seized the chance to augment the garrison:

> The French had time to supply it with all manner of provisions, and stores in abundance. Marshal Boufflers also had got in with a good body of troops; so that the garrison consisted of 14,000 regular troops, besides a number of inhabitants [militia] that were of service on many occasions.

Any proper attempt at such a formidable fortress required a large siege train, and the Allies were still denied the use of the waterways of northern Flanders. Marlborough wrote: 'That which hinders us from acting with vigour is that as long as the French are masters of Ghent we cannot make use of either the Scheldt or the Lys.' Arrangements were made to bring forward the siege guns and ordnance by road from Antwerp through Brussels and on to the army. This was to be a period of great convoys, with hundreds of wagons trundling southwards, while French armies hovered malevolently on either flank of the march. Meanwhile, Marlborough and Eugene had to contend not only with the Duc de Vendôme's army, still dangerous behind the Ghent-Bruges canal, but with the army of the Duke of Berwick, newly arrived from the Moselle. Vendôme might be winded, but Berwick was always dangerous.

Marshal Boufflers had been sent by Louis XIV to take command of the town and citadel of Lille. The veteran soldier arrived on 29 July 1708, attended by only a small escort, but their saddlebags bulged with *louis d'or* (gold coins) with which to pay the arrears of the troops of the garrison. Preparations to improve the defences of the place were immediately put in hand, with trees and copses around the town being cleared to a distances of 800 metres. Marlborough wrote on 30 July to Sidney Goldolphin: 'M. de Boufflers is come to the government of Lille. I hope he will have better success than he had at Namur [which Boufflers failed to hold in 1695], if we were once so happy as to get our cannon.' Progress in the preparations for the siege was slowed by the persistent lack of access to the waterways of the region while the French held Ghent and Bruges; on 3 August 1708, the Duke wrote to Secretary of State Henry Boyle:

> The difficulties we have been struggling with for this fortnight and more, to get the greatest part of our heavy artillery to Brussels, which being happily effected, the prince [Eugene] is going to-day with 25 battalions and 25 squadrons from hence, to strengthen his army, in order to bring the artillery forward.

In such an advanced posture, well inside the borders of France, Marlborough understandably had a constant concern for the rear areas, the regions through which the lines of supply and communication for his army ran. Vendôme, secure behind the Ghent-Bruges canal, was the immediate threat, and Marlborough wrote to William Cadogan in Brussels: 'For God's sake, do not risk the cannon, for I would rather come with the whole army than receive an affront.'

By 4 August 1708 Eugene's 50,000 strong army had moved to Ath to cover the first convoy coming southwards from Brussels. This vast, cumbersome column, hauled by 16,000 horses and mules, set off on 6 August, heading on the road towards Mons but then swinging to the west to link up with the Prince. Marshal Berwick, whose troops lay at Douai, found Vendôme lethargic and almost impossible to work with, and nor could he fathom the Allied moves in time. Marlborough was able to write to the Secretary of State again, on 9 August:

> I am very glad to acquaint you that the train of artillery is come safe to Ath, where it has passed the Dender, the enemy not having thought fit to make the least attempt to insult it on the march. I hope it is now past all danger, and that we shall have it in hand in three or four days, the Prince of Savoy, under whose care it is, having with him an army of near fifty thousand men, including the reinforcements he has had from hence. The French are now making lines without the town of Ghent for the security of that place, and it is said they have cannon coming to them from Dunkirk.

The following day the huge convoy was within reach of the Allied army, and the French had lost the chance to strike effectively at the wagons and guns as they trundled forward. Partly through good management and daring, and partly through French ineptitude and misjudgement, the convoy came safely through to Marlborough's camp, arriving at Menin on the evening of 12 August. In the meantime, the Marquis de Tarazena, so tiresome and troublesome to Marlborough in the victorious aftermath of Ramillies, was once again being rather a nuisance. The Duke, even with so many other demands on his time, felt obliged to write to Colonel Miklau, whose Hessian cavalry had been helping to cover the passage of the convoys:

> Having been advised of the protests of M. le Marquis de Tarazena of the necessity to have more cavalry to secure the town of Anvers [where Tarazena was governor], when your squadrons are returned from Brussels, I wish you to send immediately two squadrons of dragoons from your corps to Anvers. p.s. The two squadrons are not to stay at Anvers longer than absolutely necessary.

Eugene moved on with his army to complete the investment of Lille on 13 August, while Marlborough covered the operation. The Duke added a note to a letter written to Count Maffei:

> The Prince of Savoy has invested the town of Lille on all sides, and the cannon have arrived at Menin within reach of the siege, which will be pressed with all possible vigour, and this may at last convince the enemy that they have lost the battle of Oudenarde.

The plan was that Eugene would command fifty infantry battalions in the siege operations (of whom at least ten would always be on duty in the trenches) while the Duke led the covering army, fending off attempts by Vendôme and Berwick to disrupt the campaign. Eugene's engineer officers took advantage of the occasion of escorting a party of ladies in leaving Lille, to scout the defensive works, while Marshal Boufflers allowed the citizens of the town to appeal to Eugene to spare them the full rigours of the bombardment. The Prince's uncompromising response was that 'A besieged town ought to be kept very close. But when he should be master of the place, the burghers might be assured of his protection, provided he should be satisfied that they had deserved it, by their impartial carriage during the siege.' Given that the town-recruited militia were actively engaged in the defensive operations, and the citizens were lawfully the subjects of Louis XIV, this was an impossible request, and it is difficult to see how such impartiality could be demonstrated. On 20 August, Marlborough once again reported progress to the Secretary of State:

> On Friday last [13 August] part of the artillery was sent from Menin to the siege, and the rest marched thither this day, having been covered by a detachment of about five thousand men, which I ordered to take posts between Lannor and Pont à Chin, to secure them against any insults from the garrisons of Tournai or the Duke of Berwick's army. This night the

Prince of Savoy designs to open the trenches, which I hope he will do with good success. Hitherto, the French have not made any motion to disturb us, and cannot do it now with the same advantage they might five or six days ago, since we are at liberty to draw off a considerable strength from the siege to reinforce our army upon occasion. M. de Vendôme and the Duke of Berwick are in the same camp, only the latter has drawn to him what troops he could from the neighbouring garrisons.

The approaches to Lille town were quickly cleared, allowing the allies to advance from the north; the fighting opened at the chapel of St Magdalen, in particular, and was vicious and hand to hand. By 21 August the nine mile-long lines of circumvallation (facing outwards from the town) and contravallation (facing inwards) were complete, and the digging of trenches began the next day. There were regular exchanges of artillery fire between besieger and the besieged; the Prince of Orange's valet had his head taken off by a French round-shot one morning while assisting his master to dress. The young nobleman sensibly moved his quarters to a safer spot, while Eugene's own breaching bombardment began in earnest on 27 August.

Meanwhile, Vendôme and Berwick had been spurred into action by tart instructions from Versailles to do something to interrupt the preparations for the siege. The Duc de St Simon wrote that:

> M. de Vendôme did not budge from the post he had taken up near to Ghent. The King wrote to him to go with his army to the relief of Lille. M. de Vendôme still delayed; another courier was sent with the same result. At this, the King, losing his temper, despatched another courier, with orders for M. de Bourgogne, to lead the army to Lille, if M. de Vendôme refused to do so. At this, M. de Vendôme awoke from his lethargy. He set out for Lille. The King demanded news of the siege from his courtiers, and could not understand why no couriers arrived. It was generally expected that some decisive battle had been fought; each day increased the uneasiness.

On 29 August 1708 the two French armies combined near to Grammont, and two days later they moved to Tournai, but Berwick could not work with Vendôme and resigned his field command; he now accompanied Burgundy as an adviser. Marching southwards through Orchies, by 5 September the French army drew up south of Lille, facing Marlborough's covering army, which had prepared to receive them, near the hamlets of Ennetières and Seclin. The Duke, with about 60,000 troops, was outnumbered by Vendôme, at least until he could pull reinforcements out from the trenches to support him. So he took up a strong defensive position with flanks secured by the rivers Deule in the west and Marque in the east. Two days later, the armies still confronted each other, and Vendôme, who urged action on his colleagues, wrote to Louis XIV in exasperation: 'I cannot resist saying that the most part of the general officers of this army care nothing about losing Lille … What I see makes my heart bleed.' However, it seems that Vendôme was dressing up his own vigour for the benefit of the King. Berwick also wrote at this time to Michel de Chamillart, warning of the dangers of making a frontal attack on the strongly posted Allied army:

> With battalions under strength we should risk not only a repulse, but even total overthrow thereafter. It is sad to see Lille taken, but it would be even more sad to lose the only army which now remains to us or which can stop the enemy after the fall of Lille.

Before long, Marlborough, seeing that his opponents were, for the time being, at a standstill, felt confident enough to send back to the trenches those troops Eugene had brought to his support. He wrote to Sidney Godolphin:

> M. de Vendôme having drawn out all the troops possible from the garrisons, and having a great train of artillery joined him from Douai, made his own army and ours believe we should have had a battle on the 5th, which was the King of France's birthday, so that Prince Eugene joined me that morning with seventy-two squadrons and seventy-six battalions; but they not moving from their camp, which is in sight of ours, we sent back the foot the same night to the siege, resolving to entrench the front of our camp which we began to do yesterday. The entrenchment is so far advanced that I have this morning sent him back all his horse, as also a detachment of 2,000 foot, to assist him in the attacking of the counterscarp this night, and for the carrying on of the siege with more vigour than hitherto; for it is certain our engineers find much more work than they expected.

Despite its formidable reputation, the extent and strength of the defences of Lille had, it seemed, taken the Allied commanders by surprise. They had underestimated their opponents, and hard days lay ahead. Steadily, though, the work of Eugene's big guns produced a breach in the outer walls, and deserters reported that Boufflers was pulling some of his artillery back into the safety of the citadel. So, plans for a great attempt on the outer-works of the town were made, and the assault went in, on the evening of 7 September. It was stoutly resisted and the casualties among the Allied troops were heavy, Kit Davies recalling: 'A most furious one it was, the enemy's fire from the outworks, which were not yet demolished, made a dismal havoc.' One of Eugene's chief engineers, Des Roques, wrote of the affair three days later:

> On Friday, the seventh instant, we made an assault on the counter-scarp, about half an hour past seven in the evening. 2400 grenadiers, and as many fusiliers, sustained by twelve battalions, being commanded to make the lodgement, on the glacis, we attacked the whole front, reaching from the horn-work, before Magdelen's Gate, along the ravelin and tenailles, as far as the other horn-work, on the right of the lower Deule. After an obstinate fight, of about half an hour, during which, the enemy sprung four great mines, which destroyed abundance of our men, we obliged them to retire into their capital works, from whence they made a terrible fire, for some hours. But, as we had the misfortune, upon the advancing towards the

enemy, out of the trenches, to lose the six engineers, who were to direct the workmen, appointed to make the lodgement on the ravelins, and before the breaches, the said workmen, by the favour of the night, dispersed themselves; So that we could not maintain ourselves, but only on the angles of the glacis of the two horn-works, and of the tenaille. This unhappy accident retards the taking of the town, which may yet hold out eight or ten days. We had, in that attack, 2000 men either killed or wounded, among whom are sixteen engineers, either in the ordinary or extraordinary. We have raised two batteries on the glacis of the horn-work, on the right, and of the tenaille; and in a day or two, we shall erect another, in order to ruin the foot of the breach, which the enemy repair every night. Yesterday in the afternoon, the enemy made a sally, in order to ruin a sort of gallery, which we are drawing from the angle of the horn-work, at Magdalen's Gate. directly to the breach, that we may not be obliged to make a second assault upon the outer-works; But our regiments in the trenches repulsed the enemy with great vigour, killing abundance of their men.

The engineer's matter-of-fact style cannot entirely disguise the sense of the breathless deathly assault, the noise and the shrieking as hundreds of men strove to seize and hold the French works in the smoky twilight of the autumn evening. Boufflers, in his despatch to Louis XIV describing the repulse of the attack, said that the Allied losses were nearer 4,000, and he may well have been correct. Des Roques went on to comment on the ever-present concern in any besieging army, the maintenance of the supply for the great guns: 'We expect, with impatience, a convoy of ammunition, which is coming from Brussels, very à propos; For, we are in great want of it.'

In the meantime, the French put in a strong and well executed counter-attack on the besiegers, resulting in a mortifying loss to Marlborough's army. Kit Davies was pursuing her part-time career as a looter, and saw a strong party of French infantry on the move, apparently unobserved by the Allied sentries. She hurried to the Duke of Argyll, who was nearby, to give warning of their approach:

> I had observed all the hedges lined [with soldiers] and the cannon ready to play on us … We had scarce got time to get into the lines for safety. Sir Richard Temple's and How's regiments were ordered to clear the hedges, and the duke would have gone with them, and probably never returned, had I not prevented him by holding back his horse; for both these regiments were cut to pieces before our horse and train of artillery came up, which soon drove them to the main body of their army.

John Deane wrote of this same incident, and the hasty, bungled counter-attack:

> August 28th [8 September N.S.] a party of about 300 of the enemy was possessed of a chateau in the front of the two armies, which proved very prejudicial to us … How's Regiment advancing first, and the way bad, with narrow bridges and close lanes so that but one or two could pass

abreast. The enemy advanced out and lined the hedges, and firing on our people did them great damage before they could come up and recover themselves, and after retired into the chateau before Temple's Regiment could come; but at last we beat them out and took some prisoners. But at length the Earl of Orkney by the Duke's order commanded the two regiments off with all expedition; which command was very seasonable, otherwise they had cut them all off or taken them prisoners. Major-General How's regiment suffered very much, having 15 officers and 13 sergeants with 116 soldiers killed and wounded. Brigadier Temple's lost very considerable likewise. The enemy's loss was but inconsiderable.

The counter-attack on the French sortie was undoubtedly a rushed and badly mismanaged affair; the British troops went in without proper planning or supports, and had quite rightly been badly cut up. The French, on the other hand, behaved with great dash and gallantry; Boufflers's garrison were tired, but were proving to be a dangerous lot.

That night the Duke of Argyll moved his quarters to a less exposed location, not too soon by all appearances, and Kit Davies offered to help provide supplies, such as candles, and straw with which to pack the mattresses. Irrepressible as ever, she also helped herself to the Duke's stock of wine, with which she refreshed some of her cronies in the nearby guard. Davies then took two of the soldiers to a nearby inn, which apparently doubled as a brothel, where, she maliciously remembered 'One of them was received with so warm an affection, that he must be ungrateful if he ever forgets it, for the favour she bestowed upon him was of a lasting sort.'

In timely fashion, the Earl of Albemarle's thirty squadrons of cavalry escorted a fresh convoy through on the road from Brussels, now relatively free from French interference, while Vendôme's army was occupied facing Marlborough to the south of the city. Such a freedom, enabling the Allies to replenish their magazines and so continue the massive bombardment of Lille's defences, was a welcome bonus to the Duke. On 10 September Vendôme again threatened an attack, and Marlborough once more summoned Eugene to join him with his cavalry. The French commander, after some manoeuvring, found that Marlborough's dispositions gave little opportunity for success, and rather meekly drew off; moving towards the Scheldt to once again try and cut the Allied lines of supply through Brussels.

Progress in the siege was frustratingly slow, as Marlborough described in a letter to Godolphin, sent on 20 September: 'It is impossible for me to express the uneasiness I suffer, for the ill conduct of our engineers at the siege where I think everything goes very wrong.' Meanwhile, the pressing call for supplies and materiel necessary to feed the operations, with the enormous daily expenditure in munitions, had now to be answered with convoys forced through from the Allied-held port of Ostend. On 28 September a large number of wagons and carts set out southwards, heading for Lille, with a powerful escort of horse and foot led by Major-General Henry Webb. The French lay in ambush, under command of the veteran Comte de la Motte, near to Plas-

Endael. After an inconclusive encounter at Oudenbourg the previous day, where a fierce battle at bayonet point between Scots and French troops took place in the market square, de la Motte's force moved to overtake the convoy near to the village of Wynendael. Webb's own account of his hurried march to receive the approaching French was subsequently printed in London, during an undignified argument over who should have the credit for the action. Rather disconcertingly he referred to himself in the third person:

> The seventh and twentieth of September. General Webb (who, as eldest [senior] major-general, commanded in Chief) received advice that Major Savary, of the Regiment of Gethem, had possessed himself of the post of Oudenbourg; whereupon, he sent 600 grenadiers, under the command of Colonel Preston, a battalion of Orkney's, under the command of Colonel Hamilton, with that of Fune, commanded by Colonel Vogt, the whole under the command of Brigadier Landsberg, to reinforce that post.

After describing how, on the morning of 28 September, William Cadogan with a detachment of cavalry left Lille to meet the convoy, Webb told how his own mounted advanced guard, under Count Lottum, brushed against a strong force of French cavalry and infantry advancing to cut the road at Wynendael:

> All the foot, consisting of two and twenty battalions, Count Lottum with his 150 horse, making the advanced guard, with the quarter-masters and grenadiers that were not detached [to march with the wagons and give close protection] were ordered to march immediately, to gain the village of Ictegem, by the way of Wynendale. As soon as the advanced guard got to Wynendale, they perceived the enemy, in the opening of the plain. Whereupon, the quarter-masters and grenadiers were drawn up in order of battle. Major-General Webb and the Count of Nassau-Woudenburg [son of Veldt-Marshal Overkirk] at the head of the 150 horse, advanced to reconnoitre the enemy, giving orders, at the same time, to the foot to advance, and form themselves, as fast as possible, in the plain. The 150 horses were left, to amuse the enemy; and, to embarrass them, the more, the quarter-masters and the grenadiers were posted in a low coppice, on that side of the plain where the enemy were expected to pass.

De la Motte's attack came in through a small gap between two stretches of dense woodland. His hastily emplaced artillery did manage to fire on the Allied battle-line, but the French commander had no room to manoeuvre properly. Webb described his very neat dispositions, making the best use of the narrow and difficult ground:

> We had scarce got six battalions into the opening when the enemy began to cannonade us, with forty pieces of cannon, whereof ten were of three bores. But notwithstanding the great fire of the enemy, the 150 horse kept their ground, which produced the desired effect, in giving the General [Webb] time, to form his foot, in two lines. The left wing was extended beyond the low coppice, as well to prevent the enemy from passing that

way, as to cover our flank. On our right flank was posted, in the wood of Wynendale, the Regiment of Heukelum; and, on our flank on the left, the regiment of the Hereditary Prince of Prussia, commanded by Colonel Rhader, with orders not to discover themselves, nor fire until they could take the enemy in flank. Some platoons of grenadiers were advanced forty paces upon the right and left, with the same orders; and the quarter-masters were also posted in a road, on the left, that crossed through the aforementioned low coppice.

The attack by the French and their allies came on with great determination: 'Count Lottum was hereupon ordered to retire and post himself 300 paces behind the foot.' Not-withstanding the efforts of the French gunners, the Allied musketry was brutally effective, cutting down the leading ranks of attackers with terrible efficiency. The fallen soldiers piled up, hindering and tripping those who pressed on from behind, and the unlucky French were, many of them, jammed together in the narrow pass between the trees, unable to deploy or use their own weapons to proper effect. Colonel De La Colonie acknowledged that the French attacks that day, for all the courage of the soldiers, had been badly handled:

> Our troops, who ought to have had detachments detailed for the express purpose of attacking the wagons and cutting the traces whilst the main body attacked the escort, entirely devoted themselves to a combat in the moorlands of Vignandal, and allowed the wagons of the convoy itself to pursue their way in all haste. Owing to this inattention to details we did not profit by our superiority in numbers, whilst the enemy on the other hand, who knew too well how to take advantage of the ground by posting themselves in the woods, always warded off our people, and eventually obliged them to retire with some loss.

Despite the desperate valour of the French infantry, the Allied musketry, hitting them both in front and from either flank, continued to break up their attacks, although some of the attackers got close enough to club and bayonet their way through the front rank, before being slaughtered by Webb's reserve battalions, which were just then hurrying into place. Kit Davies spoke of the action in which her man played an active part:

> The enemy appeared in sight. They formed the infantry into four lines, and the horse in as many, and entered the defile to attack the escort; but they were no sooner within the ambush but they were saluted with a general discharge on either hand, which put their right and left into a thorough disorder. The enemy pushed on, and put two of our battalions in disorder; but the Swiss Regiment of Albemarle, under the command of Colonel Hirtzell, advancing upon their horse, that were endeavouring to penetrate, engaged them long enough to give time to the General, and Count Nassau, to bring up the Regiments of Bernsdorf, Gauvain and Lindeboom … The enemy, supported by so many lines, made another attempt to penetrate.

Meanwhile the precious wagons of the convoy trundled along southwards, often in sight, glimpsed through the trees, of the striving French soldiers. Cadogan had come up with his cavalry, and suggested a counter-attack on de la Motte's disordered force, but Webb decided against this:

> Major-General Cadogan, who came up some time after the action began, offered to charge the enemy, in their disorder, with two squadrons of horse, the other four, which he had sent for, not being arrived until seven at night; but it was not thought advisable to expose so small a number to charge the enemy, who had brought up all their horse to favour their retreat. The battle lasted two hours, and was very hot, in which we had 912 officers and soldiers killed or wounded.

This was plainly no minor affair, with close on 1,000 Allied casualties, and the losses among the French and their allies were much higher, being put at over 3,000, including hundreds of prisoners. Kit Davies was able to take part in the looting of the dead as the two armies, one tired but victorious, the other battered and defeated, went their separate ways: 'I got a fine bay horse with silver-capped pistols and laced housings and pistol bags. I sold the horse to Colonel [Gustavus] Hamilton for nine pistoles, and my pistols to Captain Brown for five crowns.'

The battle at Wynendael was a significant success, not only because the convoy delivered enough powder and shot for two weeks more bombardment, but de la Motte's effort was almost the first venture out of entrenchments by the French since the defeat at Oudenarde, at least one that led to an action. Unfortunately, offence was unintentionally given to Webb, whose success it truly was, because Marlborough's dispatch to London, which described the action, rather carelessly mentioned the involvement of Cadogan and his detachment of cavalry in a disproportionately prominent way. Prince Eugene had been wounded earlier in the month, and Marlborough was now both commanding the covering army and supervising the siege operations in the trenches. The hastily written dispatch, which caused such ill-feeling, may have been a result of this work overload. However, on 29 September the Duke had written to Webb with generous praise for the outcome of the battle:

> Mr Cadogan is just now arrived, and has acquainted me with the success of the action you had yesterday in the afternoon against the body of troops commanded by M. de la Motte at Wynendale, which must be attributed chiefly to your good conduct and resolution. You may assure yourself I shall do you justice at home, and be glad on all occasions to own the service you have done in securing this convoy upon which the success of our siege so much depends.

Webb was not mollified, and the snub he felt that he had been given was never quite forgotten. Not everyone in his small army had performed as well as might have been expected though, as a subsequent court-martial heard that an officer had 'Been seen to bow himself down close to the ground for a long time' during the exchanges of fire.

On the same day that this battle was fought in the woods at Wynendael, Marshal Boufflers, whose own expenditure of artillery ammunition and powder had also been enormous, attempted a desperate measure to resupply his gunners. Robert Parker described the exploit:

> The Duke of [Chevalier de] Luxembourg undertook it. He took 2,000 choice horse, each of which carried behind him a bag of powder, containing almost 100 weight. The [troopers] put green boughs in the hats [the Allies' field symbol], and marched with the Duke in great order from Douai. About the dusk of the evening they came up to the outer barrier of our circumvallation line, and pretending to be a party of German horse, that had been out on an expedition, and were returned with some prisoners, the officer opened the barrier, and let them in; from thence they rode on gently to the next officer's guard, where there was no barrier, and asking some questions which the Duke did not like, they clapped spurs to their horses, and rode in full gallop through the intervals of our camp towards the town, but the officer ordering his guard to fire, it gave the alarm, and the Quarter-Guards turning out, and the soldiers of the camp running to their arms, all fired upon them. This set many of the powder-bags on fire, and the fire in the crowd, catching from one to another, many of them were blown up. In the end Luxembourg with about 1,000 of them got safe into the town.

The success at Wynendael, which ensured much needed supplies for the Allied army, and Luxembourg's simultaneous desperate resupply exploit, illustrates very well the problems under which the opposing commanders laboured. The lines of supply and communication for Marlborough, in particular, were dreadfully vulnerable, for he was operating deep in French territory, with powerful enemy forces lying in the rear of his army, held off only by his own constant vigilance. At the beginning of October he wrote to Duchess Sarah:

> By the French having taken all the posts along the Scheldt, makes it almost impossible for our letters to go that way without falling into their hands; and that by Ostend is very near as dangerous, so that we are obliged to be on our guard of what we write, if we would not have them know it; so that you must not expect particulars as to news.

On 4 October the Allies attempted once again to force the defences of Lille, taking advantage of an untypical lapse in vigilance on the part of the garrison. An officer's letter giving a report of the assault was reported in the *Amsterdam Gazette* five days later:

> Yesterday, a little after noon we carried sword in hand the rest of the two tessailes and the ravelin. A sergeant of the Royal Regiment of Scots [Orkney's] advancing the foremost, observed that the French were not on their guard, as not expecting to be attacked, and called to our engineers and workmen to hasten to him, upon which the grenadiers advanced and found little resistance from the French, who were surprised, part of them were put to the sword and several of them who attempted to escape by

swimming, were drowned so that very few of 'em got into the town. The captain and forty men who were in the tenaille, were made prisoners. We found in the works 5 pieces of cannon, 100 pounds of powder, 2,000 weight of ball, 250 rations of bread and other provisions. We immediately attempted to make a lodgement but before we could cover ourselves, the enemy fired so terribly from the ramparts, that we had 50 men killed and 100 wounded, among the latter are Lieutenant-General Wilkins, Brigadier Wassemaar, and Colonel Zeden, but neither dangerously. This brave action of the sergeant who was also slightly wounded, was seen by the Prince of Nassau [Orange] and other generals, and the prince recommended him to the Duke of Marlborough, who made him a lieutenant that same day.

Plainly, rewards could come for valiant service, and the ranks of the officers of the Allied army contained numbers of men of quite humble origins. The assault on Lille went remorselessly on, and John Deane wrote that:

On the 19th [September O.S.] in the morning we made another attack upon the remainder of the outworks as yet un-taken, except a ravelin into which several of the enemy retired as fast as they was beat out of the other works. On the 22nd of Sept [O.S.], a detachment of 8 grenadiers of a [each] company throughout the army made an attack about 11 a clock in the forenoon upon the same ravelin; we blowed up a mine in the middle of them, they were so surprised that they made but small resistance, our people rushing so furiously upon them which drove them into the water so that very few escaped, but what was either drowned or blown up. We had likewise a great many killed and wounded, the enemy firing so prodigiously from the walls of the town.

Gradually, under such pressure, day in and day out without a rest, Boufflers's defences were crumbling; he beat a parley on 22 October 1708, and surrendered the town three days later. The weary survivors of his garrison moved into the immensely strong citadel. The Duc de St Simon wrote that 'Marshal Boufflers offered a discharge to all the soldiers who did not wish to enter the citadel, but not one of the 6,000 he had left to him accepted it.' Eugene, greatly impressed by the valour of the defenders, granted the Marshal good terms for the capitulation of the town, without even reading the document in detail. 'Marshal Boufflers can demand nothing of me that he should not ask, or that I should not grant', he declared. John Deane, in rather more down-to-earth fashion, wrote with some feeling of the rigours of the siege experienced so far:

We have paid dear; for this murdering siege, it is thought, has destroyed more than [the siege of] Namur did last war, and those that were the flower of the army. For what was not killed or drowned were spoiled by the hellish inventions of throwing bombs, boiling pitch, tar, oil and brimstone with scalding water and such like combustables upon our men from the outworks, and when our men made any attack. Especially the English grenadiers [who took a foremost part in assaults] have scarce six sound men in a company.

During the course of these operations, 67 year-old Veldt-Marshal Overkirk died, and his place as the field commander of the Dutch troops was taken by Claude-Frederick de Tserclaes, Count Tilly.

On the same day that the town of Lille was surrendered, the French stormed the Allied-held outpost at Leffinghe, lying on the valuable supply route from Ostend. This reverse, although minor compared with the success at Lille, caused considerable consternation in the Allied camp, as the garrison was reportedly taken quite unawares, and a number of the soldiers were butchered after having surrendered. However, the French operation was very well handled, and the loss of Leffinghe, although only temporary, added to Marlborough's concerns over the continued supply of his army. The Duke wrote to Major-General Erle, in command at Ostend, in the second week of November:

> I did not receive your packet of the 2nd forwarded by M. Veglin till yesterday, and see by it you have but an imperfect account as yet of what passed at Leffinghe, though it appears too plain, particularly by Capt. Wynne's letter to his uncle, that our people were surprised, and had made no disposition for their defence. As soon as they can be exchanged, it must be strictly examined into, that those who are to blame may be punished according to their deserts. I am very sorry to see so many of your men sick, but I hope this fair weather, while they have little or no duty, may recover them apace.

The reports of the loss of Leffinghe, in fact, were rather unfair on the garrison, as the French had assaulted the barricaded front of the village, while pushing a strong party of grenadiers around the rear of the position, thereby taking the defenders by surprise. The officers may have been hungover after a late-night drinking bout, as was rumoured, but the small garrison had fought until overwhelmed.

The difficulties in provisioning the Allied army persisted, and were a constant worry. On 7 November Marlborough wrote from camp at Rousselaer to Brigadier-General Evans, whose detachment had been gathering 'contributions' in the vicinity of Ypres since 21 October:

> Our necessities for corn increasing every day, I have ordered my Lord Stair to march to Dixmunde to see what can be got from thence and the country on the other side of the river [Yser], and therefore desire you will order seven battalions of your corps to march thither immediately under the command of a colonel to observe his orders. They will be joined by three battalions and four squadrons from Courtemarcq, besides the horse his lordship takes from hence. You will use all the diligence you can in sending the forage to the camp, because I know not how long I may be able to leave you at Langemarcq.

The Duke also wrote to Baron Fagel with orders to send three battalions and four squadrons, under command of two colonels, to support Stair's foraging expedition. As he plainly intended, Evans took the command of the troops sent out across the river, and the following day Marlborough found himself patiently answering queries on the practical steps needed to gather the crops, writing to the Brigadier-General again:

> I have received yours of last night, and have given orders that sacks be sent immediately, either by the bread-waggons or the troopers, from hence for each of the five hundred horse with you; so that as the corn comes I pray you will let it be sent hither from time to time, under the care of a careful officer.

However, the ill-discipline of some of the troops so engaged caused Marlborough to issue a steely rebuke to Stair on 10 November regarding his apparent lack of control of the operation:

> Having since seen a letter from your quarter complaining of the great looseness and disorderly conduct of the troops that are with you, particularly the horse, in plundering the churches, and all the whole country round about, I cannot forbear sending you this to desire that all possible care may be taken to prevent it, and that some examples may be made immediately by execution, and public notice of it given to the country that they shall be indemnified, otherwise I fear we may in great measure be disappointed of the hopes we had of a good quantity of corn from your parts. I believe it would likewise be necessary that a guard be posted at the bridge with a careful, severe officer to search the troopers and others, and to take from them whatever they have plundered in the country, in order to its being restored to the owners.

Despite such exhortations, Stair had hatched a plan to use the troops collected for the gathering of supplies to try to surprise one or other of the rather isolated French garrisons in the area. Marlborough wrote to him again on 11 November, with a word of caution:

> The endeavouring to surprise Furnes, or Knock, would, I fear, but interrupt our main business, which is the getting of corn, and it is great odds if you succeed. If you could surprise Gravelines it would be of much greater consequence, by opening us a communication with England; but I am afraid it is too far out of your reach.

All the while, the foraging expedition was having to spread its activities ever wider, so great was the demand by the besieging troops for sustenance, which was not coming through either from Ostend or Brussels in sufficient quantities. Reports came in that the French were again trying to disrupt the gathering of supplies, and Marlborough wrote to Baron Fagel on 12 November: 'Should the enemy approach with a large corps, you shall reinforce my Lord Stair with such troops that you consider are required.' The Duke remained concerned at the lack of discipline in Stair's detachment, writing the same day to the Earl:

The provost shall march tomorrow to Dixmude, whither you may send him your orders, and pray acquaint the officers with you that, as this service is of the greatest consequence, I expect they should be doubly diligent in keeping their people under good discipline and punishing all offenders with the greatest severity. As to what you mention of Furnes [the attempt to surprise the garrison], we may think of it when this main business is near an end.

The Duke went on to stress, once again, the importance to the army of the expedition. Perhaps appreciating that Stair's adventurous nature inclined him to more aggressive action against the various French outposts, rather than just mundane crop gathering, he held out the prospect of a further, more congenial, task:

I am very glad the country-people seem so well affected to us, for by their means you cannot want intelligence of the enemy's motions from Nieuport or other parts, which must be watched. I have sent Hookwater, one of the commissioners for the bread, who will be to-morrow morning at Dixmude, to bespeak the two thousand sacks and to give receipts to the country-people for the corn in order to its being paid for. He is to observe your orders, and I must take leave to repeat to your Lordship that not one minute's time be lost in transporting it thither.

Marlborough's concern grew, as reports of French troop movements towards the foraging parties continued to come in. In a letter to Stair on 13 November, from the camp at Rousselaer, he wrote:

We have just now advice of some [French] troops, both horse and foot, that are marched from Bruges to Nieuport, that you may be upon your guard, though you must have heard of it before now, and I do not doubt will take proper measures. I have sent this morning a thousand horse to Dixmude for corn, and shall send more as I hear it comes in.

Three days later, the Duke, in his anxiety, could not refrain from writing again to Stair:

I had this morning from M. Montagnes, who is with you before now, that you were drawing all your troops together the better to enable you to oppose any designs of the enemy, for which purpose M. Fagel has likewise sent you a reinforcement, but that this motion of the troops had hindered any corn from being brought in to Dixmude all day yesterday, upon which your Lordship must give me leave to continue my insistances that you use the utmost diligence in sending the corn by all possible means while this fair weather lasts, as a matter you know to be of the last consequence to us.

The corn was safely delivered in the end, but not without some alarms and stiff skirmishing, and Marlborough wrote to Stair on 15 November after receiving news of one such action: 'If you take any more prisoners, you should not give them leave to go home so soon; it can only tend to the giving intelligence to the enemy, and hatching mischief against us.'

Finding that he could not starve Marlborough and Eugene out, even when they were sitting deep in French territory, the Duc de Vendôme now rather belatedly undertook an audacious project to draw the Allied army off from the citadel of Lille. He moved to threaten Brussels and Antwerp, putting his troops in position at all the crossing places over the Scheldt. The loss of the two cities would place the southern provinces of Holland in fresh danger, and the States-General would be sure to demand the return of Marlborough's army to restore their security. All the Duke's campaign plans, even at this late stage, might yet fall into ruins. The Elector of Bavaria, now returned to the campaign in Flanders, fondly hoped that the citizens of Brussels, in particular, retained an affectionate memory of him as Governor-General, and would respond to his summons. Marlborough, however, was neither to be daunted by the new threat, nor distracted from the pushing forward of the siege, and he rose to the occasion with one of his masterpieces of grand tactics. The Allied army was put on the march towards the Scheldt, leaving a scratch force in the siege trenches. Colonel Molesworth wrote that Marlborough took care not to let his opponents know of his intentions:

> It was given out that the army was to move to the neighbourhood of Courtrai and from thence to be distributed into cantonments where they might refresh until the citadel of Lille were over, and then that the passage of the [Ghent–Bruges] canal would certainly be attempted. This farce was so well managed that our whole army was imposed upon by it, and I am confident all our Generals, except those few whom it was necessary to admit into the bottom of the design, really thought it was intended (as was given out) to cantoon and refresh the army for a while.

In fact, the Allied army was soon coming on in four great columns, one commanded by Eugene and three by Marlborough, towards the river crossings. The Colonel went on to describe the passage of the river:

> It was so ordered that when any one of these bodies had made their passage and lodged themselves on the other side, whichever of the others met with more than ordinary difficulties and opposition should repair to the bridges of that body that had passed, and likewise make their passage there.

Kit Davies, serving still as sutleress with her husband's regiment, remembered that:

> The Duke of Marlborough, who had found means to pass the river at Kirkhoven [Kerkhoff], attacked the enemy so briskly at Berchem, that two hundred were slain, six hundred made prisoner and the rest put to flight. The Allies had a free passage to march to the relief of Brussels.

While Marlborough and Eugene marched forward, on 22 November the Elector of Bavaria imperiously summoned the Governor of Brussels, Colonel

Pascal, to surrender or face bombardment, a storm, and the sack of the city. The Elector drew attention to the lack of numbers of the garrison, and the poor state of the defences: 'His Electoral Highness knows, that the commandant is not in a condition to defend himself, with the few troops he has; wherefore if he obliges His Electoral Highness, to begin the attack, he shall have no capitulation, for himself, or his garrison.' Pascal, a tough soldier, was not to be bullied, and replied with admirable and forthright coolness:

> The commander of Brussels is very unfortunate in not having the honour of knowing Your Electoral Highness. He dares assure you that he will do all that a man of honour ought to do, that he is satisfied with his garrison, and that he has the honour, with profound respect, to be Monseigneur, Your Electoral Highnesses' most humble servant.

The Elector's bombardment was of short duration and failed to impress Pascal. Donald McBane had been in Brussels, recovering from wounds received in the siege operations before Lille. He found himself drafted into service with an artillery battery, hastily set up to help defend the city:

> I had sixteen men to assist me; the French broke ground very near our works, which obliged us to stand to it; we continued five days cannonading one another; they burned several houses with their bombs; the sixth day they stormed us with twelve hundred men; we beat them off and killed an hundred and sixty of the French. We sallied out upon them and levelled a great deal of their works; after this the enemy desired the favour of General Murray who commanded our forces to grant a parley until they carried off their dead men, which was granted.

On 27 November, as the Allied army poured over the crossings of the Scheldt, the Elector had to withdraw towards Mons, and did so in such haste that he abandoned both his guns and his wounded. With Brussels no longer under real threat, Marlborough could turn back to the siege of the citadel of Lille; the Duke's lines of supply were, at last, free of serious interference. Meanwhile, in London, Queen Anne was mourning the death of her husband, Prince George of Denmark, and another of Marlborough's staunch supporters had left the scene. The sorrowing Queen had written on 20 November: 'You too [as I] have lost in him a true friend, who cherished your interests on every occasion.'

The defence of the citadel of Lille could not last. Marshal Boufflers signed the articles of capitulation in the evening of 9 December 1708. The 64-year-old Marshal and his surviving troops were accorded the honours of war in recognition of their fine performance and, two days later, were permitted to march away to Douai without giving their parole. Kit Davies remembered:

> The garrison marched out, following their baggage; the marshal, who was in the rear, conversed near half an hour with the Prince of Frise [John Friso, Prince of Orange]; all the officers saluted him with their half-pikes, which salutes he returned with his hat.

It had been an epic defensive operation, and the victorious Allied army paid a severe, possibly too high, price for the city – 'That pearl among fortresses' – a fact acknowledged by Louis XIV when he wrote handsomely to Boufflers on 13 December 1708:

> The Marquis de Coesquen gave me last evening the letter that you wrote to me from the citadel of Lille on the 10th of this month, with the copy of the capitulation that you signed in accordance with the orders which you received from me in my letter of the 1st of the month. It is what I could wish in the extremity in which you find yourself, and Prince Eugene has done justice to you and the whole garrison. I cannot sufficiently praise your vigour, and the pertinacity of the troops under your command. To the very end they have backed up your courage and zeal. I have given the senior officers special proof of my satisfaction with the manner in which they have defended the town. You are to assure them, and the whole of the garrison, that I have every reason to be satisfied with them. You are to report to me as soon as you have made the necessary arrangements for the troops. I hope these will not detain you, and that I shall have the satisfaction of telling you myself that the latest proof you have given of your devotion to my service strengthens the sentiments of respect and friendship which I have for you.

The French had, of course, not been able to save Lille, the capture of which was a significant achievement for Marlborough and Eugene. Still, the Allied effort, admirable though it was, had been enormous, expensive in men, munitions and time, and had not won the war for them. Boufflers returned to Versailles where he was warmly received by the King; his defence of Lille had tied down the Allied army for over four months. This in itself was a major tactical victory for the French – they had again traded ground for time, allowing their army, so exhausted and disconsolate after the shameful mismanagement of Oudenarde, to recover, in some measure, its fighting spirit. In London, the news of the fall of Lille was received on the same day as that of the capture of Minorca by Earl Stanhope, but there was not the same jubilation that had accompanied earlier victories.

As winter came on the pace of operations slackened, but soon after the fall of Lille, Kit Davies recounts an incident that caused considerable consternation and gossip throughout both armies when it became known:

> I observed an officer strolling backwards and forwards in the intervals of the camp; I fancied he had a mind to steal some of our horses, and for that reason watched him narrowly; at length I saw him lead off a mare, belonging to a poor woman, into a ditch, and with her commit, by means of the bank, the most detestable sin that can enter the thoughts of man. Colonel Irwin and another officer, that belonged to Ingoldsby's regiment, happening at that instant to pass by, caught him in this act, seized and gave him into the custody of the provost, where he remained till the duke, who had left the army, returned, when he was tried, condemned to the

gallows, and executed accordingly. The mare which this officer was enamoured with, was shot.

The Allied army now moved, in rapidly deteriorating winter weather, to retake the towns of northern Flanders, which governed the important waterways of the region. Davies again:

> Winter was already begun, and the frosts very sharp. We, who imagined it would be carried no further, found ourselves deceived; for the duke could not think of leaving Ghent and Bruges in the possession of the French ... While everything was preparing for opening the trenches [at Ghent], which was done on the 13th, and on the 14th, a detachment was sent to attack the Red-house on the canal of Sas van Ghent, where, as it is a place of importance, the French had left a garrison of two hundred men. These forces immediately raised their batteries, and made so furious a fire on the 15th, that the garrison having in vain offered to surrender, on condition that they might go off, were compelled to yield as prisoners of war.

She goes on to recount an incident that shows the perils present in even such fairly secondary operations, at a time when the year's campaign seemed to most to be almost at an end:

> My husband in the siege [of Ghent] was one of the forlorn hope, a body of men under the command of a lieutenant, ordered to lay ropes and direct the cutting of the trenches ... The ropes being lain, he with his companions were retired into a turnip field, and lay flat on their bellies, expecting the trench, which the workmen were throwing up, to cover them.

Kit had equipped herself with some beer, spirits and bread to refresh the men in the field, and made her way forward with her basket and bundle. She was accosted there by a young officer of her acquaintance, who was in something of a state:

> A spent musket-ball had grazed on, and scratched, his forehead, which his fright magnified to a cannon-ball. He desired I would show him to a surgeon, but his panic was so great, that I believe, had he been examined at both ends, he stood more in need of having his breeches shifted than his wound dressed. In his fright he left his hat and wig, but they being found and restored to him, and he at length assured his wound was no way dangerous, recovered his small share of spirits, but never his reputation.

The unfortunate officer was certainly not the first, or the last, man to foul his pants under enemy fire. Davies at last got to reach her husband and his comrades as they shivered in the frost among the turnips, and there they stayed with the bottles 'very comfortable', until the trench was ready.

Louis XIV plainly expected the French garrison in Ghent to make something of a fight for possession of such an important place. On 6 December 1708, as the capitulation of the citadel at Lille loomed nearer, the French war minister, Michel de Chamillart, had written to Comte de la Motte, the French commander north of the Ghent-Bruges canal, with rather pointed encouragement to hold onto the town as long as he could:

> The preservation of Ghent is of so great an importance that you can never take too many precautions. Although not strong in itself, Ghent can be attacked only by narrow and difficult passages; you have sufficient troops to enable you to sell this conquest at a dear price to the allies, should they persist in their design. You have good officers, capable of seconding you; you have had the misfortune to have commanded at Ostend when the enemy reduced it in a few days [in 1706 after Ramillies], and the misfortune of not having succeeded in the combat at Wynendael; it is for your interest, in the present occasion, to merit, by your conduct, the rewards of his Majesty to which you have been so long aspiring. If you are besieged, you must use all possible means to protract the siege, insomuch that it may cost the Allies very dear, and dispute the ground inch by inch, as Marshal Boufflers has done at Lille. I know the difference betwixt the fortifications of Lille, and those of Ghent; but there is in the latter a good covered way, which is equally good everywhere. I tell you nothing as to the preservation of the troops; you have in my opinion, a long time before you ought to think of their preservation, and I have reason to believe that they will serve with so much distinction and affection under your command.

Despite this exhortation to great deeds, and the reminder, both of his own failure at Wynendael in September, and of the strategic importance of these two towns, de la Motte, apparently despairing of relief by Burgundy or Vendôme, rather tamely evacuated the area at the end of December. Marlborough could now write to Godolphin announcing the delayed, but successful, outcome of his army's operations:

> I sent yesterday [30 December 1708] an express to Ostend to acquaint her majesty that the troops of Ghent were to march out on Wednesday, if not relieved before. This place will secure the conquest of Lille, and give us great advantage for the next campaign ... I have this morning sent a trumpet with letters to the governor and town of Bruges, offering the same capitulation as given to Ghent.

Three days later the Duke, content to have brought an exhausting campaign to a close, was able to give further information to his friend in London:

> I was yesterday from ten in the morning till six at night, seeing the garrison of Ghent and all that belonged to them march by me. It is astonishing to see so great numbers of good men, to look on, and suffer a place of this consequence to be taken, at this season [mid-winter, when operations were most difficult] with so little loss. As soon as they knew I had possession of the gate of this town, they took the resolution of abandoning Bruges. This campaign is now ended to my heart's desire.

With the return of the two towns into Allied hands, the campaign could at last be brought to an end. As John Deane put it 'Thus, after a very long, tiresome, mischevious and strange, yet very successful campaign, we are safe arrived in garrison.' It was none too soon, as the bitterest winter in memory had settled over Western Europe, the land being gripped by a terrible frost, and major rivers frozen over. Famine raged through France, and Louis XIV and his Marshals were in despair at the military situation; Marlborough, with an army significantly smaller than his opponent's, had not only triumphed in open battle, but had invaded France and seized her second city; this at a time when the Captain-General was quite unwell, in the grip of migraine headaches. It was plain to the French King that peace had to be obtained, no matter what the cost to France.

All now seemed certain for a victory dictated by the Grand Alliance; France was virtually bankrupt, the harvest in 1708 had failed, and there was unrest in many hungry towns. Supplies of corn had been purchased in north Africa, but these had fallen into the greedy hands of the Royal Navy ships prowling the Mediterranean out of the newly captured ports of Gibraltar and Port Mahon. The French armies, most significantly those along the northern borders, had been outwitted and outfought. Louis XIV was prepared to agree to all the onerous terms with which he was presented by the Allies, except for one. This was Clause 37, clumsily included in the peace preliminaries which were presented to his envoys, and requiring the French King to use his own troops to depose his grandson, if Philip V refused to vacate the throne in Madrid. Despite his desperation, Louis XIV rejected the terms entirely on that one point, and the war went on: 'A French King may make war upon his enemies, but should not do so on his grandchildren.' Even Marlborough recognised that the Clause was an arrogant and clumsy error; he wrote 'If I were in the place of the King of France I should venture the loss of my country much sooner than be obliged to join my troops for the forcing of my grandson.'

The terrible winter of 1708–1709 at length gave way to a sodden spring, Christian Davies remembering that 'Not a man in the army had a dry thread on his back.' In the opposing camp the Duc de Vendôme did not survive in his command in Flanders, now that Lille was lost and Ghent and Bruges so tamely given up. The veteran campaigner was summoned to Versailles where, St Simon remembered, the Marquis de Puységur had been complaining to the King about his recent behaviour and conduct:

> On his return from Flanders, Vendôme had audience with the King, but only one, and that a short one. The King, who knew and had proved by long experience not only Puységur's ability but his honesty and exactness, had his eyes suddenly opened to the true character of the man who had so artfully been represented as the hero and guardian angel of France. He was mortified and ashamed of his gullibility. The end came swiftly, Vendôme was thrown out of the service, sold his military equipment, dismissed his household, and retired.

However, Vendôme was reinstated shortly afterwards, and went to campaign, quite successfully it must be said, in Spain before dying of food poisoning in 1711. The French army in the Low Countries was now under the command of flamboyant Claude-Louis-Hector, Duc de Villars, who arrived to find the soldiers in a sorry state. St Simon wrote:

> In Flanders, the armies were lacking in everything. All possible efforts were made during the early part of July to send money and transport wheat by sea from Brittany and by road from Picardy. Nevertheless the money and the bread arrived only in small quantities, and for long periods the army was left to forage for itself on a much narrowed frontier.

In order to pay for the armies in the coming campaign, there was a call for the nobility to patriotically give up their silver plate to the Treasury. As St Simon remembered 'All this talk about silver made a great stir. No one dared not to offer.' The Chancellor, Pontchartrain, disliked the notion because:

> He represented the loss of prestige to the government, who might appear to be using this shift as a last resource. The King read the list [of those who gave up their silver] with care, and promised, again verbally and in general terms, to return an equal weight to the donors when his affairs permitted (which no-one believed).

On the exposed northern border of France, Villars was just the man for such a precarious moment. Careless of convention, and irrepressibly energetic, the Marshal commandeered civilian bread and wheat supplies to feed his troops, and pledged his own credit to see them paid. Slowly the spirits of the men revived, and recruits began to flock to the colours – soldiers had to be fed after all. Villars was luckily unhampered by having an opinionated and ineffective royal prince at his side, and robust enough to ignore most of those instructions from Versailles that did not fit his plans, as Robert Parker remembered:

> He would not accept the command, if the Duke of Burgundy was sent with him; for Vendôme had laid on him the load of all the misfortunes of the last campaign. Villars was looked on at this time as the best general in the French service. He was certainly a gallant, enterprising man. He was intolerably vain and full of himself.

On the other side of the tactical hill, the Allied armies were gathering for their summer campaign. The failure of the peace negotiations (a surprise to everyone including Marlborough) had delayed preparations for a new campaign, when it seemed there would be no need for one. The late close to the previous operations meant that there was precious little time to achieve anything very much before the fresh onset of cold weather. So, late in 1709, no plan for a deep thrust into the heart of France was practical, but there were several important French fortresses to be reduced, clearing the way for a possible grand advance in 1710. Also, the potential loss of a major fortress, Mons perhaps, Douai or Tournai, might tempt the French army out into the open to give battle. A victory in the field over the French would yield high dividends for Marlborough, and his critics might be silenced. This would be some compensation for having to adopt rather modest objectives in this short campaign season of 1709, which compared sadly with the magnificent vistas that had appeared to stretch before his victorious army in the golden aftermath of the triumph at Oudenarde the previous July.

At about this time, as the Comte de Merode-Westerloo recalled in his memoirs, one of his subordinates bungled a minor operation. The Comte was obliged to engage in urgent negotiations, and exercise some legal niceties, in order to save the necks of those of his soldiers who had fallen into French hands in the sorry affair:

> The enemy wanted to hang two of my dragoons that they had taken prisoner, as sometime soldiers in the Spanish army [that of King Philip V, before the battle of Ramillies]. I at once sent off a trumpet to claim their release on the grounds that they had changed their allegiance by due forms of law, but they were already awaiting court-martial. I sent my trumpet back to Count Bergeyck [the local French commander] with a message that if he had the men hung, who had been formally confirmed in their present allegiance by the legal powers of their legitimate sovereign, I would for my part hang all those who had not quitted the enemy's service as men who had failed to return to their proper duty [in other words, prisoners who had remained loyal to Philip V rather than declare for Charles III]. It so happened that a few days before we had captured a [French] cornet of horse and two troopers. He was dining at my table that particular day, and after I had risen from the table I said to him very gravely – that I regretted I had some bad news for him. I was going to have him hanged on the morrow.

The cornet was promptly given pen, ink and paper with which to plead to the French commander for an exchange, which was agreed to within a few hours. As the Comte remembered: 'The outcome of this incident was to give our troops a certain assurance that [they] would otherwise have lacked.'

Meanwhile, the Duke of Marlborough's position and influence in London was increasingly fragile. Sidney Godolphin was unwell and out of favour; he could not last long in his position as Lord Treasurer. The Duchess had, for some years now, been losing the friendship of Queen Anne, partly as a result of her fiery and seemingly uncontrolled temper. Clever and jealous enemies, fearful of the influence and power of the Duke, had now become the friends and confidantes of the Queen, and were active in Parliament. Duchess Sarah was dismissed from all her offices and appointments at Court, and the Duke, for all his pleading with the Queen on her behalf, could not get her reinstated.

Those envious of Marlborough's success and position, and suspicious of his motives, grew stronger. A good campaign in the Low Countries, a smashing victory in the style of Blenheim or Ramillies, was required in 1709, and would perhaps restore everything for the Duke's position and reputation in London.

Chapter Nine

A Murderous Affair – Tournai, the Battle of Malplaquet and Mons, 1709

The French army commander in the Low Countries, Marshal Villars, could not lightly risk a battle in the open in the early summer of 1709; his army was weaker in numbers than that of Marlborough, and the French soldiers were underfed and ill-equipped. Their shaken morale was reviving, the stout and long defence of Lille had demonstrated that, but the recovery was steady, after the arduous campaign of the previous autumn, and the rigours of the harsh winter. The Marshal's flamboyant personality cheered the troops, as did the way he bullied army contractors into supplying bread and uniforms for his men, but, of necessity, the French commander clung to his lines of defence. Marlborough's own plans to draw Villars out into the open were in progress, and Robert Parker wrote:

> The French had, with great expense and labour, thrown up new lines, from the Lys to the Scharp [Scarpe]; and Villars drew up his army behind them at Pont à Vendin. On the 18th of June [O.S] our generals advanced up to him, and made preparations for attacking him in his lines. Upon which Villars drained all his garrisons near him to give them a warm reception; particularly from Tournai he drew 3,000 of his best troops. This was what our generals wanted.

A note was received by Marlborough, from his confidential informant in Paris, late in June:

> I have seen the letters of 29th [May] from Flanders which show that M. de Villars is encamped in a very favourable position, that the morale of the army is good, that Villars has withdrawn all the garrisons from Mons, Tournai and Ypres, and has sent them to join the main army. M. de Villars suspects some of his staff officers of giving the enemy information of his plans.

Marlborough had subtly decoyed Villars, who shifted his troops to the south of Lille, between Douai and La Bassée, and the artillery train of the Allied army began to move to Menin, as if to threaten Ypres or Bethune. No sooner had the French commander weakened the garrison at Tournai to reinforce the apparently threatened sector, than Marlborough struck at that very same town with his now accustomed speed. Marching through the night the Allied soldiers, according to Parker, 'Found themselves before Tournai, which was invested immediately, and that in such a manner, that it was impossible for Villars to return the troops he had drawn from thence.'

However, the Comte de Merode-Westerloo wrote in critical terms about the opening of the new campaign: 'Our twin heroes did nothing with their formidable army until 27 June when they invested Tournai – a step they should have taken before besieging Lille had they truly applied the principles of war.' Despite such criticism the operation was neatly handled, and a plainly wrong-footed Villars learned too late Marlborough's true intentions. The Duke wrote to the Secretary of State that same day with the details:

> Upon repeated advices that the Maréchal de Villars had finished his lines, and the continued rain having not only made the roads very bad, but likewise the approach to his entrenchments along the river very difficult, and part of our heavy cannon being come to Menin, which had given the enemy some jealousy that our design was upon Ypres, whereby they neglected Tournai so far as to send part of the garrison to strengthen their army, it has been thought most advisable to undertake the siege of that last place: in order whereto we sent our heavy baggage yesterday morning to Lille, and at nine in the evening the army decamped. We marched the whole night, and early this morning invested the town on all sides. The garrison is commanded by M. Surville, a Lieutenant-General, who was wounded at the siege of Lille, and has the reputation of a very good officer. We are told it consists only of twelve battalions, whereof several are said to be weak, and of five squadrons of dragoons.

The siege proved to be a severe test for the Allied army, despite the reported weakness of the garrison. Colonel Jean-Martin De La Colonie described the place as 'One of the strongest and most regularly laid out in the kingdom. M. de Maigrini, the famous engineer, had devoted all his knowledge to the construction of this citadel.' The French defenders fought with magnificent tenacity, and casualties on both sides were severe. Parker commented:

> Prince Eugene undertook to carry on the siege and the Duke to cover him. The Marquis de Surville, who commanded the garrison of Tournai, made heavy complaints at the Court of France, that the best of his troops were drawn from him; however, he made a gallant defence for a month, then surrendered the town, and retired into the citadel.

A flavour of the severe nature of the operations, and the extensive tunnelling and mining that was undertaken, is given in a letter written by Marlborough to the Secretary of State on 12 August:

> We are obliged to carry on our attack on the citadel with great caution, to preserve our men from the enemy's mines of which they have already sprung several with little effect. Our miners have discovered one of their

galleries at each attack, but dare not advance to make the proper use of this discovery because of the enemy's continual fire of small shot under ground. We are preparing to roll bombs into these galleries in order to dislodge them.

Kit Davies remembered that the underground fighting was often carried on with 'Pickaxes and spades, more dangerous than swords.' A report in *The Tatler*, dated 24 August 1709 (O.S) gives further details of the continuous and hazardous pace of the siege operations:

We hear from Tournay, that on the night between the twenty second and twenty third [N.S], they [the Allied soldiers] went on with their works in the enemy's mines, and levelled the earth which was taken out of them. The next day, at eight in the morning, when the French observed we were relieving our trenches, they sprung a larger mine than any they had tried during the siege which killed only four private centinels. The ensuing night we had three men and two officers killed, as also seven men wounded. Between the twenty fourth and twenty fifth [N.S], we repaired some works which the enemy had ruined. On the next day, some of the enemy's magazines blew up; and it is thought they were destroyed on purpose by some of their men, who are impatient of the hardships of the present service. A deserter, who came out of the citadel on the twenty seventh [N.S] says the garrison is brought to the utmost necessity; that their bread and water are both very bad; and that they were reduced to eat horse-flesh. The manner of fighting in this siege has discovered a gallantry in our men unknown to former ages; their meeting with adverse parties under ground, where every step is taken with apprehension of being blown up with mines below them, or crushed by the fall of earth above them, and all this acted in darkness, has something in it more terrible than ever is met with in any other part of a soldiers' duty.

The citadel of Tournai, which had been the work of one of Vauban's most accomplished pupils, proved to be a very formidable obstacle. Robert Parker went on to describe the severity of the operations:

Our approaches against this citadel were carried on mostly under ground, by sinking pits several fathoms deep, and working from thence, until we came to their casements and mines. These extended a great way from the body of the citadel, and in them our men and the enemy frequently met and fought it out with sword and pistol. We could not prevent them however from springing several mines, which blew up some of our batteries, guns and all, and a great many men.

Donald McBane also wrote with some feeling of the trials of the fighting in the trenches before the forbidding citadel:

They planted a gun directly on a flank through the wall, with one shot they killed forty-eight men, I escaped the shot, but one of the heads of the men that was shot, knocked me down, and all his brains came round my head. I being half-senseless put up my hand to my head, and finding the brains, cried to my neighbour that all my brains were knocked out; he said were your brains out you could not speak.

As usual, Kit Davies was a familiar figure in the entrenchments, and one day she begged the chance to fire one of the siege guns, for a wager, to try and hit a windmill that harboured French sharpshooters:

> Major Pettit, before I fired, bid me take care the cannon did not recoil upon me, or break the drums of my ears, which I had forgot to stop (tallow was the usual material for this) I was in too much haste to get the guinea and not minding the caution, I was beat backwards, and had the noise of the cannon a long while in my ears. The officers could not refrain from laughing at seeing me on my backside.

Peter Drake had wisely given up a rather hazardous failed career as a privateer on the high seas and, newly released from gaol and sentence of death in England, he once again sought to enter the French service. He had some business to transact in Tournai, but obviously could not get into the blockaded town; so instead he volunteered for service as a gentleman trooper in the Scots company of the elite Gendarmerie:

> The quartermaster took me to his tent, fitted me with the regimentals, which were scarlet, silver laced on the sleeves and pockets, with a carbine and sword-belt laced. Thus I was fixed in the Gens d'Armes, and I had an exceedingly good horse, which cost six hundred livres.

While Drake was arranging his affairs in this way, as soon as the capitulation of Tournai was assured, Marlborough moved swiftly against the smaller, but important, fortress of Mons. The seizure of this place would, among other things, almost complete the expulsion of the French from the Spanish Netherlands. Louis XIV was alert to the danger, and wrote to Marshal Villars urging him to save the place: 'Should Mons suffer the fate of Tournai, our case is undone. You are by every means in your power to relieve the garrison. The cost is not to be considered.' With as competent and aggressive a commander as Villars, such an appeal was tantamount to a direct instruction to go out and give battle. The Marshal was not slow to put his army into motion, which began moving forward from its lines of defence on the Sensée river.

Already, on 3 September 1709, Marlborough had sent a strong force of cavalry and infantry under George Hamilton, 1st Earl Orkney, past Mortagne to mask the relatively small fortress at St Ghislain on the Haine river, in order to clear the way to Mons and to provide flank protection for the Allied army as it moved forward. The Duke wrote to Queen Anne that day: 'The army is marching in hopes we may be able to invest Mons before the enemy can throw in any succours.' Prince Frederick of Hesse-Cassell moved on 5 September to close up to Mons itself, his troops wading across the Haine river as they did so, in hourly expectation, as Jemmy Campbell of Stair's Dragoons (previously Hay's) wrote, of 'being attacked by the French cavalry.' The following day it was learned that the French really were preparing to come forward from their defensive lines, this being confirmed by the capture of the extremely talkative Marquis de Cheldon, who plainly saw no harm in divulging the French commanders' intentions.

Peter Drake remembered that 'On the eighth of September, Marshal Villars received an account that the Governor of Tournai had caused the chamade, or parley, to be beat; that night the French army marched, in order to post themselves near the woods where this battle was fought.' Before long the two armies lay only a few miles apart, separated by a dense but irregular belt of woodland formed by the Bois de Bossu, Bois de Sars, and Bois de Lanières. Villars was moving to challenge Marlborough, and save Mons, and he was cleverly using the woodland belt to shield his movements from observation. Villars was soon joined by Marshal Boufflers, who rode to serve in the army as a volunteer: 'He did not come with any character [formal role] but to receive his commands for the King's service.'

Marlborough afterwards wrote of this advance by the French army: 'We were alarmed with the enemy's marching to attack the Prince of Hesse; upon which the whole army was immediately put in motion.' The danger was plain: if Villars moved quickly enough, he might catch the Allied advance-guard, on the south side of the Haine river, isolated from the main body of Marlborough's army as it marched along from the siege-works before Tournai. Strung out along the muddy roads, the Allied troops were hastening forward to invest Mons, although Marlborough had left a substantial corps, under command of Lieutenant-General Henry Withers, to complete mopping-up operations in the captured fortress of Tournai, and to cover the vulnerable trains of the army as they struggled onwards. By 8 September, the Duke was able to achieve a concentration of most of his army to the east of the woodland belt near to Mons. Eugene with the left Wing covered the Bois de Bossu in the north, nearest to St Ghislain, while the Duke moved with the right Wing the six miles southwards, to observe the Gap at Aulnois near to Malplaquet, between the Bois de Sars and the Bois de Lanières. This would guard the intended siege operations against any French movement around the left flank of the Allied army. Preparations were also made to storm St Ghislain if the garrison refused a summons to yield the town.

As Marlborough's army marched towards Mons, Kit Davies was keen to make the most of her opportunities to obtain booty:

> When we left Tournai, and before the investing of Mons, as the army marched towards the French lines, I chose to go with the camp colour-men, who attended by the forlorn hope, march at so great a distance before the army that they are often cut off before any force can come up to their assistance; which, though it makes it the most dangerous post, it is the most profitable, if there is any plunder to be got, as there are but few to share it.

However, she was concerned at the uncharacteristically low spirits of her husband during the march:

> He was extremely melancholy, and told me this engagement would most
> certainly be the last he would ever see: I endeavoured to laugh him out of
> this notion, but he insisted on it that he would be killed … In our march,
> so heavy a rain fell, that we were ankle deep, and seeing a little child of one
> of my husband's comrades, I took it up lest it should be lost in the deep
> clay. At night, when in sight of the enemy, our army halted, and lay that
> night on some fallow ground, on which were many heaps of dung, and he
> was a happy man who could get one to sleep upon.

Davies went off to help plunder some local cottages and, well provisioned with
her spoils, took the child safely back to her father who was, however, found lying
ill on the ground with fever. Having little option but to leave the infant to an
uncertain fate, she then rejoined her husband and his comrades on the dung-hill:

> I went in search of my husband; and after a considerable time, as there
> was so great a fog I could scarce see a yard in front of me, I met one of our
> regiment. I asked for my husband, and he showed me him fast asleep, with
> his head on his comrade's backside.

The following morning, Monday 9 September 1709, Marlborough and his staff
observed Villars's army closing up to the gap opposite to Malplaquet. With the
French commander plainly committing himself in this way, the Duke fell back
a short way eastwards, to the hamlet of Aulnois, where the Dutch infantry had
halted. In this way he might entice the Marshal through the woods and into the
open country near to Mons, where the French would be vulnerable to an attack.
The Duke quickly summoned Eugene from the Bois de Bossu, and the Allied
army concentrated there at the Gap of Aulnois to face the French. Villars was
not so rash, and only advanced to occupy the Gap that evening, but did not
venture beyond the trees. Rather strangely, the Marshal then detached his
reserve cavalry, under the Chevalier de Luxembourg, to the south to cover the
Gap opposite Mauberge, a town that was under no real threat.

In the Allied camp, a council of war was called, and the question was whether
an attack the following day, 10 September, was practical. Any delay would enable
the French to improve what was already a naturally strong position between the
woods, and with only a narrow access to the Gap available, the ability to
manoeuvre for a better position was virtually non–existent. However, the terrain
was unfamiliar to almost all the assembled generals, and on the right flank in
particular, near the Bois de Sars, the many small creeks and ditches there cut up
the ground and made it very boggy underfoot. Prince Eugene commented on
this in a letter he sent to the Emperor that night: 'Since we do not know the lie
of the land, we dare even less take any risks. The terrain is very uneven, and cut
up by many small brooks and ponds swollen by the bad weather.'

The other option was not to attack at all, but simply to take up a defensive
position and block Villars in the Gap, while the operations against Mons
proceeded. However, the Allied commanders had longed to get the French out
of their defences for so long, to fight in the open, that this course of action was
apparently hardly considered.

Some time would also have to be expended in getting the Allied artillery into place; the big guns, so essential for the support of any assault, would not arrive until the next day. An added consideration was that Withers's corps would not get to the field before 11 September. This powerful mixed force of cavalry and infantry were not to be involved in any opening moves in a general action, and could be let loose upon the flank of Villars's army once battle was in progress. These two factors, the delayed arrival of the guns, and Withers's march to the battlefield, seem to have been most decisive in the hard decision to delay an attack until the Wednesday.

Colonel De La Colonie, whose brigade was moving forward with the French army as it neared the woodland belt, now found a tedious task suddenly given to him:

> He [Villars] broke up his camp on September 7th, and directed his march along the woods of Sart [Sars] and Jean-Sart to a little place called Malplaquet, within easy reach of Mons, so that the enemy had to engage him before beginning the siege. Owing to this march, a piece of work fell to my share as unexpected as it was fatiguing. Nothing had been said to me as to the order of march, and I had gone peaceably to bed; but I hardly got there when I received an order to report myself at midnight at the centre of the first line to take over the command of six hundred men detailed to escort the baggage of the army. I was obliged to pack my things as quickly as possible, and betake myself to the point named where I was given instructions for this embarrassing commission, which I carried out but taking a different route to that of the rest of the army.

The Colonel was plainly quite put out at being given the job to do, and added the rather obvious truth that:

> Escort duty over waggons in the presence of the enemy is a troublesome affair. In addition to the confusion that usually reigns among them, care has to be taken to protect them from visits on the part of the enemy, which means continuous watching with fear of surprises; in such cases an officer's loss of reputation has often depended upon a momentary negligence. Two nights and a day did I spend in this agreeable exercise, and on the evening of the second day [9 September], after having left the baggage train in a place of safety, I rejoined the army, which had just encamped in the plain of Mons.

As Marlborough did not mount an attack on 10 September, the French had ample time to entrench their position, and they put this to good use. De La Colonie remembered:

> As soon as we realised that we were not going to be attacked that day the whole of the infantry set to work to entrench themselves in the best way possible, reckoning that the crisis would come on the morrow. The only infantry that were without any cover at all from the enemy's artillery was the Bavarian brigade [De La Colonie's own command], who held a

portion of the parapet in rear of the Garde Français, whilst in rear of us again was the Maison du Roi, who were equally exposed.

Across the Gap of Aulnois, a line of nine stout earthen redans was constructed by French pioneers, and equipped with artillery to sweep the narrow approaches climbing the gentle boggy incline between the woods. Nearby, Bleiron Farm was barricaded and loop-holed for defence, and turned into a small fortress. In the Bois de Lanières, on the French right, infantry under Comte d'Artagnan constructed breastworks and abatti obstacles, and a large battery was established between the wood and Bleiron Farm, concealed from observation but firing along a dip in the ground across the front of the trees. Over on the left of the French position, the infantry commanded by Comte d'Albergotti and the Marquis de Goesbriand, constructed three lines of breastworks reaching deep into the Bois de Sars, and jutting outwards into the Gap in a curious formation that would become known, notoriously, as 'the Triangle'. A fourth line of entrenchments were begun in the more open ground to the south of the copses, near to La Folie Farm, but these were not complete in time for the commencement of fighting the following day.

The French cavalry formed up on the open ground of the Plain of Malplaquet, several hundred yards to the south of the Gap. Although apparently in dead ground to the Allies on the far side of the woods, events would prove that the horsemen were not immune from their cannon-shot which, having skimmed the French breastworks, bounced remorselessly on across the plain itself. Villars's dispositions were good, making the most of a naturally strong position, but all his infantry were committed to holding what was, in fact, a rather narrow frontage across the Gap of Aulnois. Both his flanks, while screened with woods, were now 'in the air' and potentially exposed to a turning movement. Any unmarked opposing force, such as that which Withers was hastening forward from Tournai, could fall upon the French flank with potentially devastating consequences once battle was joined. The woods themselves gave the illusion of cover, but they were not particularly dense, and many trees were felled to add to the French defensive works.

During the evening of 10 September 1709, as the toiling soldiers rested from their labours, an informal truce was arranged and, according to Peter Drake: 'There was kind of cessation for the rest of the evening, and the officers and soldiers of both armies spoke and shook hands with each other; and it was rumoured that there were overtures of peace on the anvil'. This was not so, and the French soon noticed that Allied officers, while apparently engaging in casual conversation, were also taking a close interest in their defensive arrangements, and the informal truce came to an abrupt end. The night before a battle was always a restless one, and the opposing armies stealthily stretched out towards each other in the darkness. Colonel De La Colonie wrote:

> The enemy began to construct a battery about half-way up the avenue [the open ground between the woods] and during the night armed it with thirty cannon of large calibre to breach the entrenchments in the wood on

our left [Bois de Sars], on which they intended to make their main attack. Thus we awaited them, lying that night in battle formation, whilst our patrols and those of the enemy kept up a constant fire whenever they came across each other.

On the other side off the field, Kit Davies recalled that the small but important French fortress of St Ghislain, sitting squarely on the line of march from Tournai to Mons, had fallen to assault that evening. Her memory of the camp gossip of this action usefully highlights the accepted convention of the time for how a garrison should properly conduct itself:

> General Dedem went off with a detachment to throw himself into St Ghislain, which the Duke of Marlborough was assured, the French garrison had abandoned; but the general in his march, receiving certain advice to the contrary, instead of two hundred foot, which he designed to send hither from Genap [Jemappe], drew from thence five hundred, and sustained them with two squadrons. Colonel Haxhusien, who commanded this detachment, sent a drum to summon the garrison, having, as he drew near the town, extended his front, that he might make a greater show of numbers; on a refusal to surrender, he gave the assault that very day; and after a quarter of an hour's dispute he carried the barricade, and advanced behind a house on the right of the battery; on which the chamade was beat; but as they had not done it soon enough, they were forced to surrender prisoners of war.

The Allied soldiers were roused from their slumbers early the following morning, to take a nip of gin or rum, before falling into line in the mist of the dawn. Facing them on the Plain of Malplaquet, Peter Drake described the scene as the French army awaited the onset of battle:

> There happened that morning a fog of the greatest density I ever remember to have seen. This gave the confederate [Allied] army an opportunity to march down pretty close to the wood undiscovered, which greatly saved the effusion of blood. Three quarters after six, the attack on the woods began with great fury, resolution and bravery.

Estimates of timings vary, rather inevitably, among soldiers about to go into battle. On the other side of the field, James Campbell remembered that 'We attacked the French army who was most strongly entrenched with a wood upon each flank, our cannon began to play about eight o'clock and the musketry a little after.'

The Allied bombardment, in fact, began at 7am, and before long the French gunners were firing in reply. Major Blackader recalled that his own regiment, the Cameronians, 'Was no farther engaged than by being cannonaded, which was, indeed the most severe that ever our regiment suffered, and by which we had considerable loss, but the soldiers endured it without shrinking, very patiently and with great courage.' As Marlborough's heavy batteries hammered the French breastworks, Eugene's German and Imperial infantry, under command of Count Schulemburg and Count Lottum, moved forward into the Bois de Sars.

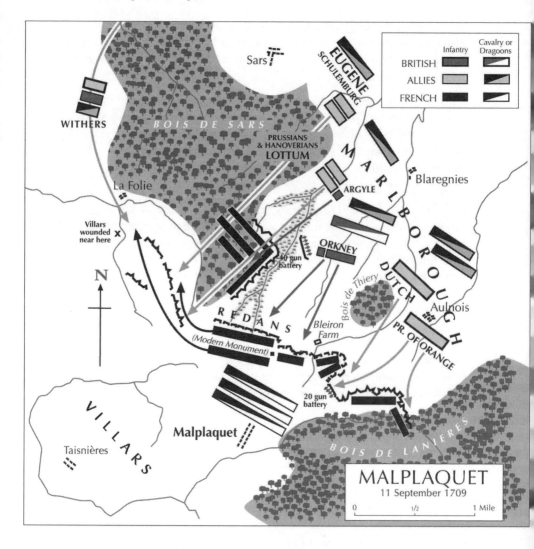

Their assault was bolstered by a German brigade drawn off from the troops screening Mons, and Temple's British brigade joined them. Desperate fighting erupted straight away, and Eugene's infantry were at first driven back by heavy musketry from the French breastworks. The Allied gunners gave excellent support, and the infantry reformed and returned to the attack, pushing the French slowly towards their rear entrenchments. Marlborough wrote that 'In the heat of the battle there was little quarter given on either side.' Soon, Eugene had to call for support, and Marlborough detached another British brigade from the centre, opposite the French redans, to add their weight to the onslaught in the woods. De La Colonie wrote in detail of the Allied assault:

> They came on at a slow pace, and by seven o'clock had arrived in line with
> the battery threatening our centre. As soon as this dense column appeared

in the avenue [the gap between the woods], fourteen guns were promptly brought up in front of our brigade almost in line with the regiment of Gardes Français. The fire of this battery was terrific, and hardly a shot missed its mark. I could not help noticing the [French] officer in command, who although he seemed elderly was nevertheless so active that in giving his orders there was no cessation of action anywhere, the cannon shot continued to pour forth without a break, played into the enemy's infantry and carried off whole ranks at a time, but a gap was no sooner created than it was immediately filled again, and they even continued their advance upon us without giving any idea of the actual point determined on for the attack.

The troops that De La Colonie watched with such fascination were the German infantry commanded by Count Lottum, who assaulted the Triangle, soon the scene of the most horrific and merciless fighting. De La Colonie goes on:

At last the column, leaving the great battery on its left, changed its direction a quarter right and threw itself precipitately into the wood on our left [the Bois de Sars], making an assault upon that portion which had been breached. It sustained the full fire of our infantry entrenched therein, and notwithstanding the great number killed on the spot, it continued the attack and penetrated into the wood, a success which it owed as much to being drunk with brandy as to martial ardour [this was a common misconception among the French soldiers].

The Colonel then commented rather acidly on the lack of steadiness among some supposedly elite French soldiers standing nearby:

Some of our best dressed troops did not think it proper to hold their ground, doubtless not so much that they were afraid of being killed as the fear of the embarrassment they might cause the state by the difficulty that would be created later on in having to replace them!! They therefore made off to a safer quarter, leaving the position to the enemy.

The Duke of Argyll was conspicuous by his bravery in the assault, going in with the British brigade attached to Lottum, which contained his own regiment (the Buffs). He stripped off his heavy laced coat, both to free his sword arm and to show his soldiers that he wore no breastplate in the hail of musket fire. Kit Davies recalled that the Duke cried to his men 'You see, I have no concealed armour, I am equally exposed with you.' Matthew Bishop described the scene as the Allied infantry crowded into the Bois de Sars:

In truth there were but very few places in that station in which we could draw up our men in any form at all, but where we did, it was in this manner; sometimes ten deep, then we were obstructed and obliged to halt, then fifteen deep or more, and in this confused manner we went through the wood.

About half an hour after Eugene's infantry went into the Bois de Sars, the Dutch corps led by the Prince of Orange attacked the French right in the Bois de Lanières. The attackers were straight away ruthlessly devastated by the concealed French battery, twenty pieces in all, near the Bleiron Farm. Their assault was renewed with the greatest courage, but the gallant Dutch soldiers, and the Swiss, Danish and Scots infantry who went in with them, were mown down in their hundreds. Colonel De Rousset, a Huguenot officer who took part in the desperate attack, and was twice wounded in the process, wrote of the assaults:

> The enemy had, in this place, three [entrenchments], one behind the other, fenced with cannon loaded with cartridges [canister-shot]. The first line advanced boldly, with their muskets on their shoulders, to within a small musket-shot. The Prince [of Orange], who had only forty battalions under his command, was to drive, from their entrenchments, eighty battalions, supported by the troops of the King's Household [cavalry], and commanded by the Marshal de Boufflers, and the Count d'Artagnan, who very well deserved a Marshal's staff, for his gallant behaviour in this action. He [Orange] was exposed to an infernal fire, which covered the earth with dead corpses, round about him; and, at the very beginning of the action, he lost the valiant Count Oxenstiern. He forced, however, the first and second line entrenchment, and had entered the third, and made himself master of the enemy's grand battery, if his troops had been numerous enough to counter the torrent of men, which Mons. D'Artagnan poured in upon him, with such fury, that his troops were obliged to retreat some paces. The Prince, perceiving this, took the Colours of the Regiment of Mey, and with as much unconcernedness as intrepidity, carried it to the entrenchment, and planted it there.

Despite such costly efforts, the Dutch and their allies were able to achieve little more than a minor and temporary lodgement in the Bois de Lanières. The French infantry reserves came rushing forward to drive them back towards the Bois de Thiery and the shelter of the Prince of Hesse-Cassell's cavalry. Count Tilly, commanding a brigade of Dutch infantry, wrote five days afterwards:

> The fire was, indeed, very violent every-where, but more especially at the attack of the infantry of the States [General], who suffered much, because of the double entrenchments which was on that side so that it was impossible to carry them, notwithstanding the good conduct and bravery of the Prince of Nassau, and the vigour of the officers and soldiers, who may all be said to have distinguished themselves, the last battalions, who supported, advancing with the same courage as those who suffered first.

On the left of the Dutch attack, the Scots soldiers of Tullibardine's Regiment struggled forward through the copses to seize a part of the French breastworks: 'We skirmished forward pice by pice' one soldier remembered. They were soon driven out again but renewed their assault without success. Their commander, the Marquis of Tullibardine, (on whose behalf Marlborough had once exerted himself to secure the regimental command) was shot down and killed while leading his men into a third attack soon afterwards. Sicco van Goslinga, the argumentative Dutch field deputy, described the scene in the Bois de Lanieres:

> The bodies of those who had been foremost seemed to have been mown down, having toppled forward in their ranks against the enemy breastworks. Behind them the ditch was so thick with corpses that no inch of soil could be seen. Add to such a sight the shrieks and groans and sighs of the badly wounded, and one can get some idea of the horror.

Lieutenant-General Jorgen Rantzau commanded a Hanoverian infantry brigade in position close to the Bois de Thiery, near the centre of the Allied line of battle. He pushed two battalions forward to assist in the attack on Bleiron Farm but these troops were soon driven back with heavy loss, as Rantzau wrote after the battle:

> Observing that the troops of the States attacked a second time the entrenchment of the enemy, and that they met with very great difficulties, I sent to their assistance (without being required to do it by any body) the battalions of Gauvain and Tecklenburg, which, with the forces of the States, got into the enemy's entrenchments, and forced them to quit it. It was there that these two battalions had all their officers either killed or wounded, expecting one Ensign, in that of Gauvain, and Captain Limburg, with a Lieutenant-Captain in that of Tecklenburg.

Deputy Goslinga galloped up at this moment, and demanded that the rest of the Hanoverian brigade be sent in against the farm, but Rantzau refused. He was quite right to do so, as his stand at the Bois de Thiery covered the left flank of Orkney's British and Prussian infantry (already weakened by the detachment of a brigade into the Triangle) as they began to move to occupy the French redans. Rantzau attracted criticism from some Dutch officers for this hard decision, and went on:

> I maintained, however, the post I had gained in advancing, notwithstanding the great fire of the enemy made upon me from a hollow way, by which the regiment de Breuil had above forty men killed in the first discharge. In the mean time, Prince Eugene sent me twice orders, by his aide de camp, to return to my former post, which I did accordingly. Quickly after that, the prince and the Duke of Marlborough passed by my post, towards the left, and Monsieur de Vlinck, Lieutenant-General, brought me orders from them not to quit the post where we were, until my Lord himself ordered us to march. We continued, accordingly, there, until all the horse and foot of the right advanced, and then we did the same,

pushing on the enemy, and drove them from the hollow way, where they still made a stand.

Despite severe losses all across the field, including Prince Eugene who was wounded in the head, the Allies were steadily achieving their aim, as the French infantry on either flank were either held in place, or driven back through the woods. John Millner of the Royal Irish remembered that 'The battalions that first attempted were entirely defeated, but being sustained by fresh troops, the enemy was everywhere forced out of their entrenchments.' The sergeant was referring to the attack in the Bois de Sars, not to the Dutch catastrophe in the Bois de Lanières, and Villars had no option but to strip troops away from his centre in order to bolster his left flank.

At this time, as a part of this redeployment, Colonel De La Colonie received orders to move his brigade away from the redans and into the Bois de Sars; he protested at the apparent folly in such a move:

> I refused to obey, and pointed out the absolute necessity that existed for our maintaining the position we were holding; but a lieutenant-general then arrived on the scene, and ordered us a second time to march off. All our remonstrances were useless.

In fact, Villars was gathering together a force of twelve battalions from the centre of his line to deliver a sharp counter-attack at the Allied infantry in the wood 'I saw that our infantry was losing ground in the wood, and I posted there twelve battalions to receive them [the Allies].' In this way Orkney's battalions opposite the redans might be split away from their comrades in the Bois de Sars. Standing near the great battery, Marlborough quickly saw the move and brought Lieutenant-General Auvergne's squadrons of Dutch and German cavalry menacingly forward, forcing the French commander to abandon the move.

As the struggle continued through the morning, the detached column under Henry Withers approached through the woods from the north-west, at about 11am. This powerful force of ten squadrons of cavalry and nineteen battalions of infantry, had come direct from the mopping-up operations at Tournai, and passed through the now Allied-held town of St Ghislain to march onto the battlefield, while the dreadful contest was in progress. Villars was present on the threatened flank, and he quickly redeployed the infantry battalions drawn from the centre, to hold the shallow ridge-line at La Folie Farm. He also sent the Marquis de Rozel's carabiniers forward to rout the leading Hessian squadrons in Withers's column. A bitter hour-long battle ensued as the Allied infantry came on again and again, striving to drive the French off the ridge and so turn the left flank of their army. Robert Parker wrote of the advance of his regiment through the outskirts of the wood, where the Royal Irish Regiment encountered their Catholic fellow-countrymen, serving in the French service with the Royal Régiment d'Irlandaise. A vicious close-range musketry contest erupted:

We came to an opening in the wood. It was a small plain, on the opposite side of which we perceived a battalion of the enemy drawn up ... When we had advanced within a hundred paces of them, they gave us a fire of one of their ranks: whereupon we halted, and returned them the fire of our six platoons at once; and immediately made ready the six platoons of our second fire, and advanced upon them again. They then gave us the fire of another rank, and we returned them our second fire, which made them shrink; however they gave us the fire of a third rank after a scattering manner, and then retired into the wood in great disorder; on which we sent our third fire after them, and saw them no more. We advanced cautiously up to the ground which they had quitted ... We had but four men killed, and six wounded, and found near forty of them on the spot killed and wounded.

The superiority of the platoon firing technique, in general use in Allied battalions, was neatly demonstrated. John Deane described the slow progress in the woods:

Then the enemy run to the third entrenchment, but our brigade followed them up so furiously that they gave them no time to draw up or form in any order, but immediately mounted that breastwork also ... We drove them clear out of the wood, and there, some of our forces, drawn up, fell upon them and broke them. And they run, all that could run ... Our brigades that drove them out of the wood was ordered to keep the wood and works that we had won until further orders.

Despite Deane's assertion of some disorder in the French ranks, Villars's infantry was in fairly good order, and they had achieved a breathing space by holding Withers off, although at a heavy cost. Matthew Bishop took part in the savage musketry contest in which the French struggled to hold their line:

My right and left hand man were shot dead, and in falling had almost thrown me down, for I could scarce prevent my falling among the dead men. The man that followed me was shot through the groin, and I escaped all, though nothing but the providence of God could protect me. Then our rear man was called up to be a front [rank man]; but the poor man was struck with a panic, fearing he would share the same fate as the others did. He endeavoured to half cover himself behind me, but I put my hand behind me and pulled him up, and told him, that I could no ways screen him ... We received a great many volleys after that, and one time I remember it wounded my captain and took my left hand man, and almost swept off those that were on my right.

The Allied infantry thronged the Bois de Sars, and Marlborough had some artillery dragged through the copses to engage the battered French battalions and the cavalry squadrons massed on the Plain of Malplaquet to their rear. Irrepressible Kit Davies was also in the woods, trying to take her husband some refreshment. She failed to find him with his regiment, and was forced to search amid the piles of dead bodies:

The shot and bark of trees flew thicker than my reader, if he has not seen action, can well imagine, not a few pieces of the latter fell on my neck, and gave me no small uneasiness by getting down my stays. My dog, at the entrance to the wood, howled in a pitiful manner, which surprised me, as it was unusual. A man nearby, who was easing nature, said 'Poor creature, he would fain tell you his master is dead'. I ran among the dead, and turned over near two hundred, among whom I found Brigadier Lalo, Sir Thomas Prendergast, and a great number more of my best friends, before I found my husband's body.

Villars now sought to gather a fresh force, under command of the Marquis de Chemerault, to strike smartly at either Withers or Eugene, and so regain the initiative over the tired Allied troops on this part of the field. Action had to be prompt however, for the centre of the French line was now almost entirely denuded of infantry, as De La Colonie described, and Orkney's British and Prussian infantry were moving forward towards the redans. The time was about 1pm.

On the southern edge of the roaring woods, Villars and his senior officers were in urgent conference near La Folie Farm, when their conspicuously mounted group was swept by musketry from some Allied infantrymen in the trees nearby. Several in the group, including de Chemerault, were killed, and Villars himself was shot through the knee. He attempted to continue to direct his troops, but, fainting from the agonising wound and loss of blood, the army commander had to be carried from the field. Peter Drake wrote of the urgent steps that followed the dire incident; Marshal Boufflers was summoned from the the Bois de Lanières, to take over the command. A crisis had come, the massed Allied cavalry were now approaching the redans, firmly in the hands of Orkney's infantry, and the French army faced calamity unless firm action was taken. At a glance, the veteran Marshal saw the immediate peril; if the Allied squadrons moved through the centre of the French position, the army would be split into two, and the infantry on either flank isolated and ripe for defeat in detail. Boufflers ordered his cavalry forward into the attack, and Peter Drake described the advance of the French squadrons:

> There was sixty-three squadrons of the French horse; the household troops and the Gens d'Armes being part of that number, to the amount of one and twenty squadrons; all of which were ordered to march down and engage a large body of the enemy's horse, who had already got within our entrenchments that were made between the two woods.

Drake gives a interesting insight into French mounted tactics at this time, where firing from the saddle, so frowned on by Allied cavalry commanders, was plainly still approved of and in use in the French army:

> The Chevalier de Janson, my captain, ordered that six men on the right, and six men on the left of his squadron (who were named for that purpose) should, on a signal given by him, detach themselves, and fall on

the flanks of the squadron we should engage, and pour in their carbine shot among them, whilst he would with the remainder of the squadron, sword in hand, endeavour to break through.

As the French cavalry came teeming forward from the vicinity of the village of Malplaquet, Auvergne's squadrons were still in some disorder after threading their way through the redans. They required a few moments to compose their ranks to receive their opponents' charge. A severe repulse for the Allies at this critical time was averted by the fortuitous presence of two squadrons of Stair's Dragoons (described by De La Colonie as the 'Scotch Guards of the Queen of England'), who were already drawn up and could take the first shock of the leading French troopers. James Campbell distinguished himself in the deadly contest in which the dragoons gained precious moments for the Dutch and Germans to gather themselves. He took the head off a French officer of the Gardes du Corps with a backhanded stroke of his sword, and was described by Earl Orkney, standing with his infantry in the redans nearby, as having behaved in the fight 'like an angel.' Peter Drake told how the Gendarmerie hewed its way through the Dutch and German cavalry opposed to them:

> We marched on to engage a third squadron, which broke in a seeming confusion, or rather opened to right and left, on purpose to draw us under the fire of Colonel Prendergast's regiment, who lay unseen by us at the reverse of the entrenchments [redans], and poured their shot among us and some other French squadrons, that had penetrated so far, which made a great slaughter … Here I was shot through the calf of the left leg, though I did not know it, which with two [sword] cuts I received before, made three wounds. Our squadron being thus broke, and I separated from them, I was riding about the field in quest of them, and I was surrounded by five Germans, who were resolved to finish me. I made the best of a bad matter; I exchanged some cuts, and fired both my pistols, but what execution they did, if any, I cannot tell.

Escaping from the deadly throng, Drake then rode inadvertently into another German squadron, just making their way through the redans to get into position. The nearest trooper raised his carbine to shoot the rather battered Irishman, but, he remembered:

> I fired my carbine, so that his shot and mine went off instantaneously, I shot the upper part off his head, and he tumbled forward; I saw his brains come down; his ball only grazed my shoulder and tore the flesh a little; but the powder blew off, and burnt the breadth of an oyster shell off my coat; and the wadding, which was tow, lodged between my waistcoat and shirt, setting them both on fire. Most of the [enemy] front rank of the squadron, if not all, poured in a volley at the same time.

The cavalry battle was fiercely contested. Although the French squadrons had been subjected to the 'overs' of the Allied bombardment all morning, and had taken losses, their dash and bravery were undiminished and they charged the

Allies no less than six times. Orkney wrote of their effort that 'I really believe that had the foot not been there, they would have drove our horse out of the field.' By about 3pm Marshal Boufflers could see that his army was no longer able to hold its position. In the face of greater numbers, it had roughly handled, and in many cases thrown back, the Allied attacks, but now the French were remorselessly being pushed off the field. Furthermore, the Allied artillery was increasingly dominating the battle, as the pieces were dragged forward into the intervals between the redans, and through the copses. Donald McBane remembered that 'Earl Orkney ordered six pieces of cannon to be drawn through the woods by strength of men.' While John Deane wrote that 'Our cannoniers did work as hard that day as ever they did since that warlike discipline was invented, and did great execution.'

The two armies were locked together all across the field, but Boufflers had not a man to spare, whereas the Allies, although tired and in some disorder after their efforts, could regroup and come on again as the afternoon progressed. Unless a clean break was achieved by the French commander, a damaging and possibly disastrous running fight might result before the French could get back to the prepared line of defence near Valenciennes. The French had to go or face destruction, so the orders were given, and Boufflers handled this most dangerous operation, a withdrawal in contact, with considerable skill. His infantry on the left approached the Bois de Sars, their musketry volleys raking the edge of the woods; the Allied infantry drew back a little, and in the interval thus gained the French began their march to the rear, their ranks depleted but in good order. De Rozel's carabiniers efficiently covered the retreat, deterring any close pursuit. On the right, d'Artagnan's infantry, in the same well-disciplined way, began to pull back through the Bois de Lanières, and they got many of their guns and caissons off the field in the process. De La Colonie wrote of the withdrawal:

> When we began our retreat, none of our infantry brigades were at all broken, always excepting the two famous regiments who had the centre of our line, and whose behaviour in quitting the field I have already remarked upon. Our cavalry were in excellent trim. Our right retired on Quesnoy and our left on Valenciennes. It is true that as soon as our line of retreat was determined upon, and our columns began their retirement, the enemy sent out a number of squadrons to keep us under observation, but they neither dared approach our rearguard, nor even made a pretence of attacking us.

James Campbell wrote in his own journal that the cavalry from Withers's column followed the retreating army for a distance and were driven off more than once. The open country allowed the French to make good time as they marched, but the withdrawal was not without its anxious moments, as De La Colonie went on to describe:

> I was with the left wing which retired by the road to Valenciennes, which for three leagues passed through a fine open country, where we met with

neither stream or defile which could afford an opportunity for the enemy's squadrons to attack our rearguard. A little further on we did reach a village, where we were obliged to cross over a fairly wide stream, which checked us for a while, but the enemy also halted, and there was some reason to fear they might attack the tail of the column during its passage [over the brook]. To meet this case, infantry were required, as our rear-guard consisted solely of cavalry. As it was the whole of the infantry had already crossed, and were continuing their march, with the exception of our regiment and my French grenadiers, who held the honourable post of rear-guard.

To the relief of the French cavalry commanders, De La Colonie's depleted brigade gave the cover necessary to fend off the Allied squadrons, while the stream was safely negotiated.

The victory for the Allies in the Gap at Aulnois was very dearly bought. Marlborough's army had suffered some 22,000 killed and wounded, 8,000 of these from the Dutch attack on the left alone. Villars's army took about 13,000 casualties, and little more than 500 of these were left behind in Allied hands as unwounded prisoners, a good measure of the disciplined order in which they got off the field. The French also got many, but by no means all, of their guns away. The shattered woods at Malplaquet were choked with the dead and wounded of the two armies, and Marlborough sent William Cadogan after the French, offering a truce so that their wagons could return and take away their fallen comrades. Peter Drake was among these; wounded and unhorsed and left behind in the French withdrawal, then taken prisoner and plundered by von Bulow's Hanoverian dragoons. He was sitting forlornly on the grass when he was noticed by the Duke of Marlborough:

> I made shift to advance five or six yards towards his Grace who, on seeing me in that condition, was so good as to stop and ask what was the matter. I told him as loud as I could that I had the honour to serve in the Gens d'Armes, and that I was a prisoner of war, very much wounded, and in danger of losing my life for want of a surgeon to dress my wounds, and begged he would please take my parole of honour, which was a favour generally granted to the gentlemen of our corps.

Drake goes on to say that the Duke turned to his Secretary, Adam Cardonnel, and 'Asked him how came all these poor gentlemen were not sent away, he having sent orders for the purpose, and desired carriages to be got ready for those that were not able to walk, for that there were no surgeons to dress our wounded.' It is not clear, from what the Irishman rather ambiguously says, whether Marlborough's concern for the 'gentlemen' indicates that he was just getting the wounded officers off the field, rather than the common soldiers. The Gendarmerie, among whose fallen Drake was languishing, were comprised exclusively of gentlemen, and that is perhaps the reason for the Duke's use of the expression. Drake subsequently underwent some fairly harrowing treatment for his wounds:

The surgeon went immediately about it, and found it a pretty hard task. The blood that ran from my wounds spread all over my body, and stuck as close as if my shirt and skin had been glued together; and notwithstanding all the pains and methods taken, with warm water, I suffered almost as much as if they had been flaying me ... One of the wounds in my head was thought by the surgeons mortal, my skull being cut open, so that the dura-matter of the brain was to be seen in dressing me.

Drake was tough, and was able to write a few weeks later that 'I grew every day stronger, and was almost quite well of my wounds, but could not yet wear a hat.'

Marlborough sent a letter on the evening of 11 September to the Secretary of State, with an account of the battle. Having mentioned Villars's advance to try and catch the advance-guard under the Prince of Hesse-Cassell, he went on to describe the audacious march of the Allied army from Tournai, the passage of the river Haine and the forming up of the armies at the woodland belt:

They sent out a detachment of four hundred horse, to observe our march, which the head of the Prince of Hesse's troops attacked, and took the Colonel who commanded them, with the Lieutenant-Colonel, and several other officers, and about fifty prisoners. Upon notice of our army's lying on this side the Hayne, the enemy stretched out the line, from Quievrain to the right, which they continued to do the next day [9 September], and yesterday they possessed themselves of the wood of Dour [Sars] and Blaugies [Lanières], where they immediately began to entrench. This motion of the enemy kept our army for two nights under arms; and, in the evening, as soon as the twenty one battalions and four squadrons [Withers's column], we were expecting from Tournai, were come within reach, it was resolved to attack them, and the necessary dispositions being made, we accordingly began at eight this morning. The fight was maintained with great obstinacy until near twelve o'clock, before we could force their entrenchments, and drive them out of the wood into the plain, where their horse was all drawn up, and ours advancing upon them, the whole army engaged, and fought with great fury until past three in the afternoon, when the enemy's horse began to give way, and to retire towards Mauberge and Valenciennes, and part of them towards Condé. We pursued them to the defile by Bavai, with great slaughter, all our troops behaving themselves, with the greatest courage. We are now encamped on the field of battle. You may believe our loss must have been very great on both sides. We have a good number of officers prisoners, but as I send this express by Lieutenant-Colonel Graham, who carries a letter to the Queen, I must refer you to my next for farther particulars. p.s. I had almost forgotten to tell you that we took St Ghislain yesterday [10 September] sword in hand, and made the garrison, consisting of two hundred men, prisoners of war.

The Duke's account, quite reasonably, does not specify the number of the casualties, for these could not yet be fully known. He does, though, rather inflate the account of prisoners taken. Marshal Boufflers, in the meantime, was in camp at Quesnoy, writing to Louis XIV to explain the result of the day's bloody fighting:

> The Marshal de Villars has, this day, received a considerable wound; but the surgeons say, there is no danger. It is a great affliction to me, Sir, that I am unfortunately obliged, to send you the news of the loss of a new battle; but I can assure Your Majesty, never was misfortune attended with greater glory. All Your Majesty's troops have acquired the greatest reputation, as well for the valour, as for their firmness and obstinacy. All the Marshal de Villars's dispositions were entirely good, and the best that could be made by the most accomplished and experienced general. He behaved himself, in the action, with all imaginable bravery and activity, and besides his good example, gave all possible good orders; but his valour, and want of care of his person, occasioned his wound, which was very prejudicial to the affair of this unfortunate day ... We repulsed the enemy more than three or four times, at both attacks [Wings], with incredible bravery. The Chevalier de St George [the Pretender to the English throne] behaved himself, during the whole action, with all possible bravery and vivacity. I heartily wish Your Majesty may be satisfied with my zeal and good intentions, I did all that possibly I could, to produce more happy effects.

The brave old Marshal's eulogistic phrases attracted some ridicule when they became known in London, the wags in the coffee houses making great fun of the long list of successes which Boufflers took care to recount to the King, while simultaneously having to explain away the French army's withdrawal from contact on the field of battle 'Though you have lost the field of battle you have not lost an inch of ground & etc.' Marlborough's own account of the trophies gained from the French, given to the Earl of Sunderland a couple of weeks after the battle, indicates that Villars's army had received a fair mauling in and around the woods, contradicting accounts that the French got off quite lightly:

> We find twenty-six standards, twenty colours, and four pairs of kettle-drums, with sixteen pieces of cannon. We took likewise near four hundred officers, of whom upwards of fourscore are of the household [cavalry]; most of these gentlemen being wounded were sent back upon their parole.

News of the battle was reported in *The Tatler* on 10 September (O.S.):

> We have received letters from the Duke of Marlborough's camp, which bring us further particulars of the great and glorious victory over the enemy on the eleventh instant [N.S.] The number of the wounded and prisoners is much greater than was expected from our first account. The day was doubtful until after twelve of the clock, but the enemy made little resistance after their first line on the left began to give way. An exact narration of the whole affair is expected next post. The French have two days allowed them to bury their dead, and carry off their wounded men, upon parole. Those regiments of Great Britain which suffered the most are ordered into garrison, and fresh troops commanded to march into the field. The States

have also directed troops to march out of the towns, to relieve those who lost so many men in attacking the second entrenchment of the French.

And, two days later:

> The loss of the confederates in the late battle is not exactly known, but it appears by a list transmitted to the States-General, that the number of the killed and wounded in their service amounts to above eight thousand. It is computed, that the English have lost fifteen hundred men, and the rest of the Allies above five thousand, including the wounded. The States-General have taken the most speedy and effectual measures for reinforcing their troops, and it is expected, that in eight or ten days the army will be as numerous as before the battle.

Understandably, the mood was made sombre by the awful scale of the conflict that autumn day, and Peter Drake also wrote of the wretched state of the local people he saw as he went to the rear to convalesce: 'The roads were lined all along with the poor inhabitants, begging from the army, which I thought as shocking a sight as ever I saw.'

That the Allied army had bought its victory at Malplaquet at a severe price was beyond question, and Orkney wrote that 'I never saw the like, particularly where the Dutch Guards attacked.' Marlborough attracted heavy criticism for his handling of the fighting that day, some asserting that he dithered and then underestimated Villars badly. It certainly seemed that the highly competent French commanders had studied the Duke's methods and little, other than Withers's march, had come as a complete surprise to them. Still, such were the resources of the Allies, and the robust resourcefulness of the Duke's army, that within days, fresh regiments had hurried into line, losses were in the process of being made good and thinned ranks were fleshed out; with hardly a missed beat, the Duke pressed on with the siege of Mons. The soldiers on both sides had to acknowledge that the French position in the dark and dreadful woods had been exceptionally strong. Credit for the Allied achievement, in forcing Villars's army off the field, and away from the relief of Mons, was given in a wittily ironic letter written by a French officer, the Marquis de Gruignan, soon after the battle. The Marquis, drily casting barbs at the performance of both the Allied and French commanders alike, wrote:

> Eugene and Marlborough ought to be well satisfied with us during that day; since until then they had not met with resistance worthy of them. They may now say with justice that nothing can stand before them; and indeed what shall be able to stay the rapid progress of these heroes, if an army of one hundred thousand men of the best troops, strongly posted between two woods, trebly entrenched and performing their duty as well as brave men could do, were not able to stop them one day? Will you not then own with me that they surpass all the heroes of former ages.

Meanwhile, operations were pressed onwards, and Captain Parker wrote in his memoirs that 'The day after the battle Mons was invested.' This underlines the tactical superiority of the Allies, but Boufflers was once again writing to Louis XIV, on 13 September:

> Your Majesty may have seen, by my letter of the eleventh instant, the unfortunate success of the action, which happened that day; and how much glory, for Your Majesty's troops, and arms, that misfortune was attended. I may, in truth, assure you, Sir, that the glory of the day, is beyond whatever I have said, or can say to Your Majesty. They [the Allies] have been well beaten, they only acknowledge they have bought, too dear, the field of battle, which the number of their troops, infinitely superior, forced us to yield to them.

It is difficult to argue with Boufflers over this very last point, but the 'beaten' Allies, as they were described, were still pressing on with the operations against Mons, while the mauled French army lay in camp nearby doing very little about it:

> The series of misfortunes, which, for some years past, has befallen Your Majesty's arms, had so humbled the French nation, that one hardly dared to own one's self a Frenchman: but I dare assure Your Majesty, that the French name was never more in esteem, nor, perhaps, more dreaded, than it is at present, in all the confederate army. Prince Eugene, and My Lord Marlborough own, that there are, on both sides, above 25 or 26,000 men killed; at least 18 or 20,000 were of theirs, which is unanimously confirmed to me, not only by all such of our officers, who, being prisoners, have been sent back, with much courtesy; but by several expresses [messengers] I have sent into their army; and even by Mr Sheldon, a Brigadier, who was taken prisoner, near Bossu, doing his duty with valour, at the head of 400 horse, and who was in their army, during the action.

Boufflers's rhetoric now rather ran away with itself and he could not resist paying himself a swift compliment: 'They speak with admiration of our fine retreat, of our good disposition, and the boldness with which it was made. They say, they have acknowledged in this action the ancient Frenchmen, and find they only want to be well led.' The Marshal had to admit to his sovereign, all the same, that the Allied campaign was moving forwards, apparently unhindered and undaunted by either their losses or the proximity of the French army:

> The enemy's army marched yesterday [12 September], in the afternoon, towards Mons, which they are going to besiege. They reckon this enterprise will employ them until the latter end of this month; and that they shall undertake nothing more, after this conquest.

Louis XIV, astute as ever, appeared to dislike Boufflers's improbable optimism at this grave time, and did not consult the old Marshal when filling the officer vacancies in the army caused by the casualties in the recent battle. The rebuke was very public, and compared starkly with the warm reception that the wounded Marshal Villars received when he returned to Versailles. The Duc de St Simon remembered: 'Villars was everywhere pitied and applauded, although he had lost an important battle, when it was in his power to beat the enemy in detail, and render them unable to undertake the siege of Mons, or any other siege.'

Mons was not a fortress of the size or strength of Tournai, let alone the massiveness of Lille, but its defences were carefully laid out, with water obstacles and well-sited artillery. The garrison commander, the Marquis de Grimaldi, was an accomplished veteran who could be depended on to do his best. In the immediate aftermath of the battle in the woods, the French also managed to slip some reinforcements, dragoons and infantry, into the place, before the Allied investment was complete. Marlborough wrote to London on 19 September with news of the preparations for the siege:

> The command of the siege is left to the Prince of Nassau-Frise [Orange], who will have three lieutenants-general, eight majors-general, and nine brigadiers under him, with thirty battalions, and as many squadrons to carry it on. They will take their posts tomorrow.

As was so often the case, the Duke's main concern was for the safety of the big guns of the siege train, writing four days later to the Secretary of State, on receiving news of French cavalry movements:

> We have made no great progress as yet towards our siege, for our artillery cannot set out till to-morrow from Brussels. Upon notice that M. Luxembourg was detached with a body of troops towards La Bussière, and M. Toulengen with another corps towards Condé, we have ordered out this afternoon forty squadrons to cover the march of the train, besides the escort first intended for that service. As soon as it arrives, we design immediately to break ground.

All was well, the guns arrived safely on 25 September, and the digging of trenches began that evening, but more than one anxious moment was suffered during the operations against Mons. William Cadogan was almost immediately wounded by a musket-ball during the digging of the trenches, and on 26 September Marlborough wrote to his wife in his anxiety:

> We opened last night the trenches, where poor Cadogan was wounded in the neck. I hope he will do well, but until he recovers it will oblige me to do many things, by which I shall have but little rest. I was with him this morning when they dressed his wound. We must have patience for two or three dressings before the surgeons can give their judgements. I hope in God he will do well, for I entirely depend upon him.

Marshal Berwick soon approached Mons with a strong detachment, to see if he could manoeuvre close enough to impede the siege operations. Failing in this, in early October he drew off, and the garrison was left to fight it out alone. St Simon commented on the poor state of the French soldiers with Boufflers at this time, going some way to explain their lack of success in lifting the siege:

> The men were without bread and pay; the subaltern officers were compelled to eat the regulation bread; the general officers were reduced to miserable shifts and were, like the privates, without pay ... Under these

circumstances it was found impossible to persevere in trying to save Mons. Nothing but subsistence was thought of.

The weather had turned foul, impeding the operations, and Marlborough wrote to Robert Walpole on 3 October: 'I shall not be properly well until I have a little quiet, or at least fair weather; it has been very rainy and tempestuous for several days past, which retards the advance of the siege.' A week or so later, the Duke could report that he had begun to drain the water out of the defensive ditch, and new batteries were successfully got into place.

In the end, Grimaldi was obliged to surrender on 20 October 1709, on terms negotiated over the previous few days. *The Tatler* of 19 October (O.S.) gave an account of the capitulation of the fortress:

> Letters from the Hague of the twenty-fifth of October [N.S.] advise that the garrison of Mons marched out on the twenty third instant, and a garrison of the Allies marched into the town. All the forces in the field, both of the enemy and the confederates, are preparing to withdraw into winter-quarters.

The atmosphere in Versailles was understandably gloomy at the loss of the fortress. Villars was still convalescent, and the Allied campaign ground apparently remorselessly on. Louis XIV was obliged to offer inducements to his troops at this time, described by Peter Drake, who detailed the scale of the bounties granted for wounds received in the recent battle:

> A reward for all those who received the least wound as well as the most dangerous, in manner following, viz., to every private soldier, ten livres, to every dragoon fifteen, to every trooper twenty, to the corps of carabineers twenty five livres, to the Corps of the Gens d'Armes fifty livres, and to all the household troops, eighty livres each, and in proportion to all the officers of the whole army who received the least hurt.

The impression is given that a simple foot soldier was valued at one-eighth of that of a trooper in the household cavalry. However, the scale of awards reflected the higher status, at the time, of those who fought on horseback rather than those who did so more humbly on foot, and their differing rates of pay. Also, only gentlemen, and the sons of gentlemen, could ever hope to serve in the elite of the French cavalry.

France had endured, and come through the year's campaign intact; the cold months ahead would afford another respite in which her armies could recover their strength once again. In the Allied camp also, there was little celebration. Quite apart from the heavy losses at Malplaquet, many of them veterans who had served long years with Marlborough and Eugene, and the resulting criticism, the campaign seemed to have achieved little when compared with earlier years. In London, in particular, Marlborough's influence was fading. However, despite all the doubt and difficulties, the New Year would see the Allied armies delving ever more deeply into northern France.

Chapter Ten

War of Attrition – Northern France, 1710–1713

In the spring of 1710, peace negotiations between the Grand Alliance and France continued, without moving forward very far. In February both Houses of Parliament in London, concerned that too much leeway was being allowed the French, had urged on Queen Anne the necessity that Marlborough should return to the Low Countries, both to participate in the peace talks, and to prepare for the new campaign:

> We, therefore, make it our humble request to Your Majesty that you would be pleased to order the Duke of Marlborough's immediate departure for Holland, where his presence will be equally necessary, to assist at the negotiations of peace, as to hasten the preparations for an early campaign.

To which the Queen promptly replied:

> I am so sensible of the necessity of the Duke of Marlborough's presence in Holland, at this critical juncture, that I have already given the necessary directions for his immediate departure, and I am very glad to find, by this address, that you concur with me in a just sense of the Duke of Marlborough's eminent services.

Once in the field, Marlborough turned his attention to those French fortresses to the south of Lille and Tournai. To take these places was a necessary preliminary to any grander campaign, thrusting deep into northern France; their elimination would reduce the threat to the lines of supply and communication of the Allied army as it moved forwards. The first town to be attempted was Douai on the Scarpe river for, once that was taken, the French defensive posture would be split into two, and the Duke could then turn either eastwards to Bouchain and Cambrai, or westwards to Ypres and Arras, as he saw fit.

On 14 April 1710 Marlborough, as was often the case at the commencement of operations, wrote to his wife of his misgivings for the prospects for the coming months:

I am very sorry to tell you that the behaviour of the French looks as if they have no other desire than that of carrying on the war. I hope God will be pleased to bless this campaign, for I see nothing else that can give us peace, either at home or abroad. I am so discouraged at everything I see, that I have never, during this war, gone into the field with so heavy a heart as I do this time.

Four days later, the Duke was able to report to the Duchess the steady gathering of his army at Tournai: 'I came to this place yesterday and tomorrow we shall have good part of the army together, so that by Monday [20th] which is the post day, I may be able to give you some account of the dispositions of the enemy.' When that letter was sent, he was also able to tell of a small initial success, on 20 April: 'The post being obliged to go this afternoon, I have nothing more to write, but that we have forced the enemy to surrender Mortagne. I hope we shall be able to march this night, so as to be able to be at the enemy's lines tomorrow.' That town had been bypassed by the Allied army on its march from Tournai to Mons, and the small untidiness had now been put right.

Those French lines of defence were guarded by 20 cavalry squadrons and 40 battalions of infantry, under the command of Marquis d'Montesquiou (formerly the Comte d'Artagnan, defender of the French right flank at Malplaquet). Marlborough expected him to make a stout defence, with potential for heavy losses on both sides, but as the Duke's army began its move forward, the French were taken off guard. The approaches to Douai were secured, and the Scarpe river was safely passed without serious fighting. Marlborough wrote to the Duchess from Lens on 21 April:

I hope this happy beginning will produce such success this campaign as must put an end to the war. I bless God for putting it into their heads not to defend their lines; for at Pont de Vendin, where I passed [the Scarpe], the Marechal d'Artagnan, was with 20,000 men, which, if he had stayed, must have made it very doubtful ... The excuse the French make is that we came four days before they expected us.

A further success could be reported the following evening: 'This day we have again obliged the French army to quit the Scarpe, so that tomorrow we shall invest the town of Douai, and then we must give some rest to the poor soldiers.' That civilities between the two armies remained a commonplace occurrence, despite the occasional bitterness of the fighting, is shown by one of Peter Drake's comments at this time: 'The officers and soldiers of each army used to walk down to their respective sides of the [Scarpe] river, and converse friendly together.'

By 24 April, Marlborough and Eugene had invested the fortress and shouldered Montesquiou's army aside in the process. Work on the long lines of circumvallation was begun on the following day, and completed three days later. The Marquis d'Albergotti, now fully recovered from his injury received when he fell from his horse at Malplaquet, was in command of the garrison.

Robert Parker, once more serving in Flanders, remembered the Marquis as 'A brave old experienced officer.' He was indeed a bold and resourceful leader, with nearly 8,000 veteran troops under him. Douai was a formidable obstacle to overcome, and d'Albergotti had the support of a strongly held outpost to the main defences of the town, in the shape of Fort Scarpe, from where the sluice gates for the river could be controlled, and the surrounding meadows flooded, almost at will. Still, Montesquiou's lack of energy with the covering army enormously assisted Marlborough in the preparations for the siege.

As in earlier operations, the difficulty in bringing forward the big siege guns delayed matters, but the trenches were opened by the toiling soldiers on 5 May. A severe setback was suffered on the night of 7 May, when the French garrison mounted a vigorous sortie, commanded by the Duc de Montemar. The trenches were surprised and two Allied regiments scattered in confusion; it took heavy fighting before the garrison were forced back into their defences. Two days later the long-awaited siege train trundled into the Allied camp – 200 heavy guns, of which no less than 80 were the big 24-pounders.

It was another two weeks before Marshal Villars had assembled his field army, near to Cambrai, in order to seriously challenge Marlborough's bid for Douai. The effects of the Marshal's leg wound undoubtedly played a part in this delay, and Louis XIV, understanding this, sent Marshal Berwick to assist Villars in the arrangements. Robert Parker said of the confrontation between the armies:

> He [Villars] seemed determined to give the Duke battle, and began to cannonade us with great fury, and this brought Prince Eugene from the siege, with as many men as could be spared. The cannonading continued until night, at which he retired out of reach of gun-shot and stood there, looking at us.

Not surprisingly, Berwick soon found his attachment to Villars's army a rather arid appointment, and when he found that Douai was likely to fall, got himself transferred elsewhere. In the meantime, the French commander feinted towards the Scheldt river, hoping to draw the Allies off, and then moved back towards Arras, looking for a chance to push reinforcements into Douai. He succeeded in neither, but the complex manoeuvring between the two armies continued for some days. Marlborough wrote to his wife, in rather weary tones, on 29 May 1710:

> The continual motions of the French army have given me very little rest for these last two nights, so that as soon as I have despatched the post I shall go to bed, in hopes of getting five or six hours' sleep; for as Marshal de Villars is now camped, I shall be obliged, for some time, to be on horseback at break of day.

However, by 1 June, Villars had concluded that the Allied army's position was too strong to be assaulted, and the next day Marlborough wrote to Sidney Godolphin: 'The Marshal made his dispositions, and marched with a resolution to attack us; but when he had viewed and seen the strength of our camp, by the advice of his generals, he camped where he now is.' Captain Robert Parker wrote of the operations against the town:

> Albergotti made a gallant defence, and disputed every inch of ground with us. He also made a great many desperate sallies, which played off a number of men on both sides. However, after a siege of eight weeks, he capitulated, and surrendered both the town and Fort Scarpe.

The submission to Marlborough came late in the month. The Comte de Merode-Westerloo heard the news and wrote later: 'While I was still at table an officer of my regiment arrived bearing tidings of the surrender of Douai on 25 June.' The cost had been very heavy – some 8,000 casualties suffered by the Allies, while 3,000 of the garrison were killed or wounded. Meanwhile, the Duke pressed ahead with the campaign, as Parker goes on to tell:

> After the surrender of Douai, our generals advanced up to Villars, to try if he would stand a battle; but he thought fit to retire behind the Sensée [river], where he secured his army, and at the same time prevented us from laying siege to Arras. Upon this we invested Bethune.

The operations against Bethune, begun on 5 July 1710, were conducted with the assistance of Peter Drake, who had recovered his health and chosen, once again, to take service with the Allies. Short of cash as usual, he volunteered for a hazardous labouring task under a Captain St Clair:

> I was told that he was the captain of the volunteers; that all those people engaged themselves voluntarily to go down to the trenches, to place gabions, a service that none was commanded on, but such as went of their own accord were received and paid a crown for every gabion they placed. My money growing short, I thought it a favourable opportunity to replenish my pockets; so without the least hesitation I entered volunteer service with Captain St Clair. That very night I went with him to the trenches before Bethune. I had the good fortune to place eleven gabions without receiving the least hurt, though a good many men were wounded, and several lost their lives. For this one night's service, I received eleven crowns and returned by three the next morning.

Such ready money was understandably welcome to the soldiery, but these arrangements did not always proceed smoothly, and shortages of equipment and materiel were apparent in the besiegers' camp. Marlborough wrote to Colonel Ross on 24 August 1710 with an instruction to get his dragoons out into the countryside to cut wood:

> I have an account that M. Schulemburg is at present retarded in his attack by want of fascines, and that the corps he has with him will not be able to provide a sufficient number by the time he will have occasion to employ them. I desire therefore that you will be assisting to him in this service,

which will be no great fatigue to your men, and I need not tell you they will be paid for it.

The following day, the Duke wrote to the Secretary of State in London, and, after commenting on the lack of fascines in parts of the siege-works, went on:

M. Fagel sends me word that he has made another lodgement on the salient angle of the counterscarp, before the bastion of St. Ignace; that he has taken a good quantity of powder out of the enemy's mines, and that he was making preparations to batter the main body of the place. We had yesterday some small advantage over the enemy here. They had sent out a good body of their horse to fall upon the Prince of Savoy's foragers, but our men received them so well, though with scarce any other weapons than their scythes, that they obliged them to retire. We took near three hundred prisoners, with a good number of horses. The Marechal de Villars was coming with the left wing of his horse to sustain his men, but, seeing our line of horse advance, thought fit to retire.

The Allied army, as soon as operations against Bethune were concluded on 29 August, moved forward to lay siege to St Venant and Aire, on the Lys river. The French had opened the sluice gates, and the area was flooded. Kit Davies remembered:

The Prince of Orange invested St Venant on 4 September with twenty battalions; as on the same day the Prince d'Anhalt-Dessau, with forty battalions, did Aire. The drains we were obliged to make at St Venant, to carry off the water, were a great hindrance to the siege, for the trenches were not opened till the 16th, at nine at night ... Three days later our guns began to play.

Private John Deane wrote too of the drudgery of the work to drain the area about the town of Aire, so that the digging of the trenches could be commenced:

August the 28th [O.S.] there was ordered six men of a [each] company without arms and seven men of a company with arms throughout the Confederate army to march with a design to cut all the marsh ditches and waters that run near and about Aire. The which did their endeavours, and turned several of the waters another way, and drained off what waters they possibly could. On the 13th [September O.S], our folks was ordered by detachments to attack the works which was thought to be very advantageous to us. And at about one o'clock in the afternoon the attack begun, and very hot work there was until about four in the afternoon; and by that time our men had gained them both. Many men were killed on both sides.

Donald McBane also took part in the desperate assaults on the defences of St Venant, where the garrison resisted furiously, determined not to give ground:

'One night I was one of the stormers of the counterscarp and half-moon, and took it with sword in hand, the shell of a grenade wounded me sore in the side'. At about the same time, Kit Davies lost her new husband, Richard Wells, as a result of one of these attacks on St Venant. His wound seemed not to be dangerous at first:

> The English being commanded to attack the counter-scarp, my husband, who was unjustly forced to do another man's duty, being in the front rank, received a musket-ball in his thigh ... I knew nothing was more dangerous for him than to catch cold, as it was commonly fatal, wherefore I stripped off my clothes to my stays and under-petticoat to cover him up warm, and his comrades carried him to the [communications] trench where Mr White, the surgeon, who searched and dressed his wound, said it was but slight, but the next day, finding the bone broken, judged it mortal. When St Venant had surrendered [30 September] our wounded men were carried to the army at Aire, before which town the Prince d'Anhalt-Dessau [had] opened the trenches in two places on the 12th of September, at night ... The stony ground, the great rains we had this autumn, and the brave defence the besieged made, contributed to the length and difficulty of the siege. The garrison disputed the ground inch by inch.

Davies goes on to describe the surrender of the fortress on 11 October 1710, after which:

> We were ordered into winter-quarters, and our wounded men was sent to the hospital at Lille where my husband grew daily worse, had his wound often laid open; but at length it turned to a mortification, and in ten week's time after he received it, carried him off.

The doughty sutleress had had enough of seeing her men-folk killed, and she did not marry again while she remained with the army.

St Venant was a second-rate fortress and unable to stand very long against a proper siege. That garrison having capitulated, all attention could then be turned to Aire, a more formidable proposition. Marlborough wrote on 1 October 'The siege of St Venant being happily accomplished, we shall now pursue that of Aire, with the greater vigour.' Delays in bringing up powder and ordnance (at least one convoy was destroyed in a French raid, much to Marlborough's annoyance), and heavy rain, hampered the operations; Robert Parker described the incident:

> While we lay at this siege, provisions happened to fall short, for a party from Ypres destroyed our boats laden with provisions and stores, as they were coming up the Lys. The country about Aire is indeed noted for its produce of all sorts of grain; but the enemy had removed it out of our reach.

John Deane wearily wrote of the protracted and expensive operations against the town:

On Wednesday morning the 20th of September [O.S.] at 2 o'clock the enemy sallied out of Aire again, but our men was ready for them and maintained the trenches and beat them off with great loss. Our folks having now raised two new batteries nearer the town, made sad rattling work among them which disturbed the enemy sorely. On the 20th and 21st our folks at the siege of Aire battered very hard upon an out-sconce [redoubt], or fort that the enemy had made without the town, and did damage to it but could not yet take it; and on the 22nd of September at 6 o'clock in the morning our folks made an attempt to attack it with a strong detachment … They found a deep water between them; and the enemy received them very boldly and killed twenty three officers and killed and wounded forty men. And our men run for shelter to a brick kiln, hardly there but the enemy followed them and chased them out there hence home to our works again.

The fighting continued for several more weeks, and slowly the besiegers' efforts wore down the resolve of the garrison. But, Deane remembered:

On the 17th [October O.S.] a great part of the garrison of Aire sallied out and did beat our men from the trenches for a while at a sad rate, and was very near taking a battery of our guns which they designed to have nailed up [spiked]. And their spade and shovel men was as busy a throwing down our works as could be; while at last our battalions hardly turned out upon them and drove them home helter-skelter; and a great many men was killed on both sides at this attack.

The Duke commented on the awful conditions for the troops in one of his letters to Sidney Godolphin: 'Our poor men are up to the knees in mud and water, which is a most grevious sight, and will occasion great sickness.' Despite such trials, the French garrison, ably commanded by the Marquis de Goesbriand, surrendered on 8 November 1710. The Duke paid a compliment to their gallant conduct: 'The garrison of Aire marched out yesterday 3,628 strong, leaving upwards of 1,600 men sick and wounded in the town. This defence was the best we have seen this year. Our foot are weak, but our horse are in a very good condition.' The capture of the two fortresses had been achieved at heavy cost to the Allies, some 7,000 killed and wounded excluding those who had fallen sick in the flooded trenches. It was as if a major battle had been fought in open field, and yet relatively little ground had been taken. The French had, again, succeeded in stalling the Allied advance deep in their fortress belt, and rather wearily the troops in the opposing armies went off to winter quarters, while Marlborough returned to face renewed troubles in London.

The Comte de Merode-Westerloo commented acidly on the way that the Allied campaign had been waged in 1710. 'We must not overlook the great number of men lost at these sieges, which were so utterly useless for the prosecution of the overall design that our leaders claimed to be pursuing.' There is more than a grain of truth in his comments, but he ignored the necessity for Marlborough to clear out the French fortress belt before moving deeper into France, and the strength of those same fortresses. Quite what different strategy the Comte would have pursued, with Villars resolute in refusing to give the Allies battle in the open, despite the repeated loss of valuable territory, and cherished fortresses, the Comte does not go on to say.

In the early spring of 1711 Marlborough took the field at the head of some 120,000 men, facing Marshal Villars's army, which stood behind the formidable defensive Lines of Non (Ne) Plus Ultra (Nothing Further is Possible – said to be a quip made by Marshal Villars's tailor, when asked to let out his breeches, although some reports ascribe the comment to Marlborough's valet, when viewing a coat of particularly dashing cut) reaching all the way from the Channel coast to Valenciennes.

The death from smallpox of Emperor Joseph on 17 April 1711, and the complex diplomatic procedures required to secure the election of Archduke Charles (otherwise Charles III of Spain), required Prince Eugene's presence in Vienna. In the meantime it was necessary for a substantial contingent of Imperial troops to move to the upper Rhine, to reassure the German princes of the Empire in this period of transition. So, on 13 June, a hot day, the Duke had to bid his good friend and comrade farewell – they would not meet again while Marlborough commanded the Allied armies. Despite this significant loss of strength, made worse by the detachment of five British battalions on a futile expedition to Newfoundland, Marlborough was quite willing to engage the French, should Villars accept battle. Louis XIV, however, had given instructions to the Marshal not to do so, appreciating that time was, it seemed certain, on the side of the French.

Marlborough, meanwhile, had turned his attention in particular to the strong French fortress at Bouchain, at the junction of the Sensée and Escaut (Scheldt) rivers. To take this place was a formidable task; not only was it a Vauban masterpiece sheltered by the French defensive lines, but the Duke would also have to contend with the activities of the more numerous French field army. Villars could be depended on to exert all his skills to prevent the fall of Bouchain. An indication of the difficulties that the French commander could throw in Marlborough's way, particularly in impeding the valuable use of the waterways in the area, is given in a letter the Duke wrote to Henry St John on 14 May 1711. The French garrison in Valenciennes had recently raided a convoy on the Scarpe, destroying several valuable laden barges and inflicting heavy losses on the escort. They now tried to lower the water levels around Douai, as Marlborough explained to the Secretary of State, Henry St John:

> The enemy having made two dams in the Senset [Sensée] near Arleux to overflow the borders of the river and stop the waters coming to Doauy, on Monday I ordered a detachment of three hundred foot covered with four hundred horse, to open the dams, which they did and returned in the night to the camp [near to Douai]; so that the water has now its free course; the enemy fired upon our men with three pieces of cannon for upwards of three hours, without doing them the least harm. Twenty squadrons of horse and six battalions of foot are ordered to encamp

between St Amand and Mortagne, to cover the men employed in clearing the Scarpe of the boats that were burnt and sunk the other day by the enemy; in three or four days we hope the river will be navigable again.

And, a few days later, in another letter to St John:

We have cleared the Scarpe of the late accident, and the boats now come up that river as formerly. We had a great convoy of boats with artillery and ammunition come up the Lys last week from Ghent; they arrived safely as far as the Pont Rouge and have continued their passage under a good escort towards Bethune, St Venant and Aire, being designed for those garrisons.

The French continued to be active, delaying and disturbing Marlborough's preparations, and the waterways, so vital to the provisioning of the Allied army, presented an inviting target. Later in May the Duke wrote to London:

The [French] garrison of Ypres marched out on Monday night, to the number of about four thousand men, commanded by Lieutenant-General Villars, brother to the Marechal. They came early on Tuesday morning to Harlebeck, and after three repulses made themselves masters of a small fort that covers the sluices which by the treaty of Contributions are to be protected. They burned part of the timbers of the sluices, and then retired with precipitation, being apprehensive of being cut off in their return by the Prince of Holstein, who upon the first notice, marched with the garrison of Lille and Menin and a detachment of horse to intercept them, but came too late; the damage is so little that we hope to have it repaired in four or five days. Yesterday the right of the army made a general forage on the borders of the Senset and the Scheldt, close to Bouchain, in sight of the enemy's army, without the least hindrance.

Marlborough went on to discuss the niceties of prisoner exchanges at this point in the war:

There is a proposal for the exchange of M. Chambrier, a Swiss brigadier in the States' service who was made prisoner at the burning of the boats the other day on the Scarpe, against M. Greder, a Swiss brigadier in the French service, but the latter being the Queen's prisoner [that is, taken by British troops], I would do nothing in it without knowing first H.M's pleasure.

To get at Bouchain, Marlborough's first task was to get past the Lines of Non Plus Ultra, if possible, without fighting a major battle to do so. To achieve this he employed a subtle and complex ruse, commencing on 6 July, by having Jorgen Rantzau seize the French fortified post forward of the village of Arleux on the Scarpe river. The Duke then strengthened the fort, but moved his main force elsewhere and apparently negligently left this minor conquest ill-garrisoned. After an initial rebuff, Villars recovered the fort on 11 July; the report in the Paris press of this assault ran:

The enemy having taken the redoubt of Arleux, defended by seventy men, and the mill, in which were only fifteen men, separated from the French Army by impracticable morasses, they worked for three weeks together, to put them into such a posture, that they could not be attacked but by a formal siege. They erected a very good fort, surrounded by three ditches which covered three several works, linked with pallisades, and put a garrison of 500 men in it, under Colonel Savary, with ten pieces of cannon; and a great quantity of ammunition, besides 130 in the mill … The [French] troops under the command of Count d'Estain, the Marquis de Coigny, and the Prince d'Isenghien marched, with so much diligence and secrecy that the post was invested, the 23rd at break of day, before the enemy had notice of the design. The besieged defended themselves very bravely, and yet the mill and the fort were taken by storm, at one, in the afternoon, and the garrison made prisoners of war, as a reprisal for the like treatment made to the French, when the Allies took that post. The officers and soldiers showed an extraordinary valour, wading through the ditches up to their middle.

Exasperated at these seemingly pointless skirmishes, well away from the main armies, the French commander then demolished the post and withdrew his troops to the southern side of the river. The loss of this forward salient, useful in giving warning of any Allied approach to the causeway crossing point at Arleux, seemed of little importance, as Marlborough had by this time also concentrated his army well to the westwards, on the plain of Lens beyond Vimy ridge. He appeared to have lost interest in the place, apart from publicly expressing some chagrin at Villars's apparent success in recovering the fort. However, should Arleux be threatened at a future point, there seemed to be no difficulty in marching back to reinforce the spot in good time; Villars in the meantime prepared to mount a cavalry raid into Brabant, so secure did he feel within his fortified lines.

Marlborough now made preparations to mount a frontal attack on the French lines from the plain of Lens, and everyone expected to fight a battle just as bloody as Malplaquet. Peter Drake wrote of the preparations for action:

There were sixteen fine villages along the front of our army between us and the French lines, which his Grace ordered to be burned and levelled, which was done, and in three days became as even as any part of the plain. This finished, the Duke ordered a great number of fascines to be made, and laid at the front of our camps. By all these preparations it appeared manifest to the whole army, even to the senior officers, that we should soon attack the enemy's lines, which must have cost much blood. Marshal Villars was making all his dispositions to give us a warm reception.

Adam Cardonnel wrote in the evening of 3 August to a friend about the impending operations:

We have marched two days to come near the enemy, and are now but two small leagues from them. Monsieur de Villars has assembled all the troops he could, and our advices even say that the garrisons of Ypres and St Omer are in march to join him. Nevertheless, we may probably attempt to force his Lines, before two days are at an end, all possible preparations being made for that end. Though the weather is not the most favourable, it having rained continually today, from noon to this hour.

Suddenly, in the early hours of 5 August 1711, the Allied soldiers were roused from their sleep and set marching eastwards through the night towards Arleux. A cavalry detachment, held in reserve near Tournai under command of Graf Reynard van Hompesch, was already hurrying ahead to secure the crossing place. The French army commander, taken completely by surprise, could merely try to catch up, scrambling to get his sleepy soldiers on the march as best he could.

By mid-afternoon, and 39 miles of hard marching later, Marlborough's army was pouring across the causeway at Arleux, watched only by the French Marshal and his small cavalry escort, who were quite unable to hinder them. This party was soon driven off by Marlborough's cavalry, and the road to Bouchain was now open. Parker wrote of the dazzling exploit:

> To our great joy, orders came along both lines, to strike our tents, and form our regiments with all dispatch imaginable; and in less than an hour, the whole army was on a full march to the left. We continued marching all night, being favoured by the light of a bright full moon, and fine calm weather. A little before day [5th August] the Duke being at the head of the march, an express arrived from General Cadogan, signifying that he and General Hompesch had passed the causeway of Arleux without opposition, between twelve and one that morning, and that they were in possession of the enemy's lines. As our foot was marching over the plain before Arras, the front of their [the French] horse appeared upon the rising ground on the other side of the Sensee [river]; but their foot was a great way behind. The front of their horse, and the foremost of our foot, marched in fair view of each other, sometimes within half cannon-shot ... had not the Sensee and the morass been between us, we could not have avoided coming to blows with them.

The troops were too busy marching to exchange shots or insults with each other, and so he goes on 'Our regiment passed over at Arleux about four in the afternoon. Thus did the Duke of Marlborough carry the Marshal's lines by dint of art and stratagem only, and without the loss of a man.' Marlborough gave his own account of the hugely successful operation in a letter to Henry St John, on 6 August 1711:

> You will have seen by my former letters I have been for some time meditating the passage of the enemy's lines. It was with that view I marched from Cote to Rebreuve and Viler Brulin, to draw the Maréchal de Villars with all his troops that way, while I was taking measures to pass on this side, having to that purpose left a good garrison at Douay and a

detachment of horse and foot with our baggage near Bethune; these, with five battalions I drew out of Lille, Tournay, and St Armand, formed a corps of twenty-three battalions and seventeen squadrons, who rendezvoused on Tuesday in the evening near Douay, under the command of General Hompesch, where Mr Cadogan and Lieutenant-General Murray likewise joined them when it began to be dark. These troops marched to Arleux, and passed at break of day without any opposition; the whole army marched likewise this way as soon as it was dark, and about nine in the morning I joined our detachment with the horse of our left, the rest of the army followed, and after marching twenty-four hours with great cheerfulness, and without halting, were all passed last night, and, as they arrived, drew up in order of battle. The Maréchal de Villars soon took the alarm, and marched likewise with great diligence most part of the night, hoping to have prevented us. Almost as soon as I got hither he appeared with the head of his army, and immediately put a hundred dragoons into the castle of Oisy, a musket-shot from this place, who were all made prisoners, and apprehending we were already too strong for him to attempt anything with the troops he had with him, he encamped at Marquion, where he had his quarters within half a league of part of our camp, extending himself from thence to Cambray, having a rivulet and a morass between us. He gave out he would attack us this morning, which made me defer writing till this afternoon. I had the army drawn out to receive him, and it were to have been wished he had done it, since we are now stronger by the detachments drawn from our garrisons, and which must soon be sent back, than it will be possible for us to be any part of the remaining campaign, but I suppose he must expect orders from court before he can attempt anything. This surprise will be the more mortifying, since you may remember the Maréchal some time ago assured the King he had taken such precautions for preserving all his lines, and was so confident of his superiority that he offered to send a third detachment to the Upper Rhine, if it was thought proper. I dispatch this by Brigadier Sutton by the way of Ostend, to give H.M. the earliest account of our success, and must pray leave to refer you to him. You may be assured nothing shall be left un-attempted that may tend to improve this advantage. If the enemy decline a battle, which in that case it will be impossible for us to give, I design to besiege Bouchain; in the meantime this success must give a great reputation to H.M.'s arms in all parts.

St John's reply, sent on 11 August 1711, was suitably appreciative. A number of letters had recently arrived from the Duke, but the account of the breaking the lines caught all his attention:

We had been this evening so agreeably surprised by the arrival of Brigadier Sutton, that you must pardon us if we could give no great attention to any accounts but those which he brought. My Lord Stair had indeed opened to us the several steps which your Grace intended to take in order to pass the enemy's lines in one part or the other; it was, however, hard to imagine, and too much to hope, that a plan which consisted of so many parts, wherein so many different corps were to co-operate together, should entirely succeed, and no one article fail of what Y.G. had projected. I most heartily congratulate with Y.G. on this great event, of which no more need I think be said than that you have obtained, without losing a man, such an advantage as we should have bought with the expense of several thousand lives, and have reckoned ourselves gainers.

Prince Eugene, still detained with the Imperial troops on the Rhine, was also delighted at the news of his friend's much needed success: 'No person takes a greater interest in your concerns than myself; your highness has penetrated into the ne plus ultra. I hope the siege of Bouchain will not last long.'

This subtle and imaginative scheme, passing the formidable French lines of defence at no cost, was a significant tactical achievement, made sweet by the evident and very public bafflement of Marshal Villars. The passage of such a formidable obstacle might have been expected, quite legitimately, to be an expensive business. Badly out-manoeuvred, Villars now drew up his field army into formation at Bourlon Wood and offered battle, but Marlborough was not to be drawn into a premature engagement, particularly as his infantry were weary from their forced march – some men had dropped down fainting with exhaustion on the way. This decision attracted some derision from the Duke's critics, apparently oblivious to the French superiority in numbers and their strongly held position, but he wrote with rare dismissiveness of their prattling: 'I despair of being ever able to please all men. Those who are capable of judging will be satisfied with my endeavours: others I leave to their own reflections, and go on with the discharge of my duty.'

On 7 August Marlborough marched towards Cambrai as if to give battle to Villars, and then turned quickly aside and crossed the Scheldt river on newly laid pontoon bridges to invest Bouchain. This manoeuvre, drawing up to the French and then moving away, neatly masked them from access to the river, preventing Villars from laying his own pontoon bridges in good time to move across and hamper the investment of the town. The complexities of prosecuting such an ambitious operation as this siege, when faced with an enemy army in superior numbers in close proximity, are well shown in a letter written by the Duke to Henry St John, a week or so later:

Since my last, we have carried our lines of circumvallation down to the Senset [Sensée], whereby we have, in a great measure, cut off the enemy's communications with the town on that side; they are now practising a new way with fascines in the morass, covered by willows, between that river and the Scheldt, which we are hard at work to prevent, and hope we may be able to succeed by tomorrow night. We had this morning two Deputies come out of the town to pray we would favour the buildings all that is possible in the siege. They inform us the enemy have increased the garrison to nine battalions, besides a detachment of six hundred Swiss, which is more than it was thought could have been necessary for the defence of the place.

The continued importance to the allied army of the use of the waterways, an asset so badly lacking in the siege of Lille three years earlier, remains very evident; for Marlborough went on in his letter:

> We have a convoy of upwards of a hundred boats come up the Scheldt from Sas to Tournay, with artillery and ammunition. The same escort is to return for a further store. p.s. Colonel Kerr received a contusion last night in the leg from a cannon ball from the town, but I hope he will soon be well again.

The same day, Marlborough had to write and beg a favour from the French commander, illustrating the niceties that existed between opposing generals in certain matters. The Duke wrote in courtly fashion to Villars:

> My son-in-law, the Duke of Montague, having many affairs calling him to spend some time in England, it would give me great pleasure if you will have the goodness to send me a passport for him to be able to go from the army of Holland to Ostend, with his escort and servants.

The Marshal, who was in just as much need of such polite concessions for his own staff when travelling about, no doubt complied with this request.

Villars was, however, still smarting at the humiliation of having been fooled at the breaking of the Lines of Non Plus Ultra. Being then unable to prevent Marlborough, despite his marked superiority in numbers, from closing up to Bouchain, he had put it about that the movements of his own army had been hampered by heavy rain and poor fields of observation. Marlborough rebutted these assertions in a letter he sent from the 'Camp before Bouchain' to the Imperial Court in Vienna, on 30 August 1711:

> Not a drop of rain fell on the army during the whole day, not until night [the weather having changed during the evening, the troops were drenched with rain], that our bridges were made over the Scheldt at eleven in the morning, and the army was on the march by two in the afternoon, the greater part having passed before dark.

As the two armies squared up to one another through the latter part of August, and shifted this way and that, each trying to find an advantage over their opponent, Peter Drake found himself cut off from his comrades:

> Towards the night the [Allied] army seemed to divide, some marching one way, and some another. I was ordered to keep in the rear, and not let any men loiter, but bring up all stragglers. On this service, the night being

dark, I lost the line of march, not knowing for above two hours where I was going with thirty men of different regiments I had picked up. At last, I saw some brisk firing at a pretty good distance, ... I came up to the place, and found some of the Dutch forces were beginning to throw up some work between them and the French, who on their part were endeavouring to prevent it. This detachment was commanded by Brigadier Collier, a Scotch officer in the States of Holland's service. To him I went, told him how and what happened to me; that I brought thirty men I had picked up; that we were come to put ourselves under his protection and receive his orders. He instantly assigned us a post under the command of a major, where we did our part in defending the work.

With daylight breaking, Drake was free to seek out his own regiment, but took the sensible precaution to get a docket from Collier, explaining his valuable service in helping to defend the Dutch redoubt that night: 'When I returned to my regiment I was closely examined where I had been all night; I told the Colonel, and showed him my certificate [from Collier], at which he told me he was well pleased at the testimony I gave of my good behaviour.'

Despite the French commander's best endeavours, the Allied siege of Bouchain – 'An upper and lower town, the latter defended by a huge horn-work' – was vigorously pressed in awful conditions. On occasions the infantry went into the attack waist-deep in water, for much of the surrounding country was inundated. In one particularly spectacular feat, a 24-gun battery was constructed in a single night by 5,000 toiling workmen opposite Wavrechin hill, with no attempt by the French to interrupt the work. Marlborough's Chief of Engineers, Colonel John Armstrong, was the mastermind behind this effort, and by the end of August an impressive 30 miles of entrenchments had been constructed for the siege. The operations were fiercely contested, and Peter Drake tells us, in commendably phlegmatic tones, of two narrow escapes he had while serving in the trenches. As he stood one day beside some senior officers near the works he wrote that:

A drake shot, otherwise a four pounder, being fired from the town tore a hand's breadth off the brigadier's boot, and blew four or five buttons off Colonel Pocock's spatterdash, broke four legs of four grenadiers of his regiment, but did no further mischief; the brigadier fell, and though his skin was not tore, nor his blood spilt, yet he was near losing his leg, and was ever after lame ... That very night, being sent by the general to order one of the engineers to come to him ... When I came within twenty paces of the engineer, a mine was sprung; whereupon he, with all that were about him, were blown up, and I flung down by the blast, and almost covered with earth, which fell like a heavy shower, but I thank God I received no hurt; I then went to my duty on parade.

Marshal Villars was not inactive by any means, and he sent a strong force of cavalry on a raid towards the Allied encampment, causing some alarm and damage, but this did not seriously interrupt Marlborough's progress. A week or so later, the Comte de Villars (the French commander's son) led a force of 5,000 horse and foot towards Douai, attempting to draw off the Allied army from the siege, but Marlborough refused to take alarm. Cadogan was sent with a strong detachment to intercept the raid, and the Comte had to scramble back within the French lines of defence to avoid being cut off. Marlborough had a firm grip on the operations against Bouchain, and on 11 September an Allied storming party captured a detached bastion in the lower town. Robert Parker saw the Duke, very close to the trenches, at this time: 'He stayed only three or four minutes, and then rode back. We were in pain for him while he stayed, lest the enemy might have discovered him, and fired at him; in which case they could not well have missed.'

Two days later the garrison could do no more. Attempts by Villars to maintain communications between his army and the fortress had failed. Marlborough announced his success at Bouchain in a letter to his friend, Sidney Godolphin, written the following day, 12 September:

> I am sure you will be very well pleased with the good news I send by Collins of our being masters of Bouchain, and that the marshal de Villars has done us the honour of being our witness of the garrison being made prisoners of war. They consist of eight battalions and 500 Swiss. The French, notwithstanding their superiority, burn all their forage in their power, in order to make our subsistence difficult.

The subsidiary comment, concerning forage, is a reminder of the ever-pressing need to provide for the huge numbers of horses with any army on campaign at the time, and the fact that there is more than one way to engage in a war. A commander may fight battles and take towns, but he has to feed his army, whether on two legs or four, each and every day without fail, or all will fall to pieces in the end.

A Dutch officer, writing to a friend about his part in the siege operations against Bouchain shortly after the surrender, described the conduct of the French, both the garrison and the field army, in rather dismissive terms:

> We are at last masters of Bouchain; the siege has been short, but very bright. The garrison was numerous, and wanted nothing; it was supported by the French army: and yet, in the sight of a hundred thousand fighting men, who endeavoured to relieve them, they were made prisoners of war ... A gun was not shot, but the Marshal de Villars saw the smoke, or heard the report of it. He tried and attempted all possible ways to force or surprise us; and if, at our passing of the Lines [of Non Plus Ultra] he forgot himself awhile, he seemed afterwards to have gathered all his vigour; recalled his pristine vigilance, and recovered his former genius and spirit, to revenge himself on my Lord Duke. But all his vivacity, all his spite, availed him nothing.

Marlborough's army lost little more then 4,000 men killed and wounded (rather more than at the startling victory of Oudenarde in 1708) in the whole vast operation, while about 3,000 of the garrison became casualties, and a similar number were taken prisoner. The Comte de Ravignau, the commander of Bouchain, and 229 of his officers, were among those taken, with twenty-four regimental standards and colours.

There now arose a dispute over the finer details of the agreement to capitulate, which illuminates a part of the etiquette of siege warfare rather well. A number of French officers protested that they had only agreed to this course on the basis that they would, in recognition of the stout defence they claimed to have made of Bouchain, become prisoners upon parole, waiting only for formal exchange with Allied officers currently in French hands. Marlborough, however, regarded them as legitimate prisoners of war, who had surrendered themselves without promise of parole or exchange, after dropping earlier requests for terms, which had been refused. Their complaints of such alleged ill-usage soon reached the ears of the French army commander, and Villars wrote in protest to the Duke on 28 September 1711:

> I have been thoroughly informed, by the Count de Ravignon, and the other chief officers of the garrison of Bouchain, of their just complaints of the word and faith infringed in the capitulation granted them by Colonel de Pagnies, commander of the Dutch Guards, by Monsieur de Fagel's order. You will see, Sir, by the enclosed copy of all that passed thereupon, and of which those brave men sent the original to the King, to vindicate themselves, for not having preferred all dangers, and even death, to the shame of surrendering prisoners of war, that the word given to them has been formally broke … I don't question, Sir, but your own glory [regard for reputation] will, upon serious consideration, engage you to send back the garrison, upon the conditions that were offered them when they surrendered.

Marlborough, however, was unimpressed by this. Having conferred with Colonel de Pagnies to make sure that nothing more than was intended had been offered the French garrison, he coolly replied to Villars:

> My manner of acting on so many occasions of this nature, ought to be to the King and the whole world, as so many pledges of my upright proceeding, and I flatter myself they will do me the Justice to believe that nothing was done, in the treatment that garrison met with, contrary to the capitulation that was granted them.

Furthermore, the Duke wrote that the field commander of the siege operations, Baron Fagel, had he been allowed to have his way, would have stormed the breaches in the defensive works already made, but that 'Those gentlemen thought fit to hang out the white flag.' He went on:

> When you have seriously considered these facts, you will do me the justice that is due to my proceedings, and if necessary, inform the King, that the complaints of those gentlemen are groundless, and that what was promised them has been literally performed.

The row, which had threatened to upset the long-standing, mutually beneficial, arrangements for the parole and exchange of prisoners between the warring parties, was allowed by the French to quietly subside, but Marlborough's enemies in England seized on the incident as an example of his bad faith.

The fall of Bouchain marked almost the end of the campaign in Flanders that year, but soon after the Duke returned to London, Villars sent a detachment to break up the sluices of the rivers around Bouchain. The fresh raid, aimed once again at denying the Allied army the valuable use of the waterways to transport guns and materiel, was promptly driven off by Cadogan and the Earl of Albemarle. Shortly before the end of the year, Marlborough wrote from St James's to Albemarle, who was still conducting 'mopping up' operations before the troops went off to their quarters for the winter:

> I have received the honour of your Lordship's letter of the 20th inst. [December]. We had an account of the precipitate retreat of the enemy, which everybody allows is chiefly owing to your Lordship's great care and diligence in drawing the troops together and marching to oppose their designs. The whole I think must turn to their confusion, besides the great loss and damage sustained by assembling so great a body of men at this season of the year. I hope the mischief they did will soon be repaired, though Count Hompesch tells me, in a letter of the 24th instant; you meet with greater difficulties than were at first apprehended; in the mean time, this frost comes very seasonably to enable you to supply the garrisons of Douay and Bouchain with forage and other necessary provisions ... I shall only add my hearty wishes of many a happy New Year to your Lordship.

This was almost the last letter the Duke wrote while in command for, a few days later, he was dismissed from all his offices and appointments by Queen Anne. The Duke furiously threw the Queen's letter of dismissal into the fire, but his reply, while undoubtedly barbed, showed that he had by then fully recovered his customary courtly poise:

> I am very sensible of the honour your Majesty does me in dismissing me from your service by a letter of your own hand, though I find by it that my enemies have been able to prevail with your Majesty to do it in the manner that is most injurious to me ... I wish your Majesty may never feel the want of so faithful a servant as I have always endeavoured to approve myself to you.

The news of the Duke's dismissal was published in the *London Gazette* on 1 January 1712 (O.S.). On hearing the news, Louis XIV perceptively remarked: 'The affair of displacing the Duke of Marlborough will do all for us that we desire.' Just who had been driving the Allied war effort forward was plain to the French King.

By this time Great Britain had tired of what seemed to have become a wasteful and pointless war (particularly as the Austrian claimant to the throne in Madrid was now happily established as the Emperor in Vienna). James Butler, 2nd Duke of Ormonde, succeeded the Duke at the head of the Allied armies early in 1712, but his skills as commander were not of the same high calibre, despite the personal bravery that he often displayed. Nor did he have the strength of character to resist the interference in the campaign exerted by the politicians in London. The French commander, Marshal Villars, was aided by infamous restraining orders placed on the use of British troops by their Government. 'It is the Queen's positive command to your Grace [Ormonde] that you avoid engaging in any siege, or hazarding a battle, until you have further orders from Her Majesty.' The order went on 'Her Majesty thinks you cannot want pretences for conducting yourself without that which might at present have an ill-effect if it was publicly known.' So, Britain's allies were to be kept in the dark over all this. Lacking the firm direction of the Duke of Marlborough, the Allied campaign in the Low Countries languished in the face of dogged French resistance, and Villars was, as a result, newly invigorated, and able recover a significant amount of the ground lost to the Allies between the action at Malplaquet in 1709 and the fall of Bouchain in 1711.

At last the British troops were ordered to march away, leaving their Dutch and Imperial Allies still in the field to face the French. At first the British troops were refused shelter in Dutch-held garrisons, whose commanders resented what they saw, with some reason, as an abandonment of the common cause against France. The Count of Nassau-Woudenburg (the late Veldt-Marshal Overkirk's son) was obliged to write to Ormonde, on behalf of the Dutch field deputies with the army:

> That being acquainted that the commandants of Bouchain and Douay having refused to admit some of his officers into those places, upon the march of his army, they had thought themselves obliged to declare, that the same was not done, directly or indirectly, by their orders, and that the said commandants should be severely reprimanded … They were ready to give every possible assistance to the troops in their march, and to do everything that could be desired of them, towards the preserving of a good understanding and union, between the Queen and their masters.

Still, the Allied campaign limped on without the British, and the French were now bold. At Denain in 1712 Villars achieved a notable victory; he surprised and overwhelmed an Allied detachment before it could be reinforced, inflicting heavy losses. The account of the action, sent to the States-General of Holland, ran:

> They fell, with so much fury, on the regiments posted there, that after one discharge, the entrenchment was abandoned. Then the enemy, breaking into the entrenchment, charged our men, on the right and on the left, broke them, and after a vigorous but vain resistance, forced them to retire over the bridge on the Scheldt: but the bridge, having been unfortunately broke by the weight of the baggage which had newly passed it, the greatest part of those who attempted to pass it, were drowned.

Violent criticism of the Allied commander at Denain, Earl Albemarle, for his failure at this action was overdone, and at least partly had to do with his close friendship with Marlborough. Prince Eugene wrote sharply to the States-General in the Earl's defence, shortly afterward the fall of Denain:

I am surprised and troubled, to hear of the injustice people do to my Lord Albermarle, and all the impertinent discourses that have been vented, concerning his conduct, in the action at Denain. I have long been sensible, that the ill-informed vulgar judge by events, and that the unfortunate are always censured by them: but I wonder that such slanders should have found reception among men of figure, as could only have been broached by his enemies. I should think myself wanting in the duty of a man of honour, if I did not testify the truth, of which I was an eye-witness. He performed, on that occasion, all that a courageous, prudent and vigilant General could do; and had all the troops done their duty, the affair would not have gone as it did; but when they run, as soon as they had given one fire, and cannot be rallied, no General in the world can help it.

As the armies of Great Britain gradually withdrew from the field, so too were the enormous financial subsidies regularly paid to her allies, and those states that had provided troops for the war against France. The campaigns began to wind down also, although they continued dangerously enough, as Jean-Martin De La Colonie remembered, when describing the French operations against the Allied-held fortress of Douai, in the summer of 1712:

The garrison was not large and gave us little trouble, but the fogs which rose every evening over the marsh, in which we had been working, brought with them miasma, which produced many diseases among our army, the least among them being obstinate fevers which gave much trouble in their curing. The majority of our officers fell sick, and for the first time in my life, I found myself no more exempt than the rest of us. However, I paid little or no attention to it. One day I was there [in the trenches] with M. d'Albergotti, who was in command, he expressed his intention of visiting our trenches and reconnoitring an outwork, which he wished to carry by assault. He had the kindness to put off his inspection until the shivering fit which had seized me had passed off, so that I might accompany him; he believed in my knowledge of fortification, and his good opinion of me nearly cost me dearly. He had taken up his position at a little opening in our trench which exposed him down to the waist, to examine some sacks of earth which the enemy had laid along the top of the palisades of the covered-way, when he was noticed, and directions given to fire upon him. On such occasions one does not remain too long in a place like this, so he withdrew quickly to allow me to make my own observations, but hardly had I taken his place than I was hit by a bullet, which, luckily for me, only passed through my hat and along the side of my head. I merely sustained a contusion, which instantly developed into a swelling the size of an egg. A trifle to the right, and my fever would have given me no more trouble.

Meanwhile, Marlborough was under suspicion at home over allegations of financial impropriety and, lacking friends and influence, was now more than ever prey to accusation and slander. The Duke only waited until Sidney

Godolphin died, and then sought permission of Queen Anne to live abroad. This request was promptly granted, and he and the Duchess travelled to Holland and Hanover. There, Marlborough was joined in voluntary exile by his trusted lieutenant, William Cadogan, who had refused to return to England with the British troops when they were recalled from the campaign. The tired war, in which the Duke had played such a prominent, unrivalled part, staggered to an untidy end in 1713 with the Treaty of Utrecht, followed by the Treaty of Rastadt in 1714.

Philip V remained on the throne of Spain, and Emperor Charles stayed in Vienna. Still, the main aims of the Grand Alliance, to keep the crowns of France and Spain separate, to divide the Spanish Empire overseas (the Spanish Netherlands passed to Austria, courtesy of Marlborough's triumph at Ramillies), and to restore the Dutch Barrier, were largely achieved.

When George I ascended the throne in London in 1714, Marlborough and his Duchess accompanied him to England, and Marlborough was reinstated in all his posts. It seems that the Duke's relations with the German King were not particularly close, however, and he took no very active part in the suppression of the 1715 Jacobite Rising, leaving this to the Duke of Argyll, William Cadogan and Joseph Sabine. Marlborough suffered a stroke, the first of several such attacks, in 1716, and this was thought to have been brought on by the early death of his favourite daughter, Anne, the rather eccentric 32-year-old Countess of Sunderland. He lived in increasing ill-health and had, gradually, to retire from public life. The Duke of Marlborough died at Windsor Lodge in June 1722, and was succeeded in the post of Master-General of the Ordnance by Cadogan.

Henry St John, Viscount Bolingbroke, although he had become a bitter critic in public of Marlborough, wrote, after the Duke's death, of his qualities:

> I take, with pleasure, this opportunity of doing justice to that great man whose faults I know, and whose virtues I admired, and whose memory, as the greatest general and as the greatest minister that our country, or any other, has produced.

The final word might, perhaps, be left to Robert Parker, an 'honest marching captain', the stalwart Irish eye-witness to Marlborough's wars; one who shared camp, campaign and march, success and disappointment alike, with John Churchill, 1st Duke of Marlborough:

> As to the Duke of Marlborough (for I cannot forbear giving him the precedence) it was allowed by all men, nay, even by France itself, that he was more than a match for all the generals of that nation. This he made appear beyond contradiction, in the ten campaigns he made against them, during all of which time it cannot be said that he ever slipped an opportunity for fighting, when there was ever any probability of coming at his enemy; and upon all occasions he conducted matters with so much judgement and foresight, that he never fought a battle which he did not gain, nor laid siege to a town which he did not take.

Chapter 11

Over the Seas to Spain – The Spanish War 1702–1713

To win a war, fought ostensibly to keep the crowns of France and Spain apart, and to determine who should sit on the throne in Madrid, it was plainly desirable to succeed in Spain itself. In 1703 Portugal had been persuaded to break with France and join the Grand Alliance, and a combined Anglo-Dutch fleet under Admiral Rooke had captured Gibraltar in the very same month in 1704 that the battle of Blenheim was fought. The Allied garrison had then withstood strenuous efforts by strong French and Spanish forces, commanded by Marshal Tesse, to retake the as yet ill-fortified place. Brigadier-General John Shrimpton wrote to Marlborough on 14 February 1705, with vivid details of the savage fighting still taking place:

> The enemy attacked us this day, at break of day, at the Round Tower and the breach above it. They began this attack with 500 grenadiers sustained by 1,000 Spaniards. They carried the Round Tower and the breach and came over the hill as far as the four-gun battery, and were possessed of that too which is within 400 paces of the castle breach which is very easy to enter and that is the last opposition on that side and had they attacked us at the same time on the covert way, the north bastion and the curtain, we should have found it very hard to have kept them out. Our garrison being not above 1,800 men and they so harassed that they have not the rest that nature requires, being always at arms or at work. The enemies have had reinforcements of four French battalions and 19 companies of grenadiers. The Marshal de Tesse is with them. They threaten us heavily with a general assault which has kept us night and day under arms. Our daily loss is 20, 30 and sometimes 40 men a day wounded or killed. The Round Tower and breach and another post lying so exposed to the enemy's batteries, were killed of the enemy in this action 150 men and a good many officers and we hear more wounded and [we] took 40 prisoners and six officers. We had 180 men killed or wounded. I must tell your Grace that our battalion of Guards [2nd, the Coldstream] diminishes a pace. We have not above 250 men fit for duty and above 200 wounded and sick. They begin to be very ragged with the hard duty and working daily.

Corporal Matthew Bishop also remembered his exploits in these operations, writing with commendable coolness:

> We found the duty extremely hard, for what they beat down by day we were obliged to clear away at night. They sent in a great many bombs, once I thought they had sent us one too many; for I was at work just in the bastion, and there came one, swift as lightning. It blew up in a moment, which made the ground tremble. I was not above a yard from it when it fell, and had I been so unwise as to have stood up when it fell, I should have been lifted up by its wings. I never minded a bomb at all only to observe its falling and step out of the way, and fall with my face to the ground.

Gibraltar was held and Tesse, for all his undoubted skill, had to admit defeat and draw off after a while. For a time thereafter the Allied campaigns in Spain prospered, although the involvement of Portuguese troops on their soil antagonised many Spaniards who might, perhaps, otherwise have declared for the Austrian claimant. The Anglo-Portuguese forces in the western theatre were led by the Huguenot Earl of Galway, while the Earl of Peterborough was sent with wide plenipotentiary powers to command the Allied army in Catalonia, accompanied by the Archduke Charles and an extensive, argumentative and costly entourage.

Early in September 1705, Barcelona was seized by Peterborough and Prince George of Hesse-Darmstadt in a brilliant exploit. Unfortunately, the highly competent and very popular Prince was mortally wounded in the night attack. An anonymous soldier in Raby's Regiment of Dragoons, who left most informative memoirs, had rather enjoyed his time in Portugal up to this point (although other units seemed to be less fortunate): 'It is a plentiful place of wine, oil and fish.' He now found that his regiment was detailed to be part of a general reinforcement of the Allied armies in Catalonia, in time for the capture of the city:

> On the 11 of August 1705 we came to an anchor down below the mould [mole] of Barcelona and on the 13 of that month we landed our small army about 3 or 4 miles below the city, but the enemy set all the straw and forage for our horses that they could on fire. We marched as if we were going to our shipping but we marched all night and took a compass round the backside of the city under the mountain called Manjoy but commonly Muniuch [fort of Montjuich, south of Barcelona], where there is a strong castle, well fortified, but having had the news our embarking again they little thought what would befall them, which they found in a little while. For before the break of day [3rd September N.S.] our foot advanced up the hill towards their works, which when the enemy found that they were not a little surprised and soon retired into the castle ... We having taking Munjuck we drew down our batteries and laid close siege to [the] city both by sea and by land and in a short time we were masters of the city.

Then, with a soldier's typical, and entirely understandable, interest in the effects of the weather, he goes on 'If they had not surrendered as they did it would have been impossible for us to have kept the field much longer for there came such heavy rains, enough to drown us.'

Peterborough then moved forward to threaten Valencia. Raby's dragoon remembered that 'We marched up the country and in hopes soon to gain the whole country, for as we marched all the country declared for King Charles.' He added with evident relish and approval: 'Catalonia is very mountainly but good corn, oil and wine it does produce, and fruits of all sorts plentiful.' On 4 February 1706, the troops reached Valencia, where the population welcomed them, declaring for King Charles III: 'Early in the morning we marched towards Valencia, a very fine city. We were not billeted but as we marched along the street they took as many as they could until all was quartered.'

The Allied army could then move to occupy Madrid, while the French claimant, Philip V, withdrew northwards towards the French border with his entourage. It briefly seemed that the Allies, no matter what was happening elsewhere in Europe, would achieve one of the principle objectives of the Grand Alliance. With Aragon, Valencia and Catalonia all falling into their hands, success appeared to be assured, and an Austrian Archduke would soon become King of Spain indeed.

Alliance warfare, in Spain as much as in the Low Countries, proved a troublesome business. Peterborough quarrelled with the Austrian courtiers, and the Archduke allowed himself to be detained in Aragon instead of pressing onwards. However, the Earl of Galway (who was undeterred by losing an arm in fighting at Badajoz) and General Das Minas advanced from the west with an Anglo-Portuguese army. Their opponent, Marshal Berwick, was unable to intercept their march and withdrew to the north. By early August Archduke Charles, Peterborough and Galway (whose troops had now entered Madrid) met to the north-east of the capital. The Earl of Peterborough, rather strangely, had not brought forward his main force from Valencia, and Berwick, now reinforced by Marshal Tesse's army, soon manoeuvred Galway's troops out of Madrid. The Marshal, no less than his opponents, found that princes could be troublesome, and while his army was embroiled in daily running battles with Galway's troops, a messenger arrived from Philip V, giving him permission to engage the enemy, if he thought it really necessary.

Faced with superior numbers, the Allies had no other option than to fall back to Valencia, and a great opportunity to conclude matters appeared to have been lost. However, the people of Madrid had been lukewarm, at best, in their reception of Charles, and the Allied lines of supply and communication with the coast were under constant threat. The animosity of much of the local populace towards the Allied troops led to atrocities and reprisals on both sides. George Villiers Carleton, an engineer officer, was travelling with Peterborough's entourage on the journey from Madrid, and told of a harrowing incident at a small village called Campillo:

His Lordship had information of a most barbarous act committed that very morning by the Spaniards at a small village about a league distant. A captain of the English Guards [the Coldstream], marching to join the battalion of the Guards, then under the command of General Windham, with some of his soldiers that had been in the hospital, took up his quarters in that little village. But, on his marching out of it, next morning, a shot in the back laid that officer dead upon the spot; and, as it had been before concerted, the Spaniards of the place at the same time fell upon the poor weak soldiers killing several; not even sparing their wives. This was but a prelude to their barbarity ... They took the surviving few, hurried and dragged them up a hill, a little without the village. On top of the hill there was a hole, or opening, somewhat like the mouth of one of our coal-pits; down this they cast several, who with hideous shrieks and cries, made more hideous by the echoes of the chasm, there lost their lives.

As soon as the news of the atrocity was received, Peterborough and a mounted party rode over to the hamlet, and Carleton, who was among them, remembered that:

As soon as we entered the village, we found that most of the inhabitants, but especially the most guilty, had withdrawn themselves at our approach. We found, however, many of the dead soldiers' clothes, which had been conveyed into the church and there hid. And a strong accusation being laid against a person belonging to the church, and full proof made that he had been singularly industrious in the execution of that horrid piece of barbarity on the hill, his lordship commanded him to be hanged.

The priest was strung up at the door of his own church. George Carleton also recounted his part in a skirmish later in the campaign, when riding with a party of dragoons under command of a Major O'Roirk (Carleton, rather unnecessarily in light of his name, describes this officer as being an Irishman):

Just before Villena, a jutting hill, under which we must unavoidably pass; at the turning whereof, I was apprehensive the enemy might lie, and either by ambuscade, or otherwise, surprise us; I, therefore, entreated we might either wait the coming of our rearguard, or at least march with a little more leisure and caution. But he, taking little notice of all I said, kept on his round march; seeing which, I pressed forward my mule, which was a very good one, and rid as fast as her legs could carry her, until I had got to the top of the hill ... I could plainly discern three squadrons of the enemy ready drawn up, and waiting for us at the very winding of the hill.

Carleton quickly took back this information to O'Roirk who, however, seemed most concerned that some other dragoons, also on the road nearby, would get all the credit from an engagement:

Our captain, as if he was afraid of their rivalling him in his glory, at the very turn of the hill, rode in a full gallop, with sword in hand, up to the enemy. They stood their ground till we were advanced within two hundred yards of them, and then in confusion endeavoured to retire into the town ... One remarkable thing I saw in that action, which affected and surprised me; a Scotch dragoon, of but a moderate size, with his large basket-hilted sword, struck off a Spaniard's head at one stroke, with the same ease, in appearance, as a man would do that of a poppy.

Having reached the coast, Peterborough, apparently despairing of trying to work successfully with the Austrians, absented himself from his command with no actual authority to do so. He went to Italy, apparently to raise funds for the cash-starved army in Catalonia, but he then returned to England. The roundabout route he took enabled him to visit Marlborough in the Low Countries, and to congratulate him on the towering achievement of Ramillies earlier in the year. The Earl's subsequent arrival in England caused some consternation, as he was thought still to be in Spain.

A rather jaundiced view of the strategic military and political situation facing the Allies in the peninsula is given in a remarkably frank letter written by Henry St John, Secretary at War, on Christmas Eve 1706, to his friend, Lieutenant-General Thomas Erle, who was even then en route to join the campaign in Valencia:

> You will find a King [Charles III] destitute of any one able and honest minister, a court without order or economy, the Portuguese difficult to be managed and made to do more good than harm, the English and Dutch dispersed, broken in spirit, and reduced in numbers, one general [Galway] tired and over-burdened, eager only to get from under the load, which however he is ordered from hence still to continue to bear, the other general [Peterborough] (if he is not gone from Spain upon some other project once more) full of pique and cavills all what is passed, accounts and all matters in the utmost confusion, and, to conclude, all the Spaniards either animated against you or at best mistrusting your strength and afraid to declare for you. These are melancholy though true reflections. Little diversion must be expected from the side of Portugal.

St John was writing frankly to a friend in a way not often seen in more official correspondence. Erle may well have been alerted to the problems he would face, but can hardly have been encouraged by the letter. Still, St John had neatly put his finger on the problem; not the inefficiency, waste and corruption of the Austrian entourage, or the fatigue of the generals and lack of harmony among the Allies; but the fact that the Spanish people, if they did not actively support Philip V (and many did), did not trust Archduke Charles to win his throne. With the exception of the Catalonians who hoped to regain lost privileges for their region, the people were reluctant to flock to his standard.

By the opening months of 1707 the Allied armies in the peninsula had been reinforced with about 8,000 fresh troops (some of whom were drawn off from Marlborough's efforts in the Low Countries). As the Allied commanders could not agree on a single, concentrated course of action, they rashly divided their forces; the Archduke and his courtiers stayed in Catalonia and those parts of

Aragon occupied so far, while Galway and the Portuguese under General Das Minas ventured into Murcia, wasting time in marching about and attacking small fortresses, apparently waiting for reinforcements from Alicante in the south, before going on towards Madrid. In late February 1707, Marshal Berwick, still commanding the armies of Philip V, was able to report a small but heartening success against the Allies who were attacking Villena, in their new but rather hesitant advance on the Spanish capital:

> I had placed M. de Zerecenda with his regiment of cavalry in an advanced post, as the fittest officer in the army to give me proper intelligence. He received advice that a large convoy, destined for the troops that were in the vale of Castalla, was to be sent from Alicante upon which, he placed himself in ambuscade at half a league's distance from Alicante, with fourscore select troops. Instead of the convoy, he saw an English battalion come out of the city, which he suffered to approach within fifty paces of him; perceiving then that the battalion was marching in a column with their arms slung, and without any suspicion of him, who was concealed in a bottom surrounded with trees, he sallied out on a sudden, and forced his way at full speed into the midst of the battalion, which had neither time to recollect itself nor to form; he killed one hundred of them and took the remaining four hundred with their baggage. He had not more than four of his horsemen killed or wounded.

Berwick added the compliment to his successful lieutenant: 'This was a very bold and brilliant action. He took his time so well, and availed himself with so much skill of his opponent's negligence.' Had his opponents properly combined their armies they would have significantly outnumbered those fielded by Berwick, but such minor disasters as this (to which particular regiment it is not recorded) must have done little for the morale of the Allied commanders, or their troops, as they wearily, and apparently aimlessly, marched along the rough roads of Spain. Unknown to either Galway or Das Minas, whose own intelligence gathering seems to have been very faulty, unlike that of Berwick, the Marshal was being substantially reinforced from France. At last the Allies called off the siege of Villena, and moved to close with the French commander to confront him in open battle.

On Easter Monday, 25 April 1707, Galway's small army was heavily defeated by the French and Spanish forces under command of Marshal Berwick, at Almanza. The approach march was arduous for the soldiers, as can be seen from a doggerel rhyme popular at the time: 'Full twenty miles we marched that day/Without one drop of water/Until we poor souls were almost spent/Before the bloody slaughter.' An initial success by the Allied army was not sustained, and Berwick was able to recover his tactical poise, and overwhelm his opponents, inflicting a severe loss on them. The Portuguese infantry fought well, on the whole, but their ill-equipped cavalry had been overthrown without difficulty, and fled, despite the desperate efforts of Das Minas to hold them together. The dragoon in Raby's Regiment wrote that:

On Monday April the 14 [O.S.] which now is the 25th, which is St Mark's Day, 1707, our advance guard marched up to them very boldly and beat them in a gallant manner all their out guards. So our army marched up in line of battle, though our men were much spent for they could get no water all the day's march before. So then the armies engaged very brisk and sharp so that at one time it was thought we should have gained the day, for our foot beat theirs and drove them, but our horse was much overpowered by reason that the Marquis Delamenes, the Portuguese General, did not come up with the rest of the army as he should have done, for thirty-five squadrons of the Portuguese horse was not engaged but turned tail and left the English to the mercy of the enemies, which was but small, and it would have been a dismal day for the English had not the Duke of Berwick, as he was our enemy, been there, for he gave strict orders that if he gained the day to give the English quarter.

As the Allied line of battle fell apart under the blows so skilfully directed by Berwick, the dragoon describes a desperate manoeuvre, not unlike that adopted by Caraman's Bavarian infantry when withdrawing from the fight at the Lines of Brabant two years earlier:

A great part of our foot was under the command of Brigadier Shrimpton did fight their way through in hollow square and they got to a mount and [negotiated] good conditions for himself and for all his men, but the rest of the army was forced to make the best of their way and escape as best they could and my Lord Galway received a wound in his head.

This defeat was a crushing blow to the Allied campaign, for nearly half of Galway's army were either killed, captured or had fled in panic and disorder. Berwick admitted only to 2,000 casualties of his own, but this is probably an underestimate. When the news of the defeat was received, Carleton remembered that 'We at first gave no great credit to it; but, alas! We were soon woefully convinced of the truth of it, by numbers that came flying to us from the conquering enemy ... I was not present in that calamitous battle.' Three days after Almanza, Galway wrote from his camp to Admiral Byng:

We have lost our artillery, and as to our foot, none is returned in a body unless a few officers and scattered soldiers. As to the horse, I believe there may be about 3,000 or more saved. You are sensible that with what we have we shall not be in a position to form an army able to protect the kingdom of Valencia. We just now resolved to pass off what we have here and at Valencia with all the diligence we can to Tortosa to see if we can with the troops his Majesty has in Aragon and Catalonia make up an army.

In the circumstances, Galway had no choice but to fall back into Valencia where he could draw provisions and support from the Royal Navy, and try and rest his depleted and demoralised army. The city of Valencia could not be saved, although Lerida, Tortosa, Alicante and Denia held out, for the time being. The dragoon from Raby's Regiment remembered that, perhaps rather surprisingly in light of the recent Allied defeat, a considerable number of deserters came into their camp at this time, and 'Being got into Catalonia we were pretty safe.'

The stubborn old Huguenot warrior, Galway, made the best of a very bad situation, helped by the drawing away, before too long, of French troops to counter Prince Eugene's ultimately unsuccessful campaign against Toulon. Soon (with remarkably little help from Archduke Charles and his lordly entourage) Galway could put a respectably sized army of some 15,000 troops back in the field. Meanwhile, the Archduke, with the remainder of the Allied forces, contented himself with passively defending what territory in parts of Aragon and Catalonia had been gained in his name, and was left to him after Almanza. Marlborough's intelligence of the state of affairs in the peninsula was good, and on 15 May he wrote to Sidney Godolphin: 'We must expect the worst, and begin to take our measures for repairing this great loss. When we come to learn directly from Spain, I fear we shall find our people confine themselves to the preservation of Alicante and Catalonia.'

The effort to place the Austrian claimant on the throne never really recovered its full momentum after the defeat at Almanza. This was despite some local successes, and a certain fatigue in Versailles at the cost and effort of the Spanish campaign. Philip V was aware of his increasing popularity with the Spanish people, and grew reluctant to be dictated to by his grandfather. The fortunes of the war in the peninsula continued to favour one side and then the other; although a stubborn Allied defence of the town of Tortosa on the Ebro river proved unsuccessful – the French lost nearly 5,000 men killed and wounded in the capture of the place on 10 July 1708. Still, Admiral Leake seized Sardinia in August that year, with valuable supplies of grain, and then went on to capture Port Mahon, in conjunction with Earl James Stanhope, on the island of Minorca. With Gibraltar already firmly in British hands, the French fleet beached or burned in the harbour at Toulon the previous year, and now Minorca secure, the Mediterranean was fast becoming a lake on which the Royal Navy could operate at will. So, with some careful management, all might be well for the Allies after all.

The severity of the fighting on the mainland of Spain meanwhile, and the ruthless way in which much of the campaign was conducted, may be gathered from the anonymous diarist in Raby's Dragoons, who left an account of a night raid carried out on the French camp in September that year:

> A deserter from the enemy gave an account in what manner they did lie and gave their signal and their parole [or password]. At which the Prince [Henry of Hess] gave out private orders for the Germans grenadiers & likewise Spanish, but for the English there was no orders. About midnight they got over the river with a guide and having their parole they were challenged but they could answer them [and] there was no mistrust, so as they came up to a sentinel giving the signal they were admitted by it and then they secured the sentinel, telling that they were the Duke of Berwick's regiment that were come to strengthen [the position]. It being dark they could not discern their livery, so having the sentinels and the guards they then went down the lines and pulling up the tentpins and

stabbing [bayoneting] of the men as they lay asleep, some turning out of their tent naked, not knowing what was the matter, and our Maccalas [Miquelets or irregular partisans] firing on them there and our men taking their colours and their arms, for they seized all their bels [stacks] of arms, and making the best of their way fearing being surprised themselves.

The bloody work on such an occasion would inevitably result in a certain bitterness, leading perhaps to a reluctance to give quarter at other times. The French commander, Marshal Berwick, despite the indignation felt in his own army at both having been taken so unawares, and the merciless slaughter of sleeping men, took care to let it be known that 'He was sensible that there was no English in the action, for if there had he was sure that they could have not been so barbarous.' However, Berwick could be brutal enough on occasions, as when he was busy with the suppression of rebellion in southern France, and had prisoners (admittedly men who had attempted his own assassination) broken on the wheel.

Despite such local successes as this nocturnal raid, matters did not prosper for the Grand Alliance. By the spring of 1709 Louis XIV was drawing troops away from Spain to shore up his own northern border, but all the same the Allies suffered a severe defeat at Val Gudina in Portugal in May of that year. Archduke Charles's attention was increasingly turned towards his possessions in Italy, immensely more valuable than poverty-struck Spain, and to Vienna, where his brother's death would, in time, make him the Emperor. His heart was less set on Madrid, where he once aspired to be King. Troops, supplies and money continued to be trickled out begrudgingly to the Allied commanders in the peninsula. Despite such failings, on 27 July 1710 the army led by Earl Stanhope soundly defeated King Philip V's Spanish troops in open battle at Almenara. Raby's Dragoons were there, and the anonymous diarist wrote that:

On Sunday 16th of July [O.S.] just as the sun was rising we got over the river, then we refreshed our horses and ourselves, and about one in the afternoon good part of our horse was got over the river and we had orders to mount our horses, which we did and marching into the plain a party was ordered out to go with Brigadier Peper to see if he could discover the enemy, which he soon did. Our horse being almost all over and our foot making all the haste they could in getting over, but the enemies squadrons began to appear very thick upon the hills, which was strong ground. About an hour before the sun set on the 16th day of July 1710, our squadrons had orders to advance, the left [of] our army being a great deal nearer to the enemy than our right, therefore our right wing was obliged to advance as fast as our horses could go. The sun then was not above a quarter of an hour high [above the horizon] when the left began to engage and the right was soon up with them, which made the enemy in amazement to see and behold how like lions our men fell upon them with sword in hand. And we advancing so fast after the enemy that our foot could not keep up with us, likewise our train [of artillery] could not no way bear up with their cannon to do the enemy any damage.

The dust and smoke of the battlefield, then as now, made identification difficult, and the dragoon recounts a tragic incident when the Allied gunners began firing in error: 'They came so near that they saw a squadron of our horse and took it to be the enemy and killed Count Nassau, a cornet and a private dragoon.' Despite such mishaps, the pursuit was pressed ruthlessly on, with their opponents in full flight:

> They were all so amazed and running all that could get off under the walls of Lerrada, leaving behind them seven or eight pieces of cannon and several waggons loaded with provision for their army and a great deal of baggage. On Monday the 13th [sic] of July all the dead was buried and the wounded taken care of well.

This success was followed with the prompt seizure of Lerida, with the Spanish troops now fleeing in disorder before Stanhope's cavalry. Raby's Dragoons were in almost constant action, as we read in an account of an action near Balbastro:

> There was presently ordered a party of Dragoons to march on foot in order to storm the church. And we had not been long in the town before we began the attack. General Carpenter at the head of us, for I see him the first man that mounted the ladder over the church walls. But half of was not got over before they beat a parley and surrendered themselves prisoners.

The dragoon commented on the enthusiastic welcome offered to the advancing Allied army, at that time, by the local populace. Early in August the town of Saragossa was reached, where the forces of Philip V tried to make a stand:

> All that night, being the 8th of August [O.S.], we lay that night upon our arms, though we had nothing to eat ourselves nor ought to give our horses for the heath we lay on have no grass but a sort of prickly weed that our horses would not eat. Both armies being in a readiness for engaging, a great many shot passing from one to the other in the night of the patrols, now on Wednesday, being the 9th of August 1710 the enemy, thinking what they must stand to for they could not get off the ground without a hazard of a battle, they thought therefore they would make the best show they could of their courage: then at the sun rising they began to cannonade us which was soon answered from us. Thus they and we held cannonading for some hours but our batteries did them a great deal more damage to them than theirs did to us.

While the bombardment went on, the dragoons had chance to attend to some personal administration before the onset of battle proper:

> About 9 of the clock in the forenoon we had orders to go to water our horses. Just then we received half a day's bread, so we got a little bread and a little water before we engaged, for it was about 10 of the clock when the signal was blown up, at which time we mounted and advanced upon them sword in hand. Cutting and hewing then down sword in hand, for their firing at us first made their horses gerr [shy away], then we broke

them in a very short time and was as able with the blessing of God to have broke any squadron that should have come against us … Most of the English horse was against the right of their army, for they knowing that the Dutch and English to be on the left of our army they placed the best of their army on the right, but, as I said, that our squadron stood and was able to meet any squadron that should come against us.

The hectic slashing contest which overthrew the French and Spanish cavalry put their whole army into disordered flight. The dragoon continued:

I had not one drop of blood drawn from me that day but my hat was all cut to bits in the crown and my coat was shot through in many places and I had balls went through my waist-belt that I had on. The enemy being gone we had to look for the rest of our squadron, which we soon found drawn up in good order and General Stanhope at the head of them … We were masters of the field; Stanhope he said unto us the reason was that he would not let us pursue the enemy might rally again. So the battle being over and the enemy put totally to the rout we stayed some short time in the field of battle and marched nearer the city … About four in the afternoon I was ordered out with the banroules [marker flags] with the quartermasters to go on the other side of the city to pitch out the ground for our regiment … The country had orders to bury the dead and they gave an account; there was slain of the enemy's army about 5660 and odd, and of ours as was giving in what each regiment had lost did amount unto 1100 men, but the enemy had left all their train and all their foot, except a few that made their escape, prisoners.

He then remembered, with some relish, that 'We lay in camp just out of the city of Saragossa and we began to have everything very plentiful. Likewise we found stores of provisions that the enemy left in the city, abundance of good bacon which was given to our army.' The dragoons moved forward shortly afterwards, but examination of the prisoners taken in the recent battle showed that numbers of Allied soldiers, previously captured by the enemy, had been persuaded to turn their coats and enlisted to fight for Philip V. The anonymous dragoon wrote that: 'We moved our camp about a league beyond the city of Saragossa by a small village where on Friday the 18 of August there was deserters shot that we took in the battle, ten of them.' Soon afterwards the city of Madrid was taken once again, in the name of Charles III: 'Friday the 10th of September 1710 [O.S.] our army moved their camp nearer to Madrid within a league and a half of it. On Sunday being the 12th of September I had leave to go to Madrid, which I did and it is a very fine place.'

Philip V and his entourage had retired to Valladolid for the time being. Despite this seemingly important success for the Allied army, their lines of supply were, as on the previous occasion when they got to Madrid, too long and vulnerable, and the population were indifferent, if not actively hostile. Of the proclamation in the city of the Archduke as Charles III, the Duc de St Simon wrote with some relish 'It was reported that a few scarcely audible and feeble acclamations were heard.'

At this point in the campaign, the French, whose attention had for some time been firmly on the military disasters on their northern borders, returned in force to the peninsula, under command of the Duc de Vendôme. He moved quickly to foil a planned concentration between the Imperial field-marshal Guido von Stahremberg and Earl Stanhope on the one hand, with the forces coming westwards from Portugal on the other; these troops were not making much progress anyway, and when this was realised Stahremberg and Stanhope fell back on Madrid. Finding that with a precarious supply situation they could not winter in the capital, the Allies left the city on 3 December, heading for Aragon. The army, in order to make foraging easier, marched in three widely spaced columns, a rather dangerous formation with Vendôme around. A week later the detachment under Earl Stanhope was caught and overwhelmed, after desperate and bloody fighting against superior numbers, in the streets of the hilltop town of Brihuega. The dragoon in Raby's Regiment, who fought in the doomed action, remembered that, the previous day:

> About 9 of the clock in the morning their advance-guard did begin to appear upon the mountains looking at us, but yet we thought ourselves secure enough and we had if we had marched out of the town then. About 12 of the clock we had orders to saddle our horses and to be in a readiness for to mount when ordered, which we did and at 3 o'clock we had orders to mount and to draw up in the castle yard, thinking still they could not harm us, but an hour before sunset their cannon did appear upon the hills. On Tuesday the 28th of November 1710 [O.S.] we had all of us orders to make fascines and to carry them into the market place and then to go with our arms in order to keep the enemy from coming into the town.

The walls of the town were old and decrepit, and the French artillery soon made breaches, although these were high up in the stone work, reportedly only accessible to men clambering onto the backs of horses before leaping over into the action. The dragoon described the battle in the narrow streets:

> We had no cannon to defend us nor to offend them, and we should have kept them out longer but now our ammunition began to be wanting that our men was forced to be careful of it, and the enemy finding it made them brisker & the bolder. By 3 or 4 of the clock in the afternoon great part of their army was got into the town and houses and made holes in the walls of the houses and knocked us down so fast as they could shoot. We blocked up the street that led into the market-place but it was all in vain, for by this time the enemy began to march in all streets and we had no ammunition, it being all spent.

Stahremberg was slow off the mark, but marched towards Brihuega through the failing light, firing signal guns as he went, to encourage Stanhope to fight on. He arrived too late to prevent a capitulation and the total loss of the Earl's detachment, which comprised many British troops. The dragoon goes on to describe the surrender:

There was orders for our drum-major to beat a parley, but it was not heard the first nor second time, but third time it was heard, and the enemy stood before all the time and when the parley was heard they came to our breastwork and talked with us. This was all agreed on by 10 of the clock on the 29th of November in 1710 [O.S.] but it was said that the reason that we got so good quarters [terms] was that the enemy knew that our General Starhremberg was coming to our relief. We surrendered ourselves prisoners twelve regiments of us, four regiments of horse and dragoons and eight regiments of foot.

Unfortunately, the 'good quarters' terms in the capitulation were not properly adhered to, and the British prisoners were subject to harsh treatment before their eventual release on parole: 'They took away all that we had except our old clothes that was on our back, which were not worth the taking. We were treated worse than dogs.'

The following day, Stahremberg mauled Vendôme's army, fighting the French commander to a bloody standstill in battle at Villaviciosa, inflicting nearly 4,000 casualties, and taking many guns. These could not be dragged off, for want of horses and mules, and so the captured pieces were spiked and abandoned, as was the Allied field train. Stahremberg gathered what was left of the Allied army in Spain about him, and withdrew into Catalonia with about 8,000 men in early January 1711. Vendôme maintained a watchful, but cautious, distance as they marched eastwards.

The early campaigns in Spain had been characterised by the deployment of several indifferently led and poorly-equipped Allied armies, who gained local successes against weak French detachments badly supported by the Spanish; there was an illusion of victory which never came about. The latter campaigns saw good Spanish troops, well supported by the French allies, out-manoeuvre and out-general the Allied armies, which were still poorly led and badly-equipped. Almost inevitably, the cause of Philip V prospered while that of Charles III steadily failed. Although Louis XIV had, in the despair of the early months of 1709, declared his intention to withdraw his troops from Spain, two years later his generals were able to conduct an increasingly successful campaign on behalf of Philip V, taking Gerona early in 1711. In May Emperor Joseph died of smallpox, and his younger brother, the Archduke, was elected to replace him. Charles left Catalonia in September that year, visiting his possessions in Italy before going on to Vienna, and never went back to the peninsula, although his wife remained there in Barcelona as Regent for some time. The following year, as Britain's interest in the war faded, Queen Anne's troops were removed from Spain, and there was a general succession of hostilities both in that country and Portugal during the autumn of 1712.

An indication of the maladministration and speculation – corruption is probably not too strong a word – that was rife in the Allied armies in the peninsula, and which drained the Treasury of Queen Anne, and dogged the efforts of able and honest commanders and soldiers alike, is given in an extract from a report prepared for the parliament in London in 1713, on the conduct of the campaigns:

> Some regiments had been paid which were never on any [Army] establishment, while others had been paid before they were established. The Earl of Galway's Spanish Regiment we have received so very uncertain an account of, that there seems to have been unnecessary expenses made on the public for providing it. Captain Henry Pullein deposes that he held a captain's commission dated April 6th 1707, given him by the Earl of Galway; that he arrived in Portugal the June following, when he heard the [Spanish] regiment had been taken prisoners, and found two or three officers there, but never saw any privates, nor did he hear that musters were ever taken. The commissary, and the paymaster-general have deposed:– That they never saw any muster rolls, but that there was a list of prisoners returned to the paymaster, after the regiment was supposed to have been taken by the enemy, wherein the name of only one private is inserted which had created the suspicion that the regiment was an imaginary one and was never actually raised.

These comments refer to an apparent 'phantom' regiment, raised and paid for in the British service where checks and balances, of a kind, did at least exist. This was not the case in some of the allied armies, where such abuses, it seems fair to conjecture, will have been worse.

A sad postscript to the unsuccessful Allied war in Spain is the fact that the Catalans never forgot their devotion to the young Austrian prince who had come to be their King, but who was now the Emperor in Vienna. Barcelona reaffirmed its loyalty to Charles III on 9 July 1713, and defied a summons from Philip V to declare their allegiance to him. After a bitter and lonely struggle, with Europe's attention on other things, Barcelona was invested and attacked by Marshal Berwick in September 1713. There was fierce and bloody fighting for the outworks, but the valiant defence crumbled. The town was narrowly spared a sack, as Berwick recalled in his dealings with a delegation of the citizenry who asked for terms, when he told them sternly that 'We were masters of the city and had it in our power to put everything to the sword.' The magistrates withdrew but the Marshal sent a message after them that the town would be stormed and sacked the next day unless they submitted:

> I then promised them their lives would be safe, and even that there should be no plunder ... The rebels retired from all their posts, and our troops having beat the generall, marched through all the streets in such order to the quarters that were assigned to them, that not a single soldier got out of the ranks.

Despite Berwick's assurances to the magistrates of the town, which he was in no real position to keep, Philip V was vengeful, and some stern reprisals for their act of rebellion were exacted against many of the prominent citizens. The rest of Catalonia was quickly subdued and the Duc d'Anjou could at last claim to be King of Spain indeed.

Appendix 1

The Aims of the Treaty of Grand Alliance, 1701

i   That Emperor Leopold I should have possession of the Milanese in northern Italy, the Two Sicilies, the Spanish Balearic Islands, and the Spanish Netherlands and Luxembourg, on behalf of his son, the Archduke Charles.
ii That a strong fortress barrier should be maintained in the Spanish Netherlands, to protect the security of the United Provinces (Holland).
iii That the Maritime Powers (England and Holland) should be permitted to trade without restriction in the Spanish Americas and the Indies.
iv That German states loyal to the Empire would receive subsidies from the Maritime Powers on supporting the Alliance. Also, the Elector of Brandenburg would be accorded the title 'King of Prussia' in return for his support.

No explicit mention was made at this time of removing Philip V from the throne of Spain (both England and Holland had acknowledged his accession in 1701), or of keeping the thrones of France and Spain separate. As the war progressed, and the Allies gained in confidence, additional aims were added. Salient among these was the notion that victory could only be assured if Archduke Charles was in possession of the Spanish throne. This could only stem from a victory in Spain itself, unless Philip V should agree to vacate the throne. The cry of 'No Peace Without Spain' originated in London after Ramillies, when anything seemed possible, and was soon heard throughout the Grand Alliance. Vast amounts of men, materiel and treasure were expended in the lost cause of forcing the Austrian claimant on the Spanish people, who were, in the main, quite content with their young French prince.

Appendix 2

The Terms of the Treaty of Utrecht, 1713

The Treaties of Utrecht, Rastadt, and Baden (1713–1715), which brought the War of the Spanish Succession to a close, are often referred to under the simple title 'Treaty of Utrecht'. The following were the main provisions of the treaties:

i   Philip V was recognised as the King of Spain and the Indies, as long as the crowns of France and Spain were kept separate (Philip had, in fact, already irrevocably renounced his entitlement to the throne of France, on accepting the Spanish throne).

ii   Naples, the Milanese, Sardinia, and the Spanish Netherlands (now to become known as the Austrian Netherlands) came under Imperial Austrian rule, although the following were guaranteed to Holland as their new 'Barrier Towns' – Furnes, Ghent, Mons, Charleroi, Namur and Tournai.

iii   France retained Alsace and Strasbourg (as allowed under the Treaty of Ryswick, 1697) but surrendered the fortresses of Kehl, Breisach and Freiburg on the eastern bank of the River Rhine.

iv   The Elector of Cologne and the Elector of Bavaria were restored to their domains (in the process Marlborough lost his principality of Mindelheim, granted to him by the Emperor after Blenheim).

v   The Hanoverian, Protestant, succession to the throne of Great Britain was guaranteed, and James III (the 'Old Pretender') was to be expelled from France.

vi   Britain retained Minorca, Gibraltar, Newfoundland, Hudson's Bay, Arcadia and St Kitts, and was guaranteed exclusive access to trade in certain Spanish ports set aside for the purpose. In addition, the fortifications of Dunkirk were to be demolished.

vii   The Kingdom of Prussia was recognised, and given overlordship of Upper Guelderland.

viii   The Duke of Savoy received Sicily, and part of the Milanese.

Bibliography

Alison, A., *Military Life of John, Duke of Marlborough*, 1848
Atkinson, C.T. (ed), *Gleanings from the Cathart Mss*, JSAHR, 1951
—— (ed) *A Royal Dragoon in the Spanish Succession War*, SAHR, 1938
—— *Marlborough and the Rise of the British Army*, 1921
Barnett, C., *Marlborough*, 1974
Bathurst, A., *Letters of Two Queens*, 1924
Brereton, J., *History of the 4/7th Dragoon Guards*, 1982
Brown, B. (ed), *Letters of Queen Anne*, 1934
Burn, W. (ed), *A Scots Fusilier and Dragoon Under Marlborough*, JSAHR, 1936
Burrell, S. (ed), *Amiable Renegade, Memoirs of Captain Peter Drake*, 1960
Carleton, G. (ed), *Military Memoirs*, 1830 and 1929
Carman, W., *The Siege of Lille, 1708*, JSAHR, 1940
Chandler, D. (ed), *Military Memoirs of Marlborough's Campaigns*, 1998
—— (ed), *Journal of John Deane* JSAHR, 1984
—— *Marlborough as Military Commander*, 1974
—— *The Art of Warfare in the Age of Marlborough*, 1992
—— *Blenheim Preparation*, 2004 (ed J. Falkner)
Churchill, W.S., *Marlborough, His Life and Times*, 1947
Courvoisier, A., *La Bataille de Malplaquet*, 1997
Coxe, W., *Memoirs of the Duke of Marlborough*, 1848
Crichton, A. (ed), *Diary of Lt Col J Blackader*, 1824
Cronin, V., *Louis XIV*, 1964
Dickinson, H. (ed), *Correspondence Henry St John and Thomas Erle*, JSAHR, 1970
Drake, P., *Memoirs of Captain Peter Drake*, 1755
Dugawe, D., *New Dictionary of National Biography*, 'Christian Davies', 2004
Evelyn, J., *Diary* (ed), 1929 and 1979
Falkner, J., *Great and Glorious Days, 2002*
—— *Blenheim 1704, Marlborough's Greatest Victory*, 2004
Fortescue, J., *History of the British Army*, 1908
—— (ed), *Life and Adventures of Mother Ross*, 1929

Frances, D., *The First Peninsular War*, 1974
Henderson, N., *Prince Eugen of Savoy*, 1964
Hibbert, C., *The Marlboroughs*, 2001
Horsley, W. (ed), *De La Colonie J-M, Chronicles of an Old Campaigner*, 1904
Johnston, S. (ed), *Letters of Samuel Noyes*, JSAHR, 1959
Kamen, H., *The War of Succession in Spain*, 1969
Lediard, T., *Life of John, Duke of Marlborough*, 1736
McBane, D., *The Expert Swordsman's Companion*, 1728
McKay, D., *Prince Eugene*, 1977
Merode-Westerloo, J., *Memoires*, 1840
Millner, J., *A Compendious Journal*, 1733
Murray, G. (ed), *Letters and Dispatches of the Duke of Marlborough*, 1845
Norton, L., *St Simon at Versailles*, 1980
Orkney, 1st Earl, *Letters, English Historical Review*, 1904
Parker, R., *Memoirs*, 1747
Petrie, D., *The Marshal, Duke of Berwick*, 1953
—— (ed), *Letters, from the Duke of Berwick to His Son*, 1954
Rowse, A.L., *The Early Churchills*, 1956
Spencer, C., *Blenheim*, 2004
St Simon L de R, *Memoires*, (edited and translated 1876, and 1958)
The Tatler magazine, June–December 1709
Taylor, F., *The Wars of Marlborough*, 1921
Trevelyan, G.M., *Select Documents for the Reign of Queen Anne*, 1929
—— *England Under Queen Anne*, 1947 (3 volumes):
—— *Blenheim*
—— *Ramillies and the Union with Scotland*
—— *The Peace, and the Protestant Succession*
Van der Zee, H & B., *William and Mary*, 1973
Verney, P., *Blenheim*, 1976

(JSAHR – Journal of Society of Army Historical Research)

Index